West African Regional
Cooperation and Development

West African Regional
Cooperation and Development

West African Regional Cooperation and Development

EDITED BY

Julius Emeka Okolo and Stephen Wright

Westview Press
BOULDER, SAN FRANCISCO, & OXFORD

Westview Special Studies on Africa

Published in 1990 in the United States of America by Westview Press, Inc.,
5500 Central Avenue, Boulder, Colorado 80301, and in the United Kingdom
by Westview Press, Inc., 36 Lonsdale Road, Summertown, Oxford OX2 7EW

Library of Congress Cataloging-in-Publication Data
West African regional cooperation and development / edited by Julius
    Emeka Okolo and Stephen Wright.
        p.   cm.--(Westview special studies on Africa)
    Includes index.
    ISBN 0-8133-7354-9
    1. Economic Community of West African States.   2. Africa, West--
Economic integration.   3. Africa, West--Economic policy.
I. Okolo, Julius Emeka.   II. Wright, Stephen, 1954-
III. Series.
HC1000.W47   1990
338.966--dc19   87-9290
                                                                           CIP

Printed and bound in the United States of America

 The paper used in this publication meets the requirements
of the American National Standard for Permanence of Paper
for Printed Library Materials Z39.48-1984.

10   9   8   7   6   5   4   3   2   1

Contents

PART 2: COOPERATION AND DEVELOPMENT

Tables

viii

Acknowledgments

The editors wish to thank the individual contributors to this volume, who worked professionally to complete their chapters within time constraints and who kept to the framework of topics and themes suggested to them. We would also like to thank Professors Leslie Rubin and Timothy Shaw for their early encouragement of the volume and their help towards its publication.

We are grateful to Rebecca Ritke, Barbara Ellington, Bruce Kellison and Lindsay Schumacher of Westview Press for their assistance and advice in preparing the manuscript and for their patience when deadlines slipped.

We would like to thank the following for granting permission to publish data and material from previously published sources: Europa Publications; Greenwood Press; the International Monetary Fund; the Jerusalem Journal of International Relations; MIT Press; Politique Africaine (Karthala); the United Nations; and the World Bank.

Finally, we would like to pay special thanks to Northern Arizona University for the use of facilities and resources. We wish to thank Emilee Mead for drawing the map of West Africa, and we are especially grateful and indebted to Annette Bowers, Julie Pickering, Carolyn McBeath and Michele Wallace of the Department of Political Science, who worked through all the various stages of the manuscript and whose energy and patience were largely responsible for seeing the volume completed.

Julius Emeka Okolo
Stephen Wright

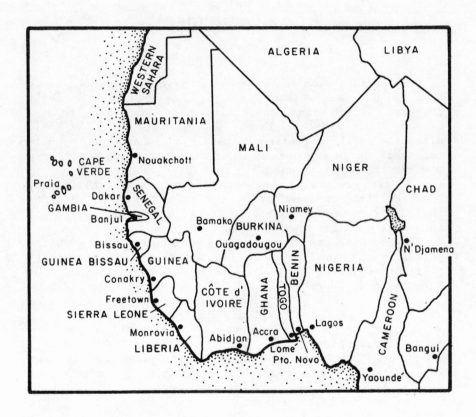

Map of West Africa

1

Introduction: Cooperation and Development in West Africa

Stephen Wright and
Julius Emeka Okolo

Regional cooperative ventures have always been considered to be viable programs to promote welfare and development within Africa. Over the last decade, however, the increasing problems and stagnation of African economies have led to an even greater awareness of the need to strengthen linkages between states and to encourage regional groupings within the continent. New organizations have been established, such as the Southern African Development Coordination Conference (SADCC) and the Preferential Trade Area (PTA), which vary considerably in scope, membership and objectives, but which aim to improve economic conditions within their member states. The Economic Community of West African States (ECOWAS), founded in 1975 and now comprising sixteen members, provides the major organizational framework for subregional cooperation within West Africa, although many other smaller organizations also play important roles within the subregion.

This volume of original contributions provides a detailed examination of what we have called "Cooperation and Development" within West Africa. While other scholarly books concerned with a similar enquiry tend to focus upon either the organizations in the subregion or else the developmental problems faced by individual countries, this volume combines both in a dual focus. The chapters contained in Part 1 discuss the prominent organizational ventures within West Africa, notably ECOWAS, the francophone organizations and the Mano River Union (MRU). This list, of course, excludes many other significant groupings, such as the Club du Sahel[1] and the (now defunct) Senegambian Confederation,[2] and although these are touched on from time to time, space limitations have prevented further discussion.

The second part of the volume contains five chapters which discuss developmental issues from a non-organizational perspective. Here the focus is upon common problems and issues which affect all or most of the countries of the subregion, and how these factors impact upon the developmental process. This dual focus, with chapters on subregional organizations as well as thematic developmental issues, offers the opportunity of a broad discussion of present and future prospects for West Africa.

Development

The word *development* raises controversy among scholars both in terms of its meaning and usage. In this volume, authors utilize the term in its widest context. Development refers not only to the improvement of traditional economic performance, measured by gross national product, per capita incomes or industrial output, but also explicitly includes an emphasis on social or *human* considerations, such as literacy levels, health facilities, life expectancy and civil liberties. Subsequent chapters in this volume consider a diverse array of development issues which affect West African countries individually or collectively. In addition, authors analyze the importance of other political and social factors, such as the role of military leaderships in promoting development, the pervasive influence of Islam in the subregion, and the status and economic impact of women in West African societies.

Wide parameters in usage for the term development have fostered dichotomies concerning its application, and authors here reflect these debates by being at times at variance with each other. Perhaps the greatest disagreement occurs over the question of whether West African cooperative ventures are shaped primarily by political or economic motivations. For instance, should an organization such as ECOWAS involve itself in a defense agreement, an apparently overt political action? Or alternatively, to what extent can decisions regarding economic cooperation be divorced from political considerations? The editors' opinion is that ECOWAS and other subregional cooperative ventures are inherently political, but that the scale of operations and objectives of each organization will be partially determined by the level of political commitment, while the success of such an organization will depend considerably upon "political will."

Another dichotomy evident in several chapters is the interesting question of whether development within West Africa is perceived in a subregional or purely national context. Are West African leaders viewing problems as subregional or national in scope, and at what level is a solution being proposed? A volume such as this may tend to exaggerate the subregional focus of development efforts, but sufficient evidence is present to conclude that development objectives primarily have national focuses, despite the apparent benefits that could accrue from collective action.

A final divergence to mention here centers upon whether governmental development strategies seek to emphasize primarily economic goals rather than the improvement of social conditions. Of course, these two emphases are not necessarily mutually exclusive, but in the harsh economic realities of the early-1990s, most West African governments have introduced structural adjustment programs, at the bidding of creditors, which have targeted specific economic goals. In the process, the programs have undermined many social goals, leading to problems such as deteriorating health care facilities and the squeezing of resources from schools and universities. For the majority of West Africans, the quality of life has deteriorated during the decade of the 1980s, but national rather than cooperative regional programs continue to be the standard response to this crisis.

West Africa: A Profile

It is not our intention to present a detailed survey of the economic structures and development programs of West African countries because that can be obtained elsewhere.[3] Our aim here is to introduce various factors which directly affect the level of cooperation between the countries, or else serve to hamper their collective aim to promote development. The geographical extent of the volume's coverage is the sixteen countries which are members of ECOWAS. These range along the West African coast from Mauritania in the northwest to Nigeria in the southeast, and include neighboring landlocked states. Non-members of ECOWAS, such as Chad and Cameroon, are also touched upon when appropriate. Statistical data for the region are notoriously poor, a factor which hampers an accurate survey of pertinent facts and presents serious hazards for the development planning process itself.

Countries in the subregion of West Africa are more different than they are similar. The most striking differences can be seen in Nigeria, whose population and gross national product are roughly equal to those of the other fifteen members of ECOWAS combined. This intraregional inequality has often hampered cooperative ventures and provoked suspicions of Nigeria's intentions within ECOWAS. Reinforcing divisions are further differences, such as the trilingual cultural heritage of anglophone, francophone and lusophone influences on countries as well as the numerous currency zones across West Africa. Such a range of cultural, historical, political and economic differences remains a serious obstacle to be overcome in the search for further cooperation and potential integration.

An additional hazard to development efforts within the subregion is the extreme political instability of many of its member states. This issue is taken up by Claude Welch in Chapter 8, but we can state that West Africa accounts for an unproportionately large share of coups d'etat within the continent, and that these coups have destabilizing and debilitating effects upon the countries and their development goals. Planning in particular becomes problematic because political fluidity detracts from the long-term stability desired for the success of these development schemes. Other problems also impede the planning process, such as the paucity of resources, inefficiency, corruption, and the lack of political will. Such a mix of factors led Douglas Rimmer to conclude that development plans in West Africa were ineffectual: "At best, therefore, central plans in West Africa have been loose envelopes of ambitions and desire within which the economies have evolved; at worst they have been totally irrelevant to what actually happened."[4] If such plans are relatively unsuccessful at a national level, then can one expect any greater level of achievement at the level of ECOWAS?

Another important area to draw attention to in this sketch of West African countries is the peripheral nature of their economies within the international economy although some, such as Nigeria and Côte d'Ivoire, could be classed as semi-peripheral. Indeed, besides uranium (Niger) and petroleum (Nigeria), the region currently has little in the way of strategic or "valuable" minerals or commodities, except perhaps for the luxury commodity, cocoa.[5] In terms of overall exports, fourteen of the sixteen ECOWAS members have a 60 percent dependence or more on just one or two commodities.[6] The region's trade pattern is one very much linked with and dependent upon the outside world, with less than 10 percent of official trade being intraregional. During the 1970s, there were high hopes that regional integrative communities in Africa would alter this predominant trade pattern, but such changes have not materialized. Furthermore, decreasing terms of trade and rising international debts have forced West African countries into greater dependency on Western nations and banks, as well as multilateral agencies. By 1988, ECOWAS members' debts totalled $62.96 billion, of which Nigeria (46 percent) and Côte d'Ivoire (21 percent) accounted for the lion's share.[7]

Table 1.1
General Indicators

	Population (m) 1987	Area ('000 sq kms)	GNP, $ per capita
Benin	4.3	113	310
Burkina Faso	8.3	274	190
Cape Verde	0.4	4	320
Côte d'Ivoire	11.1	322	740
Gambia	0.7	11	290
Ghana	13.6	239	390
Guinea	6.5	246	320
Guinea-Bissau	0.9	36	180
Liberia	2.3	111	450
Mali	7.8	1,240	210
Mauritania	1.9	1,031	440
Niger	6.8	1,267	260
Nigeria	106.6	924	370
Senegal	7.0	196	520
Sierra Leone	3.8	72	300
Togo	3.2	57	290

Source: *World Development Report 1989* (New York: Oxford University Press/World Bank, 1989); *Africa South of the Sahara 1987* (London: Europa, 1986); *Global Studies Africa* (Guilford CT: Dushkin, 1987).

Regionalism in West Africa

Orthodox economics favors the creation of regional integrative blocs to promote industrial growth and trade between countries based largely upon the principle of comparative advantage. Integration, as opposed to mere cooperation,[8] would in the West African context lead to a substantial growth in intraregional trade, increased industrial programs planned at a subregional rather than purely national level, and potentially a stronger economic status vis-à-vis the outside world. In addition, these positive economic factors would help to provide a more influential political voice in world affairs for the member

6

countries.

While there are some positive signs of success for West African integration, and these are discussed in subsequent chapters, many scholars have begun to question the real potential of integration schemes throughout the Third World.[9] There is evidence to suggest that the classical objectives of trade diversion and trade creation do not automatically come to fruition, while successful integration does not necessarily reduce dependency. Within West Africa, the lack of political will combined with the paucity of joint industrial projects and skilled human resources have all led to the painfully slow pace of growth and integration. Furthermore, there appears to have been little progress made towards the avowed goal of breaking dependent relationships with the West and limiting the role of transnational corporations (TNCs). Ralph Onwuka concluded a recent study by commenting that "it is obvious that the TNCs, aided by resident compradors, have in most cases continued to exploit the economic deficiencies of the host countries."[10]

Evidence of continuing dependence has contributed to louder calls from many quarters for self-reliance and self-sustainment, both at the national and West African levels, with the objective that such an emphasis would help to restructure West African economies in an introverted rather than an extroverted manner. The economic problems associated with such a policy reorientation are vast, and many of them are discussed later, but the political difficulties are also considerable. Claude Ake has argued convincingly, as others have after him,[11] that the African bourgeoisie has much to gain from the status quo, and much to lose from an attempt to alter radically the neocolonial relationships which benefit the elite groups. Indeed, the current strategy of ECOWAS appears to be a shaky compromise in that it combines what were thought to be mutually exclusive options, namely the maintenance of strong external links with the West and the steady (yet slow) expansion of intraregional linkages. These issues are discussed further in Chapter 6 by Timothy Shaw.

West Africa contains a plethora of overlapping intergovernmental organizations which are handicapped by many problems, notably a lack of resources and political will to cooperate more fully. The legacy of colonialism has been to divide the subregion into distinctive cultural, political and economic zones, and the resulting cleavages have provided severe obstacles for the integrative process to overcome. These obstacles were recognized to be very serious in the 1960s, when one scholar predicted:

> ...economic integration is likely to proceed at a very slow pace, if at all, in the foreseeable future. It is also unlikely that co-ordinated industrial development plans will succeed in breaking the vicious circle of underdevelopment where national development plans failed. This does not imply that a few countries with rich natural resources and large domestic markets could not succeed in making rapid progress under conditions of political stability and dynamic leadership. However, such progress would be of little benefit to the other countries of the region.[12]

While this analysis was presented some seven years before the establishment of ECOWAS, the creation of that organization has not, as yet, brought dramatic benefits. Scholars such as Renninger,[13] Ezenwe[14] and Asante[15] among many others have all found beneficial aspects of ECOWAS, but have generally concluded that the organization has brought only marginal improvements to West Africa. Guy Martin was extremely pessimistic in his conclusion to a recent study:

> Ultimately, the major beneficiaries of ECOWAS seem to be the foreign businessmen and the West African comprador bourgeoisie; the net losers are the bulk of the population in the member states in whose name and to whose benefit integration is supposed to be realized.[16]

ECOWAS provides the focus for the majority of chapters in the first part of this volume. Julius Emeka Okolo analyzes many of the pertinent issues in Chapter 2, where he discusses the origins, goals and current operation of the organization. He examines in depth the motivation and maneuvering of Nigeria, which was largely responsible for the creation of ECOWAS and without which it would be of less significance. Okolo traces the important diplomatic agreements and intraregional problems of the organization, and provides positive analysis of its benefits.

An ongoing difficulty within ECOWAS, however, has been the implicit incompatibility of its sixteen members, both in terms of economic characteristics and diverse colonial legacies. The greatest rivalry traditionally centers upon the relationship between the francophone group, the Communauté Economique de l'Afrique de l'Ouest (CEAO), and the wider ECOWAS system of which the CEAO is an integral part. This uneasy association is analyzed by Daniel Bach in Chapter 3, where he also examines the role of other significant

francophone organizations within West Africa. Bach concludes
that the francophone members are not as responsible for the
slow progress of ECOWAS integration as many others submit,
although he does accept that the presence of a distinct
political/linguistic group within a wider organization poses
problems for ECOWAS's cohesion and growth. It is possible to
argue, as Rimmer does elsewhere,[17] that these divisions
within ECOWAS provide a positive stimulus to intraregional
trade because it is over national borders that incentives
such as price differentiation and currency convertibility
gains are to be found. The unofficial trade (or smuggling)
which thrives on such factors, and which provides
considerable income to a number of countries, would naturally
be threatened by any relaxation of trade barriers as promised
under ECOWAS development programs.

These cross-cultural problems faced by ECOWAS are also
evident in other micro-organizations within West Africa, and
Amadu Sesay provides a discussion of these and other issues
within the Mano River Union (MRU) in Chapter 4. The MRU
comprises three countries, namely Liberia, Sierra Leone and
Guinea, but despite its small size, the organization has been
unable to fulfill its promise of integrative cooperation.[18]
Sesay analyzes the problems faced by the MRU, and offers a
number of potential remedies, but he concludes that the
prospects for the MRU are not very promising.

The final three chapters in Part 1 provide broader
perspectives on the integrative efforts of ECOWAS and,
indirectly, other subregional integrative groupings on the
continent. In Chapter 5, Phoebe Kornfeld presents a detailed
analysis of the intra- and extra-regional growth of ECOWAS
over its first decade. The study is specifically confined to
this period both for practical reasons concerned with
availability of complete data, but also to highlight the
organization's failure in its first ten years to break from
its position of dependence vis-à-vis former colonial
metropoles, and to indicate the magnitude of the task that
still lies ahead of ECOWAS in the 1990s. Timothy Shaw, in
Chapter 6, builds upon Kornfeld's arguments but also broadens
the discussion to include a number of other themes. Shaw
compares the objectives, progress and political economy of
ECOWAS with those of SADCC, and then considers both
organizations in terms of their vertical interaction with the
international economic system. His conclusions provide a
provocative challenge to orthodox studies of regionalism when
he contends that ECOWAS member states may not be pursuing--
and may not want to pursue -- the correct strategy to produce
a strong, viable and self-reliant subregional grouping.

Oliver Knowles completes Part 1 with a balanced assessment of the performance of ECOWAS since 1975. Using his intimate knowledge of the workings of ECOWAS, Knowles provides a succinct account of its institutional and infrastructural difficulties, but he is able to conclude positively that the organization has achieved more than could have been expected given its many constraints, and Knowles offers a number of suggestions to improve its efficiency. Possibly the most important change needs to be in political will, and the desire to make ECOWAS work. Turning rhetoric into reality remains both the priority and the problem.

Trends and Problems in West African Development

The second part of the volume contains five chapters which discuss pertinent and controversial aspects of the development process within West Africa. Two basic themes underpin these chapters: firstly, that there are numerous problems and development debates which are common to countries throughout West Africa, and that these provide a useful focus for comparative study of government reactions and policies; and secondly, that cooperation and the pooling of resources could be increased at a non-organizational level (bilateral or otherwise) to improve the chances of successful attainment of the region's development goals. Significantly, if bilateral cooperation is not evident at a satisfactory level, then this raises doubts as to the future vitality of the integrative process in West Africa.

Social Issues

The areas chosen for discussion in these chapters are diverse but cannot possibly begin to cover the complete range of potential subject matter. One important area often touched upon, but which does not have a chapter devoted to it, perhaps requires some emphasis here. This concerns the level of *social* development reached by West African countries, and can be measured in terms of the basic human needs (BHN) philosophy, or else quantitatively by the Physical Quality of Life Index (PQLI).[19] Table 1.2 provides the raw data to show that, on the basis of the PQLI, the level of "development" attained within West Africa is very poor, with some countries being among the world's poorest. Here is a good example of common problems shared by all West African countries, where a cooperative approach could help to

Table 1.2
Social Indicators

	Life Expectancy Female	Male	Adult Literacy %	Deaths/ 1000 births
Benin	52	49	26	116
Burkina Faso	49	46	13	138
Cape Verde	62		48	82
Côte d'Ivoire	54	51	43	96
Gambia	36		25	198
Ghana	56	52	53	90
Guinea	44	41	29	147
Guinea Bissau	41		31	149
Liberia	56	53	35	87
Mali	49	46	17	169
Mauritania	48	44	18	127
Niger	46	43	14	135
Nigeria	53	49	42	105
Senegal	49	46	28	128
Sierra Leone	42	40	29	151
Togo	55	51	41	94

Source: *World Development Report 1989* (New York: Oxford University Press/World Bank, 1989); *Africa South of the Sahara 1987* (London: Europa, 1986); *Global Studies Africa* (Guilford CT: Dushkin, 1987)

improve the standard of living throughout the subregion. But to date, little coordinated effort across West Africa appears to have been exerted to promote dynamic change. Energies are instead spent on promoting industrial cooperation and joint-venture schemes, which have faced political resistance and whose economic viability in regional and global terms has been questioned.[20]

If West Africa's socioeconomic problems appeared insoluble in the late-1980s, they will seem even more so in the decade to come. Inequalities of wealth and income do not appear to be narrowing, and the poverty-stricken majority within West African states seems likely to continue to suffer from structural adjustment programs. Plans to alleviate some of the suffering, introduced in Ghana and Nigeria in 1988 and 1989 respectively, may only scratch the surface of the problem.[21]

Although virtually all West African states have introduced

population control/family planning programs, no noticeable
progress has been witnessed in any country. Nigeria's
population alone is anticipated to grow by some sixty million
in the next decade. These population pressures will place
unbearable pressure on already struggling economic
infrastructures, especially when one realizes that over 50
percent of West Africa's population is below the age of
eighteen. In 1989, the Organization of African Unity
designated the 1990s as the "Decade for the African Child" in
recognition of the problems involved in this area. A
critical problem centers upon the handling of West African
youth, who are emerging in increasing numbers into a
shrinking job market.[22] Urban drift and underemployment --
socioeconomic problems certainly not new to Africa -- are
intensifying and set major challenges for West African
policy-makers.

Other Trends

An important feature of West African society is the
prevalence of political instability, which has resulted in,
and been reinforced by, numerous coups d'etat and military
governments. The widespread nature of military rule provides
the basis of enquiry for Claude Welch in Chapter 8. Welch
provides a provocative analysis of the military's role in the
development process and argues persuasively that military
leaders are not necessarily any more pro-ECOWAS than civilian
ones, nor are they more gifted at promoting development
efforts within their countries or at a subregional level.
Welch also contributes to the earlier discussion by Okolo of
the ECOWAS defense arrangements, and comes to the conclusion
that they are more encouraging on paper than in practice.[23]

One of the most significant repercussions of Africa's
economic crisis in the 1980s has been to address in a
critical manner the problems of agriculture in general, and
food production in particular. Calls for greater self-
sufficiency in food output as well as coordinated attempts to
reduce the threat of famine have stimulated and challenged
subregional organizations to seek ways to promote further
cooperation in this arena. In West Africa, ECOWAS is only
one of a number of organizations working to alleviate this
problem. Those afflicted by severe climatic problems in the
Sahel region, for example, have formed their own
institutional framework for this endeavor.[24] Some scholars
have argued that agricultural self-sufficiency at a national
level cannot succeed economically because of the limited

range and volume of products.[25]   Where attempts have been
made to pursue autarchic policies, these appear to have had
a primarily political, rather than economic, motivation.

A policy which is both rational and feasible focuses upon
potential self-sufficiency achieved through cooperation at
the West African level.   The success of such a program
depends upon various factors, but notably the nature and
number of commodities found within the subregion, the level
of official and unofficial trade flows to date, the political
goodwill to promote such a policy, and the infrastructural
deficiencies which could diminish the chances of success.
Mary Burfisher and Margaret Missiaen provide a comprehensive
study of the agricultural sector in West Africa in Chapter 9.
The authors concentrate on the key commodities and draw
attention to the fact that growth in intraregional trade has
been recorded in a number of sectors, even though the figures
involved may be small and possibly misleading.   Such analysis
is hampered by the paucity and unreliability of data, as well
as by the presence of large amounts of unrecorded trade.
Whatever the past and present obstacles to greater
cooperation in the agricultural sector, it is obvious that
this is a crucial area on which hangs the future of
individual nations as well as the spirit of regional unity.

Spirituality of a different kind is discussed by William
Miles in Chapter 10, where he considers the various roles
that Islam plays in promoting economic development in West
Africa.   This is a refreshing and thoughtful approach to
religion, which is often studied either in terms of conflict
and division between denominations, or else as to the impact
of Islamic fundamentalism.   Miles does discuss these
important issues, but within the framework of development,
and he casts a wider net for his own overall analysis of
Islam, which encompasses over half of the subregion's
population (as well as half of the continent's total
population) and which has followers in virtually all of the
West African states.   Miles is convincing in his argument
that Islam plays a forceful and positive role in the
development process and that this impact is evident at
several overlapping levels: helping development within
individual countries themselves; as a medium for the
promotion of cooperation between countries of West Africa;
and in terms of strengthening the linkages between West
Africa and aid/development agencies of the Middle East.

Africa's economic crisis has provided the opportunity and
necessity to reevaluate the position, role and influence of
women in the developmental process.   Many individuals
reassert the importance of women's movements in the colonial

struggle (as we witness also today in South Africa), while international organizations such as the United Nations, the Commonwealth and the Organization of African Unity make major statements about the need to correct development programs to favor women. It is unfortunately true to say that little progress has been made to date to improve women's economic and political status in West Africa, and their crucial contribution to development remains largely unrecognized. Barbara Callaway, in Chapter 11, presents an overview of women and the development agenda in West Africa. She draws our attention to many of the problems, such as the general absence of women from the development planning process and how female productivity is hampered by poor (male) administration, but she also considers areas of divergence between women's movements and aspirations in different societies. Her conclusion, however, is straightforward: women's integration into the mainstream of political and economic life is a prerequisite for real development to take place.

Although this goal is accepted by many as an obvious necessity, the strategy to be adopted to achieve it is disputed. In the face of resistance from many quarters, women's organizations are becoming increasingly radical in their challenge to the status quo. One notable example is the Women in Nigeria (WIN) movement, which was established in 1982. The WIN Document, published in 1985, provides an explicit definition of WIN's radical character by explaining that women suffer double exploitation by gender as well as by class.[26] Whether women will be able to overcome these double obstacles is unclear, but it seems likely that greater regional cooperation between women's movements will take place in the coming years.

Regional cooperation by working class movements and class exploitation are themes explored by Jon Kraus in the final chapter. Far from seeing progress in representation and cooperation by organized labor unions, Kraus stresses that these were stronger in the early years after independence and that governmental pressures in recent years have served to weaken and mute the voices of workers. This trend is indicative of the growing repression within Africa which has been accentuated by the economic crisis, but which also emanates from the increasing militarization of governments and the "structural violence" exerted by militaries against populist movements.[27] The healthy growth of regional interaction witnessed in other areas has not been repeated to the same extent in labor relations. We are left to ponder whether such negative pressures can be reversed by a more enlightened view of cooperation at a West African level.

Conclusion

The editors have brought together in this volume a balanced and interesting analysis of political and socio-economic developments within West Africa, with chapters providing a blend of constructive criticism and assessment as well as suggestions for future programs. Although there have been various setbacks to regional cooperation in Africa as a whole, most notably with the demise of the East African Community, there remains considerable optimism concerning the "second generation" organizations such as SADCC, the PTA and ECOWAS.

Within West Africa, difficult hurdles remain for organizations such as ECOWAS and MRU, while there are equally serious obstacles in the path towards "development" and "growth," however defined, for individual countries. Subsequent chapters offer solutions to some of the current problems, but also pose fresh questions for future enquiry.

Notes

1. For a discussion of the Club du Sahel see Anne De Lattre and Arthur M. Fell, *The Club du Sahel: An Experiment in International Cooperation* (Paris: OECD, 1984).

2. For a general account of Senegambia see Peter Robson, *Integration, Development and Equity: Economic Integration in West Africa* (London: George Allen and Unwin, 1983), Chapter 7, pp. 124-140. The confederation collapsed in acrimony in August 1989.

3. Perhaps the best account is Douglas Rimmer, *The Economies of West Africa* (London: Weidenfeld and Nicolson, 1984). See also Keith Hart, *The Political Economy of West African Agriculture* (Cambridge: Cambridge University Press, 1982); and J.O.C. Onyemelukwe, *Industrialization in West Africa* (London: Croom Helm, 1984).

4. Rimmer, *The Economies of West Africa*, p. 221.

5.   Hart, *The Political Economy of West African Agriculture*, pp. 151-153.

6.   UN Africa Recovery Programme, *Briefing Paper*, 3, October 1989, p. 9.

7.   UN Africa Recovery Programme, *Briefing Paper*, 1, June 1989, p. 2. By the end of 1989, Nigeria's debt was estimated to be $30.5 billion.

8.   For a detailed discussion of the importance of this distinction see S.K.B. Asante, *The Political Economy of Regionalism in Africa: A Decade of the Economic Community of West African States (ECOWAS)* (New York: Praeger, 1986), pp. 9-10.

9.   Robson, *Integration, Development and Equity*, pp. 6-16.   Also E.C. Edozien and E. Osagie (eds.), *Economic Integration of West Africa* (Ibadan: Ibadan University Press, 1982); and S.K.B. Asante, "Development and Regional Integration since 1980" in Adebayo Adedeji and Timothy M. Shaw (eds.), *Economic Crisis in Africa: African Perspectives on Development Problems and Potentials* (Boulder: Lynne Rienner, 1985). For a general discussion of the performance of regional groupings in the Third World, see *The Courier* (Brussels), 112, November-December 1988, pp. 47-85.

10.   Ralph I. Onwuka, "Transnational Corporations and Regional Integration" in Ralph I. Onwuka and Amadu Sesay (eds.), *The Future of Regionalism in Africa* (London: Macmillan, 1985), p. 168.

11.   Claude Ake, *A Political Economy of Africa* (Harlow: Longman, 1981), pp. 160-162; also, Paul M. Lubeck (ed.), *The African Bourgeoisie: Capitalist Development in Nigeria, Kenya and the Ivory Coast* (Boulder: Lynne Rienner, 1987).

12.   Nicolas G. Plessz, *Problems and Prospects of Economic Integration in West Africa* (Montreal: McGill University Press, 1968), p. 79.

13.   John P. Renninger, *Multinational Cooperation for Development in West Africa* (New York: Pergamon Press/UNITAR, 1979).

14.   Uka Ezenwe, *Ecowas and the Economic Integration of West Africa* (London: Hurst, 1983).

15.   S.K.B. Asante, *The Political Economy of Regionalism in West Africa*.

16.   Guy Martin, "Regional Integration in West Africa: The Role of the Economic Community of West African States" in Emmanuel Hansen (ed.), *Africa: Perspectives on Peace and Development* (London: Zed/United Nations University, 1987), p. 175.

17.   Rimmer, *The Economies of West Africa*, p. 153.

18. See Robson's discussion of the MRU in *Integration, Development and Equity*, pp. 70-85.

19. For discussions of these see Morris David Morris, *Measuring the Condition of the World's Poor: The Physical Quality of Life Index* (New York: Pergamon/Overseas Development Council, 1979); and Frances Stewart, *Planning to Meet Basic Needs* (London: Macmillan, 1985).

20. See Onyemelukwe, *Industrialization in West Africa*.

21. For an excellent study of poverty in general in Africa, see John Iliffe, *The African Poor: A History* (Cambridge: Cambridge University Press, 1987).

22. See Jennifer Seymour Whitaker, *How Can Africa Survive?* (New York: Council on Foreign Relations, 1988), especially chapter 4.

23. See also Tom Imobighe, "ECOWAS Defence Pact and Regionalism in Africa" in Onwuka and Sesay, *The Future of Regionalism in Africa*, pp. 110-124.

24. For an indepth analysis of the Permanent Interstate Committee for Drought Control in the Sahel (CILSS) as well as the Club du Sahel see De Lattre and Fell, *The Club du Sahel*.

25. Rimmer, *The Economies of West Africa*, pp. 235-246; also Hart, *The Political Economy of West African Agriculture*.

26. *The WIN Document: Conditions of Women in Nigeria and Policy Recommendations to 2000 AD* (Zaria: WIN, 1985); also Women in Nigeria (eds.), *Women in Nigeria Today* (London: Zed, 1985).

27. See Miles D. Wolpin, *Militarization, Internal Repression and Social Welfare in the Third World* (London: Croom Helm, 1986).

PART ONE

Regional Organizations

2

The Development and Structure of ECOWAS

Julius Emeka Okolo

The Economic Community of West African States (ECOWAS)[1] has been described as the first potential success for Third World integrative enterprises.[2] ECOWAS was created by the May 1975 Treaty of Lagos by states formerly under British, American, French and Portuguese colonial domination and which are still influenced by the languages and traditions of the former metropoles. With the exception of Ghana, Côte d'Ivoire, Nigeria and Senegal, the rest of the member states are yet to arrive at the intermediate stage of economic development.

ECOWAS was created, therefore, out of a desire to wrest the West African region from external dependence and economic backwardness. In effect, the community presents several distinctive features, which make it different not only to other African regional economic integrations but also to many other economic integration schemes among Third World countries. This chapter is devoted to a discussion of the evolution of the community and an examination of its structure. It does not intend to provide an exhaustive analysis of the distinctive features of ECOWAS. Rather it examines the most important elements essential for an understanding of the objectives, perspectives, direction, achievements and prospects of ECOWAS.

Origins of ECOWAS

West African regional integration has a considerably long and checkered history. During the heyday of Pan-Africanism in the late 1950s and early 1960s, "micro-nationalists," who opposed Kwame Nkrumah's radical "continental nationalism," had proposed some form of gradual movement toward African unity through economic and technical cooperation at the subregional level. Some, particularly the leaders of the francophone countries, envisaged from their common historical experience that they would derive much benefit from cooperative development. Several efforts at creating economic unions were thus made during and since that period. Such efforts included the River Niger Commission (RNC), the Chad Basin Commission (CBC), the Union Monétaire de l'Ouest Africain (UMOA), the Union Douanière de l'Afrique de l'Ouest (UDEAO), the West African Clearing House (WACH), the Entente Council, the Organization of Senegal River States (OERS), the Senegambian Integration Scheme (Senegam), the Communauté Economique de l'Afrique de l'Ouest (CEAO), and the Mano River Union (MRU).[3] Some failed, some survived; but the initiatives were often limited in their scope and membership, sometimes made open only to immediate neighbors or former French colonies. But the idea of integrating the entire West African subregion prevailed. ECOWAS is the latest and most significant West African effort at integrating all states of the subregion into a viable economic unit.

The first attempt to promote the idea of a West African economic community was made by President William Tubman of Liberia in his inaugural speech of 7 January 1964, in which he introduced the notion of a free trade area in West Africa.[4] With his country's backing, he arranged a series of bilateral and multilateral talks with the heads of state and governments of other countries in the subregion to promote and elicit support for his proposal. On 24 August 1964, representatives of four West African countries -- Guinea, Côte d'Ivoire, Liberia and Sierra Leone -- met in Monrovia to consider the possibility of creating a free trade zone. At the end of the meeting, the representatives favored the creation of a West African free trade zone open to other states, and established an Interim Committee of Ministers and Experts to study the problem of creating a free trade area and submit its recommendation to the four governments by January 1965. At a meeting from 15-17 February 1965, the ministers of the four participating states drew up an agreement to create an interim organization to be superseded by a more permanent Organization for West African Economic Cooperation. The agreement was signed in May 1965 in Freetown. Among other things, it charged the interim organization with the responsibility of planning the establishment of a multilateral system of economic cooperation of a regional character, with a view to removing trade barriers and encouraging the harmonious development of the cooperating states in every field.

The apparent, if limited, success of the Liberian initiative pushed the United Nations Economic Commission for Africa (ECA) and the Food and Agriculture Organization (FAO) to encourage a conference on coordination of industries which had taken place in Bamako on 14 October 1964. The conference was to examine the principles which would guide the future coordination of various industries, such as cement, food, steel and textiles in West Africa, in such a way as to maximize the benefits to the states of the region.[5] National goals and interests, however, thwarted the effort as representatives of participating states disagreed on the principles that would have guided the establishment of a number of industries, particularly iron and steel. An opportunity for laying a strong foundation for regional economic integration was, therefore, missed.

Yet ECA remained undaunted. It inspired the creation of ECOWAS through its mid-1960s division of Africa into regions for purposes of economic development. In its projected West African grouping, it included fourteen West African countries.[6] In October 1966 and April-May 1967, the ECA called specialized meetings in Niamey and Accra. The first meeting was to discuss the projected economic association, and the second led to the signing of an Article of Association of the proposed Economic Community of West Africa and the formation of an Interim Council of Ministers. In November 1967, the council met in Dakar and prepared the ground for the heads-of-state meeting of April 1968 in Monrovia. The summit resulted in the establishment of the West African Regional Grouping. But the success was limited: only nine of the fourteen countries attended the meeting and signed the protocol.[7] A conference that was to be held in Ouagadougou in March 1969, at which a West African Common Market treaty was to have been signed and sealed, never materialized. Renewed efforts to create a community would have to wait several years.[8]

The formal launching of ECOWAS came at the end of a visit to Togo in April 1972 by General Yakubu Gowon, Nigeria's head of state.[9] He and his Togolese counterpart, President Gnassingbé Eyadéma, issued a communique announcing their decision to create an economic grouping, "an embryonic West African Economic Community between their two countries."[10] The two leaders set up a commission of experts, which met at Lagos in June to make recommendations on the proposed grouping. The conference agreed to work out broad areas of cooperation in such matters as transport and communications, trade, industry, money payments, and movement of factors between Nigeria and Togo. It recommended the abolition of transit tax, which constituted an impediment to the development of trade; and, most importantly, it mandated General Gowon to call a summit conference of West African leaders to discuss the proposed community.[11]

Within eighteen months of its first meeting, the Nigeria-Togo commission of experts had produced a draft treaty. It was first considered by ministers of West African states at a meeting in Lomé in December 1973, where basic principles for the creation of ECOWAS were adopted. Following subsequent meetings in Accra in February 1974 and Monrovia in January 1975, the treaty establishing ECOWAS was adopted by a ministerial meeting. It was signed by the original fifteen ECOWAS member states at Lagos on 28 May 1975. The first five protocols annexed to the treaty were signed at Lomé on 5 November 1976. With these, ECOWAS was born.

Why and How ECOWAS

West Africa occupies a land area of some 6.1 million sq. kms., extending from Mauritania in the northwest to Niger in the northeast, Nigeria in the southeast, and the Gulf of Guinea in the south and southwest. Included in this area are the three landlocked states of Mali, Niger and Burkina Faso, the island of Cape Verde, and twelve coastline states -- in all, the sixteen participating countries of ECOWAS. The region is endowed with many mineral resources: petroleum, of which Nigeria is the world's sixth-largest producer, iron ore, tin, lead, zinc, bauxite, gold and diamonds. Large tracts of arable land are as yet uncultivated, but agricultural products are the principal foreign exchange earner in most of the countries involved. These products include cocoa, of which Ghana is a major world producer, coffee, groundnuts (peanuts), palm oil and kernel, and pineapples. The region's population in 1990 is estimated to be 195 million.

The West African region as a whole is nonetheless poor and economically underdeveloped. Most of its countries still have an annual gross national product (GNP) per capita of less than $600, which economists agree constitutes the poverty line. Economic activity concentrates heavily on primary production: extractive industries and agriculture for export. The contribution of manufacturing to gross domestic product (GDP) averages only about 8 percent.

Intra-West African and international trade patterns show minor horizontal interaction among ECOWAS members and the vertical relationship between them and the industrialized countries, primarily the former colonial powers, Japan, and the United States. Evidence of the heavy external dependence of the region abounds in the fact that in 1980, 2.72 percent of total West African exports and 3.78 percent of imports went to other countries in the region, compared with 89.17 percent and 83.18 percent, respectively, to the industrialized countries.[12] Trade among the sixteen countries prior to and since the signing of the ECOWAS treaty accounted for less than 10 percent of their total foreign trade (Table 2.1). Only the three landlocked states of

Table 2.1
Proportion of Intra-ECOWAS Trade To Total Trade:
Selected Years 1968 - 1987

Country	1968	1972	1976	1980	1982	1984	1987
Benin	--	--	6.7	8.7	3.6	5.3	6.2
Burkina Faso	42.5	28.3	19.0	21.2	25.7	33.0	27.3
Cape Verde	--	--	1.8	8.0	0.1	0.1	2.1
Côte d'Ivoire	3.6	4.0	6.3	6.6	9.1	9.5	11.3
Gambia	4.2	3.4	3.6	6.0	9.3	7.3	17.6
Ghana	1.6	6.3	6.6	12.0	6.5	13.5	6.0
Guinea	1.0	4.0	0.6	0.7	0.6	0.2	1.6
Guinea-Bissau	--	--	4.6	6.3	3.8	3.0	5.3
Liberia	1.4	0.5	0.9	1.9	0.5	0.4	1.7
Mali	20.6	33.6	23.8	26.0	25.0	25.3	29.7
Mauritania	2.3	6.8	6.6	0.5	5.2	15.9	4.0
Niger	20.2	9.7	20.4	7.5	18.0	23.8	15.4
Nigeria	0.8	1.7	1.2	1.1	1.3	2.2	2.6
Senegal	5.0	13.1	8.7	11.1	11.6	12.8	12.8
Sierra Leone	0.5	5.0	8.7	9.0	1.4	1.5	7.1
Togo	2.5	2.7	4.4	5.0	10.4	2.5	-
Mean	6.7	7.4	7.7	8.2	8.3	9.8	9.4

Source: Calculated from data in International Monetary Fund, *Direction of Trade Statistics Yearbook, 1981, 1984, 1985 and 1988* (Washington, D.C.: IMF, 1 May 1981, 23 April 1984, 30 April 1985 and 30 April 1988).

Burkina Faso, Mali and Niger conducted more than 20 percent of their external trade with the ECOWAS countries during any of the years prior to the creation of the community and thereafter. Moreover, the region's external dependence is evident by its members' heavy reliance on external loans from the industrialized countries, particularly in the West, and international financial institutions for their development requirements. The debt burden of ECOWAS states is shown in Table 2.2. The debt burden is better appreciated when it is considered that the average regional GNP per capita is some $354 and the average debt per capita is $298, a difference of only $56 between the per capita income and the per capita debt.

Table 2.2
ECOWAS States Total Debt Burden 1987-88 (US $ Billion)

Benin	1.13
Burkina Faso	0.86
Cape Verde	0.13
Côte d'Ivoire	13.56
Gambia	0.32
Ghana	3.12
Guinea	1.78
Guinea-Bissau	0.42
Liberia	1.62
Mali	2.02
Mauri-tania	2.04
Niger	1.68
Nigeria	28.71
Senegal	3.69
Sierra Leone	0.66
Togo	1.22
TOTAL	62.96

Source: UN Africa Recovery Programme, *Briefing Paper*, 1, June 1989, p. 2.

It is clear that although the ECOWAS countries occupy a region that constitutes a geographically contiguous area for purposes of integration, they did not actually look toward one another for the satisfaction of their basic needs. Additionally, the countries are characteristically divided by differential levels of economic and political development, ideological orientations, natural resource endowment, social composition and structure, and diversity of currencies. The West African region is also marked by long-standing political and territorial disputes among countries. There is the complex and unresolved quarrel between Togo and the Republic of Benin, a product more of insecurities and personal rivalries between them than of real economic and political differences.

There are also the now relatively dormant frontier disputes between Côte d'Ivoire and Ghana and between Nigeria and Benin. Not to be ignored are the irredentist movement among Ghana's Ewes; Togo's suspicions of Ghana since the assassination of President Sylvanus Olympio in 1963; the long-standing suspicion of Nigeria by Côte d'Ivoire; traditional rivalry for leadership between Guinea and Senegal that led to recriminations and an end to the Organization of Senegal River States after the alleged Portuguese invasion of Guinea in 1970, which President Sékou Touré believed was aided and abetted by Senegal; and the often forgotten rivalry between Senegal and Mali, which partly contributed to the collapse of the Mali Federation.[13]

The answer to why the West African countries decided to create ECOWAS, in spite of their differences, is partly explained by economic and political considerations. Conscious of their potential collective economic strength, they visualized that in order to enhance industrial development, they must have access to a regional market. It was in fact the exigencies of economic underdevelopment that infused the leaders with what Ernst Haas has aptly called "a shared conception of how and why they need one another." And under the whip of external dependence, economic integration becomes, in the words of Joseph Nye, the way to "get out from under."[14] More explicitly, the main political consideration was the need to have an institutional instrument to maximize the bargaining position of the smaller and weaker West African states vis-à-vis the bigger and more powerful industrialized nations of the world and, particularly, to extricate the region's economy from western neocolonial control.

The process which led to the signing of the treaty consisted of some skillful and patient diplomatic maneuvers spearheaded by General Gowon.[15] First, he personally visited several West African states and endeavored to sell the idea of the community to the leaders. Dr. Okoi Arikpo, then Nigerian Foreign Minister, also visited several states including Côte d'Ivoire, with which Nigeria had broken off diplomatic relations in 1968 following the former's recognition of Biafra during the civil war. In Côte d'Ivoire, Dr. Arikpo and Mr. Arsene Assouan Usher, the Ivorian Foreign Minister, laid a foundation for finally solving the problem existing between the two countries by stating that they would recommend to their governments negotiation of a treaty of friendship and cooperation and the forming of a bilateral committee of experts to examine the possibility of establishing a joint commission of cooperation that would deal with economics, transport, finance, law, politics, culture and agriculture.[16] Thus Nigeria was able to settle its problems with Côte d'Ivoire and so removed a potential stumbling block in the way of generating a consensus toward the creation of the community.[17]

Fear was expressed by some leaders of francophone states that Nigeria, by virtue of its population size and economic and political weight, could dominate the subregional grouping. To demonstrate that it had no desire for domination, Nigeria from the very beginning had associated Togo, the smallest of the francophone states, in the sponsorship of the community. But this did not fully assuage the fears of such leaders as Senghor of Senegal and Houphouët-Boigny of Côte d'Ivoire. Indeed, the former had initiated and the latter supported the transformation in April 1973 of UDEAO to the Communauté Economique de l'Afrique de l'Ouest (CEAO), grouping the francophone countries of the region.[18] While the ostensible reason for creating CEAO was economic -- the establishment of a unified customs system, the organization of industrial development on a regional basis and the eventual free circulation of goods and capital among member states -- the real reason was political: the achievement of what the late President Georges Pompidou of France had called "a just equilibrium" between the francophones and anglophones. Pompidou, reportedly reacting to the Nigerian West African unity moves, had stated during a 1972 visit to Niger that "it is only logical that francophones and anglophones cooperate more fully," but he added cryptically that a just equilibrium could be achieved if the francophones "harmonize their efforts so as to counterbalance the heavy weight of Nigeria."[19] It was thus to strengthen their bargaining position in a cooperative venture with the anglophone West African states that the francophones acted to create CEAO.

Sensing the fissionable tendencies inherent in the creation of parochial organizations while an all-embracing regional organization was being seriously considered, Gowon tactfully sent a message to the Bamako Conference of CEAO wishing it success in its deliberations "true to African aspirations." He followed this up with a visit to Hamani Diori, President of Niger and Chairman of CEAO as soon as the president returned from Bamako. Diori would later say that "as far as we are concerned, Niger cannot ignore the economic weight of its powerful neighbor, Nigeria, with which we have very ancient links."[20]

Later still, at the end of his return visit to Nigeria, he stated that CEAO should be regarded as a "first step" towards the creation of a "virile all-embracing economic union" which would incorporate English- and French-speaking countries in West Africa. He noted that any economic union which left out Nigeria and other English-speaking countries in West Africa would be unrealistic.[21] Togo, which had formed the embryonic economic community with Nigeria, did not sign the CEAO treaty. Also, Togo, Benin (Dahomey) and Niger had since 1970 been receiving substantial grants from Nigeria to help balance their budgets and reduce their economic dependence on France, and so worked to defeat the argument that integration would bring disadvantages to the francophone states. Their position created a division within the CEAO group to the advantage of a wider grouping.

Another consideration was the important issue of membership in the proposed community on which differing views developed. One group of states to which Nigeria belonged argued that the new community should consist of the states stretching from Nigeria to Mauritania. This area would include all sixteen states that eventually became the original members of ECOWAS. Another group led by Senegal argued that the community should be a "grouping of all states on the Western side of Africa facing the Atlantic."[22] This grouping would include, in addition to the fifteen states, Cameroon, Equatorial Guinea, Gabon, Zaire and Congo. Nigeria's stand ultimately prevailed as its government stressed that it was in keeping with the OAU and ECA that any economic community in Africa should begin at subregional level. Nigeria warned that any attempt to allow a country from outside the West African subregion to join the community at a stage when a strong regional foundation had not been laid would only create problems.

Finally, there was the issue of how soon the proposed community would be developed. There was a general agreement that several years were needed before concrete arrangements could be made. Senghor and the ECA's Adebayo Adedeji opined that the community would have to be developed gradually in view of the differences existing among West African states, and that at least five years would be needed for the development. This view was generally accepted.[23]

The negotiations were approached with caution and every possible diplomatic tact. The result was a mutual compromise that was necessary to get the new community off the ground. A major hurdle was also scaled by the fact that the highest government officials were involved in the planning and creation of ECOWAS. In this way, conditions unfavorable to political support were nipped in the bud, and the work of experts was simplified.

Of no less importance was the support of private business enterprises for the formation of ECOWAS. Most significant was the strong lobby mounted by the Nigerian Chamber of Commerce, Industry and Agriculture among its counterparts in other countries of the region, crystallizing in the creation of a Federation of West African Chambers of Commerce, Industry, Mines, and Agriculture, which threw its weight solidly behind economic integration.[24] Anticipating prospects of expanded regional trade and extensive opportunities to compete more favorably against transnational corporations and other foreign firms, indigenous West African industrialists and commercialists grouped together to foster common economic interests.

The objections and fears expressed by the smaller, less-developed states that they might be placed in a disadvantageous position in a regional grouping dominated by Nigeria were not ignored. When Niger's Head of State, Lt. Col. Seyni Kountché, asked that the proposed community should "take into account the varying degrees of development of member states,"[25] he was expressing the view held by the leaders of most states. Ultimately the less-developed countries were assured of special considerations and concessions, especially in matters that affected their vital interests.

General Gowon's considerable diplomatic acumen, the harmony of interests which developed among the business community, relevant segments of national bureaucracies, and top political leaders combined to produce the conditions favorable for ECOWAS integration. By the time discussions progressed to the climacteric of treaty signing, it was by and large a *fait accompli* since the crucial background work had already been accomplished.

The ECOWAS Treaty and Its Implementation

The process that led to the signing of the ECOWAS treaty was tortuous, but West African leaders made compromises by adopting a subregional treaty that would allay the fears of member states and satisfy their different aspirations. The ECOWAS treaty provides a process through which integration can be enhanced, spells out the objectives of the community and the means for achieving them, and stipulates the institutional structure to give effect to the community.

Broadly adumbrated, the objectives of ECOWAS are promotion of accelerated and sustained economic development and the creation of a homogeneous society leading to the unity of the countries of West Africa, the elimination of all customs and other duties on trade among member countries, and the establishment of a common customs tariff and a common commercial policy toward third countries. In short, the main objective is "the rapid and balanced development of West Africa."[26] And the treaty emphasizes that the objectives are to be achieved "by stages."[27]

The Community's Institutions

The treaty makes extensive provisions for institutions charged with administering and directing the affairs of the community, namely the Authority of Heads of State and Government, Council of Ministers, the Executive Secretariat, a number of Technical and Specialized Commissions,[28] and a Fund for Cooperation, Compensation and Development.

The authority composed of all the sixteen leaders of the member states stands at the top of the institutional structure and, as the supreme organ, makes policy decisions. It meets once a year with an annual rotation of chairpersons among the members. Naturally, each head of state endeavors to pursue national interests in meetings of the authority. Next in the hierarchical order is the council, which is made up of two ministers from each member country and meets twice a year. Its chair also rotates. It is charged with the responsibility of monitoring the functioning and development of the community, making recommendation to the authority on the efficient and harmonious development of ECOWAS, and supervising all subordinate institutions.

The executive secretariat, headed by an executive secretary who is assisted by two deputy executive secretaries and a financial controller, performs the main administrative and executive functions of ECOWAS and services all the other institutions. It also initiates and proposes policy measures and programs to the technical commissions. The executive secretary is appointed jointly by the authority and council for a term of four years and can be reappointed only for another term of four years. The secretary can be removed from office by the authority upon the recommendation of the council. The appointment of the two deputies[29] and the determination of their terms and conditions of service and those of other officers of the executive secretariat are under the control of the council, which shall, "subject to the paramount importance of securing the highest standards of efficiency and technical competence," have due regard "to the desirability of maintaining an equitable distribution of appointments to such posts among citizens of member states."[30]

The treaty expressly specifies that all officers of the secretariat "in the discharge of their duties, owe their loyalty entirely to the Community."[31] Thus, they are expected to function, according to the accepted rule of international secretariats, as uninstructed bureaucratic and technical experts whose positions are insulated from the politics and diplomacy of their states of origin. This independence accorded officers of the secretariat is expected to enhance integration by allowing technical issues to be removed from politics, depending, of course, on the general attitudes of member states and the skills, decision-making style,[32] dynamism, and overall outlook of the secretariat officials.

Each of the specialized and technical commissions is made up of experts from all member countries, and their duty is to draw up programs and supervise their implementation. The commissions prepare reports and submit recommendations to the council through the executive secretary. In addition to the office of the financial controller, who does the internal auditing, there is the office of the external auditor responsible for external auditing of the finances of the community.[33] Moreover, there is a Tribunal of the Community, whose composition, competence and other matters are decided by the authority. The tribunal interprets the provisions of the treaty, settles disputes referred to it, and ensures "the observance of law and justice."[34]

It is significant that the community has established a body which will authoritatively interpret the treaty and other ECOWAS rules. It is not clear, however, how the tribunal, given its other charge to ensure the observance of law and justice, makes its interpretation binding on member states in the absence of a supranational law-enforcement agency.

The Fund for Cooperation, Compensation and Development

The fund has a head office under a managing director appointed by the council for a term of four years. The managing director serves as the chief executive and legal representative of the fund, and is assisted by a deputy managing director who is appointed and dismissed in the same manner. A board of directors, composed of a minister from each member state assisted by an alternate and other experts, is charged with the responsibility of ensuring the proper management of the fund.

Originally, it was not clear whether the fund was created as a temporary special feature whose operation was to be limited to the initial years of the development of the community, or whether it would be institutionalized in the treaty. Thus both the fund and the secretariat became embroiled in conflict, initially concerning the degree of independence to which the fund was entitled, and later escalating into personality clashes between members of the fund and secretariat. The issue was resolved during the 1979 summit by deciding that the executive secretary heads the administrative structure of the community, and that the fund is an operations unit for the proper management of fund resources and the financial instrument for the implementation of community policies. The treaty was amended to include the fund as one of the institutions of ECOWAS.

It has been observed that "equitable distribution of cost and benefits and the adoption of a common strategy towards foreign investors are the most important factors for determining the prospects and future cohesion of ECOWAS."[35] It should be asked what type of climate has been created for the distribution of costs and benefits within the group to promote equity and elicit maximum cooperation among members.

The establishment of the Fund for Cooperation, Compensation and Development is an answer to this question. Its primary tasks include funding regional development projects and disbursing compensation to member states that suffer losses as a result of trade liberalization and location of community enterprises.[36] Articles 25 and 26 of the ECOWAS treaty also provide for compensation for loss of revenue from tariff reductions and for safeguard measures where, in pursuit of the objectives of the community, serious disturbances occur in the economy of member states. Article 2 of the Protocol on the Assessment of Loss of Revenue provides, among other things, "compensation to member states which have suffered losses as a result of the location of a community enterprise" and promotes "development projects in the less developed member states of the community." Some member states are dissatisfied with their contribution to the fund, which they claim is unequal since it is assessed on the "basis of a coefficient that takes into account the gross domestic product and per capita income of all member states." It was on the basis of the latter provision that Nigeria in 1977 paid 32.8 percent of total contributions; Côte d'Ivoire and Ghana paid 13 percent and 12.9 percent respectively; Burkina Faso, Guinea-Bissau and Cape Verde, which are among the least developed members, contributed 2.6, 1.5, and 1 percent respectively.[37]

In view of the wide differences in members' contributions, some observers believe that conflicts will arise between beneficiaries of the compensatory scheme and regular contributors, who may not always qualify for compensation. Others contend that in time ECOWAS will be viewed by its various members as an association of perpetual beneficiaries and benefactors. A tendency to cheat by falsifying figures on intracommunity transactions in order to qualify for compensation would become pronounced should member states look for quick rewards rather than take a long-term view of the benefits of cooperation. Also, some member states are unable to contribute regularly to the fund, and the fund may not enjoy the political autonomy necessary for easy disbursement.[38] Such factors could paralyze the community, especially when expected rewards do not materialize and there is unwillingness to make sacrifices.

From a different perspective, however, the compensatory scheme is an important equalizing element in the integrative system. At the initial stages of integration, the more developed member states may appear to bear a heavier burden than the less developed, but in the long run they are likely to gain more from trade liberalization when the community becomes fully operational. Leaders of member states have not lost sight of this fact.

Free Trade and Common External Tariff

In the past, expanded intra-West African trade faced economic, political, institutional, sociocultural and infrastructural problems.[39] The European Community's (EC) link with West African countries, especially the francophone states, fostered unwillingness on the latter's part to cooperate with other countries in the region. They preferred to continue to enjoy their trade preferences with the EC, an association which encouraged dependency on European states for the supply of manufactured goods. Many West African countries that attempted to promote industrialization tried to do so through the imposition of high tariffs, which only increased the price of goods and reduced their competitive ability. The net effect was to discourage intra-West African trade, particularly with nonassociates of the EC. These problems, coupled with the multiplicity of currency systems and exchange rates and the high prices and low quality of products manufactured in the subregion, slowed the growth of trade among West African states.

ECOWAS members started by recognizing that the character of their integrating scheme must be defined by the common external tariff more than the elimination of tariffs and nontariff barriers to regional trade, because it is the common external tariff that determines the protection granted to regional industry (whether or not the integrating scheme is to foster a further stage of import-substituting industrialization) and the character and nature of the new stage of industrial development. Intracommunity trade liberalization was to be accomplished in two stages. The first stage, devoted to organizational issues and provision of the executive secretariat with information about customs duties, was to have been accomplished by 1977. The second stage would have required member states across the following eight years to reduce and ultimately to eliminate import duties in accordance with a schedule drawn up to avoid disruption of the revenues of member states.[40] The requirements of this second stage should have been accomplished by 1985. A common external tariff was to be established by 1990, and duties on imports from third countries were to have been simultaneously eliminated. However, meetings between 1976 and 1979 failed to adopt a trade liberalization scheme and to establish a common external tariff. Announcement of the trade liberalization program had to wait until the authority's summit in May 1980.

The authority distinguished three categories of goods: products manufactured by enterprises accorded community status, products manufactured in a member state already accorded preferential treatment under the CEAO or the Mano River Union, and all other products. Tariffs on the first group were to be eliminated by 28 May 1981. Tariff liberalization on the second group was to start on the same

date for industrially more advanced members (Ghana, Côte
d'Ivoire, Nigeria and Senegal), which were to eliminate all
barriers by 28 May 1985; less industrially developed members
had eight years (up to 28 May 1989) to lift barriers. The
third category, the bulk of the ECOWAS tariff schedule, was
subjected to a more gradual process of intraregional tariff
reduction. Tariffs on this group were to be completely
removed by the industrially more advanced countries over a
period of six years beginning on 28 May 1981; less advanced
members had eight years starting from the same date.[41]
Tariffs on all categories were therefore supposed to be
completely eliminated by 1989. Nontariff regional barriers,
also scheduled for complete elimination by May 1985, were
left to the discretion of member states, raising serious
doubts as to their abolition. In fact, by 1989 the third
category of tariff reductions had not been made, nor had
nontariff barriers been removed.

The ECOWAS treaty provides for the creation of a common
customs tariff in respect of goods imported into member
states from third countries within five years of the end of
the trade liberalization program.[42] On the basis of the
program adopted by the authority, a common external tariff
was originally expected by May 1994. No definite program
has been decided to date, but the treaty does say that the
common external tariff shall be erected "gradually." Since
intracommunity trade liberalization was already well behind
schedule in 1989, the abolition of differences in member
states' external customs tariffs will occur much later than
anticipated.

Differences between individual countries' preferences and
those of other subregional organizations, reflecting the
problems and politics involved, caused the delay in the
community's trade liberalization program. Most member states
derive their revenues from indirect taxes, primarily import
and export duties; and, before the birth of the community,
marked differences existed between these countries in the
importance and structure of tariffs and quantitative
restrictions as sources of government revenue.[43] Regional
tariff harmonization removes the flexibility of national
authorities to raise revenues for national needs and imposes
constraints on their freedom of action. The cautious
movement toward trade liberalization, therefore, represents
a political compromise between those fearing a loss of
national revenues -- which would create domestic economic and
political problems -- and those wanting much quicker
implementation.

ECOWAS provisions for freeing trade are markedly different

from those of several other Third World integrative groupings. The Montevideo Treaty, which created the Latin American Free Trade Association (LAFTA), set a twelve-year transitional period to intraregional free trade, but the target date was repeatedly postponed. Moreover, the treaty made no provision for automatic tariff reductions, which were left to annual negotiations carried out on an item-by-item basis. Although LAFTA's objective was the eventual freeing of all trade, tariff reductions soon slowed and hardly any progress has been made recently. The Central American Common Market (CACM) provides the only example where intraregional trade tariffs were abolished swiftly -- within a set timetable of only five years. In the Andean Common Market (ACM), the approach to free trade is more rapid and automatic than in ECOWAS, but quantitative restrictions on intraregional trade have been retained to a large extent, and the establishment of the common tariff has been postponed. As indicated, in ECOWAS the objections of members of CEAO and the Mano River Union have resulted in the postponement of the decision on the target date for freeing trade.

However, at its 1989 summit in Ouagadougou, the authority adopted a proposal for a pilot scheme of free trade in twenty-six industrial products to take effect in January 1990. This did not begin as planned because in order to qualify, countries had to pay all their outstanding dues to the organization. Given the ailing economies of most West African states, this seems unlikely, although Nigeria is apparently keen to implement the liberalization program. Few private sector participants have been forthcoming, however, and ECOWAS is yet to address squarely the establishment of a common tariff structure.

Free Movement of People

Within the customs area there is, in principle, to be free movement of persons, goods, services and capital. The ECOWAS treaty contains only one provision that touches the individual in the community: citizens of member states are to be regarded as "community citizens." Nonetheless, the elimination of obstacles (visitors' visas, resident permits, etc.) to their freedom of movement, residence, and commercial and industrial activities within the territory of another state is to be carried out by agreements between the governments concerned.[44] No details were given on the matter of free movement of persons in the final communique of the April 1978 Lagos meeting. The authority, however, decided in

principle to adopt a multilateral agreement on the free
movement of persons within the community and directed the
council of ministers to propose a text to be considered at
the next summit.[45]

At the Dakar summit of May 1979 the authority considered
and signed a protocol on the "Free Movement of Persons, Right
of Residence and Establishment," which, in spite of its
title, promised very little in terms of immediate
accomplishments.[46] Visa requirements were removed only in
respect of "community citizens intending to stay for a
maximum of ninety days in another member state." Decision
on the crucial matters of residence and establishment was
postponed, the protocol having stipulated that "a phased
programme for effecting the Right of Residence and
Establishment should be drawn up, taking account of the
effects on member states of the abolition of visas during
the first phase."[47]

Free movement is the only popularly known aspect of
ECOWAS, since few achievements have been made in other
sectors. It generated hostility in several states where the
labor force felt threatened by the specter or the actual
invasion of foreign job competitors. This hostility was
particularly widespread in Ghana and Nigeria, two of the more
developed countries of the community. In time, the former
would rationalize the closure of its border in September 1982
and the latter its expulsion of illegal aliens in 1983 and
1985 as necessary and expedient measures for counteracting
economic and security strains. These strains, they said,
were caused by the influx of community citizens after the
abolition of visas under the ECOWAS protocol.

Since these actions the question of member states'
attitudes toward the community has become more sensitive,
and both the Ghanaian and the Nigerian governments have gone
to great lengths to demonstrate that their actions have not
detracted from their support for ECOWAS. The issue is
important to the organization, which cannot hope to achieve
its objectives without grass-roots support. In May 1982,
Ghana and Nigeria had strongly supported a decision by the
authority to adopt a "public enlightenment" program, using a
periodical and ECOWAS clubs to "disseminate the results of
the different activities of the community as well as progress
made in the implementation of the integration measures taken
by the authority."[48] Since the expulsion orders, Nigeria has
endeavored to explain that it was acting legally and that the
excessive number of illegal immigrants was "one of the remote
causes" of its social problems. President Babangida's three
years as chair of ECOWAS at the end of the 1980s also

attempted to display Nigeria's enthusiasm for the organization. Ghana has considered that "the global economic situation is such that no country will allow large numbers of foreign nationals living illegally on its economy."[49]

There is little evidence, however, that the governments concerned have been successful in convincing expelled community citizens or their compatriots at home of their good intentions. Although the press in many member states gave much attention to the protocol, it was not in force in 1989, a decade after being signed. Moreover, evidence suggests that the press and the wider public supported official actions. Without the backing of the majority of member states, popular support of the protocol remains a distant and elusive goal. In spite of the problems of the first phase of free movement of peoples, the ECOWAS authority at its meeting in mid-1986 at Abuja in Nigeria approved the implementation of the second phase of the protocol.[50] But this has also not been implemented by some member states. Liberia, for instance, takes the position that it could not presently implement the second phase, which gives citizens of ECOWAS the right to reside in member countries and establish businesses, until the Liberianization policy allows Liberians to get priority consideration for employment and business opportunities, among other things.[51] The majority of countries, faced by chronic economic conditions at the beginning of the 1990s, refuse to open their economies to new pressures. However, the protocol's continuing approval within subsequent meetings since 1986 indicates a token of continued commitment to the community.

Sectoral Industrial Development Planning

Apart from compensatory and trade liberalization schemes, ECOWAS is embarking on sectoral programs of industrial development. The treaty emphasizes that the programs are designed to facilitate smoother industrial development, so as to ensure a "uniform industrial climate in order to avoid unhealthy rivalry and waste of resources."[52] In effect, natural resource potentials will be the basis for allocating each member state an industrial project, which should be undertaken either jointly by member states or between ECOWAS and foreign investors.

Sectoral development planning, as Arthur Davies has noted, will not leave any member state lagging behind, since all will eventually have specific industrial projects undertaken by the community. Indeed, in the interests of balanced and

harmonized development, special treatment is to be accorded
the relatively less developed members irrespective of
economic cost in order to prevent wider economic disparities.
Moreover, sectoral planning will promote complementarity in
production rather than wasteful competition, which is
destructive to the developmental goals of the integrative
enterprise.[53]

In the early years of its operations, ECOWAS activities in
the area of industrialization were part of its preparation of
medium-term (five-year) programs for various sectors for
promotion of greater intraregional trade. The sectors
included agriculture, telecommunications, transport and
postal services.[54] Prudently, the community's industrial
program had been restricted to two principal phases: the
gathering of existing and necessary data on the region's
industry and the formation of the legal framework for
regional industrialization. Thus the program first addressed
barriers to a community approach to industrialization,
especially the need to harmonize the role of foreign
investment and other restrictions in each country.[55]

More recently, industrial cooperation activities have been
based on a development program adopted by the community in
November 1986. The program's three objectives are the
consolidation of achievements in the industrial sector and
the strengthening of cooperation between existing industrial
enterprises to lead to the optimal use of investments; the
provision of support from the secretariat to member states to
train senior staff for the industrial sector; and the
eventual harmonization of industrialization plans of member
states to rationalize the establishment of new industrial
enterprises within the subregion.

The participation of the private sector has been
encouraged by the formation of a West African Manufacturers
Association at the instigation of the ECOWAS secretariat.
Greater prospects are now available for market sharing,
coordination of production and, in some cases, the joint
participation of governmental, community and foreign
investors in industrial enterprises. Some specific examples
of such enterprises are a cement factory built in Benin; a
palm oil plant in Ghana; a fruit and vegetable processing
plant in Guinea; a surgical cotton wool factory in Senegal;
and smoked fish industries in Sierra Leone. All these
projects utilize local products with capital coming from the
respective governments, the ECOWAS fund and external
investors. Other projects are being planned, but problems
remain in the widepread development of such schemes.

In time ECOWAS member states will start bargaining toward

the implementation of sectoral industrial development planning. They must draw lessons from the defunct East African Community (EAC), whose regional industrial planning was marred by the unwillingness of its members to transfer aspects of their political sovereignty to regional institutions. They must also strive to develop a community spirit, including a long-term view of the benefits to be derived by staying in the community as against the short-term costs of membership. Integrative incentives are, perhaps, more abundant than in the EAC, but all will depend on willingness to compromise in favor of the less privileged members[56] and on how much "sacrifice of sovereignty" member states are willing to make in order to minimize the strain and tension of *regional* as opposed to *national* development planning.

Defense Pact

The ECOWAS treaty contains no specific provision for cooperation on defense. During its meeting in Lagos in 1978, however, the authority adopted a Protocol on Nonaggression intended to create a "friendly atmosphere, free of any fear of attack or aggression of one state by another" to facilitate cooperation.[57] This protocol was the first purely political decision taken by ECOWAS. As already indicated, the West African region has had its share of Africa's frontier disputes, sometimes involving violent clashes among citizens of neighboring states. There have also been accusations of plots to overthrow governments and problems of internal instability thought to be masterminded by external forces. Moreover, the ECOWAS tribunal, whose establishing provisions do not make its acceptance mandatory on member states, is inadequate as an instrument for ensuring the regional stability called for in the nonaggression pact.

Agreement on nonaggression could generate trust among member countries, but is insufficient insurance against external aggression and externally supported domestic insurrection, which could still constitute threats to the community's stability. At the Dakar summit in 1979, the authority noted with approbation two defense pact proposals submitted at their own initiatives by President Senghor of Senegal and President Eyadéma of Togo, and directed the chair of the council of ministers and the executive secretary to "convene a meeting of a technical commission of ministers composed of Ministers of Foreign Affairs, Defence, Finance, and Economic Affairs as well as Chiefs of Defence Staff to consider the said documents and submit a harmonized draft defence pact to the next meeting of the summit."[58] The group met in May 1980 but failed to reach agreement on a defense pact, owing to strong objections to the proposal from Cape Verde, Guinea-Bissau and Mali.[59] The matter was referred to the authority, which had a scheduled meeting in Lomé a few days later.

During the Lomé meeting, Senghor stressed the importance of the defense pact. Warning that "there is no development without security," he advised that it might be "even normal to leave those countries which do not want to join and let those wishing to do so negotiate a defence pact." Eyadéma declared the need to maintain peace and stability "at all cost" and pointed out the benefits of the defense pact, including the freedom ECOWAS members would enjoy from the absence of "permanent obsession of war and aggression" and the peace of mind that would result from each state's knowing that "it need not fear its neighbour, which is ready to fly to its aid in the event of any aggression."[60] In the end the authority formed an eight nation ministerial committee to produce a final draft of the defense pact, which was signed by all states except Cape Verde, Guinea-Bissau and Mali.[61]

The Protocol on Mutual Assistance and Defense provided that units from the armies of ECOWAS countries will constitute an allied force of the community (AAFC) under a force commander. Ministers of defense and foreign affairs of member states constitute a defense council under the current chair of the authority, and the chief of staff from each state will form a defense commission. A deputy executive secretary for military affairs is appointed whose functions include updating plans for the movement of troops, logistics and initiating joint exercises, preparing and managing the military budget of the secretariat, and studying and making proposals to the executive secretariat in respect of matters relating to the personnel and equipment.[62]

Three categories of hostile military action that ECOWAS will handle are identified under the protocol. The first is aggression from a non-member state. At the request of a member the authority shall meet and decide on the expediency of military action and entrust its execution to the force commander of AAFC within forty-eight hours of a member's request.[63] In such a case of external aggression ECOWAS forces will go to the defense of the member. The second is conflict between two member states. The authority shall meet urgently and take appropriate action for mediation. This action shall primarily be in the form of deploying the AAFC as a peacekeeping force. The third is internal conflict in a member state. When such a conflict is actively maintained and sustained from the outside, the authority will take action as in the case of external aggression, but if the conflict remains purely internal, community forces shall not intervene.[64]

The defense pact has since become operative upon ratification by more than seven states, and the ECOWAS treaty has already been amended to include the defense council as one of the principal institutions of the community and the defense commission as one of the technical and specialized commissions.[65] The pact is an innovation of ECOWAS and has no counterpart in the EAC, the Customs and Economic Union of Central African States (UDEAC), or the integrative groupings of Latin America.

The pact provides no standing army. Rather, the ECOWAS army exists only when needed in emergencies. But troops with different traditions, languages, training and equipment have scant chance of forming an effective fighting force without more continuous training and socialization than are envisaged. There is an added problem: how will ECOWAS handle external aggression against a francophone member state that has formal military ties with France, particularly where France intervenes militarily?[66] Additionally, ECOWAS will have to find the funds to finance a military administration and arm a defense force -- not easy tasks given the poor economic condition of the region. Nonetheless, after more than twenty-five years of unsuccessful advocacy for the establishment of an African high command, an African subregion has made a positive initiative in the direction of a security arrangement.

Opportunities were offered by the Mali-Burkina Faso frontier mini-war of December 1985, the Togo affair of September 1986, and the Senegal-Mauritania violence of mid-1989 for the defense pact to be put on a sound footing. The first was an outgrowth of a twenty-five year old dispute over the mineral rich Agacher border zone. The second was an apparent attempt to overthrow the government of Togo, which the latter felt involved some complicity (which was strongly and flatly denied) by the neighboring states of Ghana and Burkina Faso. And the third was the result of both long-standing frontier disputes and friction caused by the presence of a large number of immigrant citizens of both countries in each other's territory. In all three cases, the opportunities were missed as the conflicts were managed and controlled by governments and institutions outside the ECOWAS defense pact.[67] In fact, in the Togo affair, President Eyadéma requested and received French troops and military hardware under the Franco-Togolese defense agreement, pointing out that the ECOWAS nonaggression pact had "proved a dead letter."[68] Such involvement of a former colonial power presents an obvious challenge to the regionally-based collective security arrangement.

Achievements and Drawbacks

After almost fifteen years of existence one may rightly expect to see very concrete achievements by ECOWAS. What it has attained is, however, modest. But Rome, as the saying goes, was not built in a day. The fact that a motley collection of West African states of different cultures, languages, colonial experiences and resource endowments was able to form a community is itself an achievement. The grouping has become a forum for enhancing understanding among member states, minimizing suspicions, and promoting intergovernmental consultations. Its obvious endeavor is to move from a purely free trade area to the level where it becomes a vehicle for promoting and accelerating economic development policy on physical infrastructural and agricultural development as well as industrialization and monetary cooperation. This is the main reason why apart from agreeing upon a trade liberalization scheme, the community also agreed on agricultural and industrial development policies, established infrastructural transport and telecommunications networks, adopted the energy program to ameliorate energy import problems of member states, and steadfastly searches for a common solution to regional monetary problems.[69] Indeed, these efforts have earned ECOWAS significant international recognition from the United Nations and its specialized agencies and other organizations in both the developed and developing world.[70]

But ECOWAS faces mammoth problems in this new decade of the 1990s. Differences between member states in terms of physical dimensions, population, gross national product and resource endowments cause jealousies and uneasiness. The multiplicity of intergovernmental organizations that exist side by side with ECOWAS divides loyalties and dissipates resources, thereby detracting from the larger grouping.[71] Economic hardship and debts combined with structural adjustment programs in the region all detract from ECOWAS. The differences in the orientations and ideologies of various governments have caused frictions and, coupled with the changes in political leadership in several states, questions have been raised as to whether the high-level political support of the formative years can continue. Additionally, although the desire to reduce external dependence provided the impetus toward integration, there has been no significant change in the low level of trade that characterized West African intraregional interaction in the past. The traditional dependence on former colonial powers has continued. Togo's invitation of French troops in the 1986 crisis mentioned earlier is an indication that the ECOWAS defense pact yet harbors potential sources of intraregional conflict as well as uncertainty as to how world powers will react to future crises in the community. Conflicts have also arisen over the (still partial) implementation of the protocol on free movement of persons.[72] The closure of their borders for a long time by Ghana and Nigeria and the latter's expulsion of illegal aliens had caused much uneasiness. And although the implementation of the second phase of the protocol on right of residence and establishment has been approved by the authority, the conditions attached to it by some member states cast doubt on its implementation.[73]

ECOWAS efforts to advance regional integration are also impeded by nationalism and national rivalries. Aspects of these, many of which date back prior to the formation of the community, have been detailed elsewhere.[74] Nationalism continues to manifest itself in the member states' attitudes toward the implementation of various decisions and protocols. National economic interests and considerations of domestic political support have predisposed governments not to allow considerations of regional cooperation to undermine national goals. Such conflicts as those between Mali and Burkina Faso; Togo, Ghana and Burkina Faso; Senegal and Mauritania; and the December 1989 conflict between Liberia and Côte d'Ivoire over the alleged destabilization of Liberia; these are indicative of the types of problems that have limited the achievements of ECOWAS.

Finally, financial limitations have contributed to the snail's pace at which ECOWAS has progressed. Because of the economic problems of the region, a considerable proportion of ECOWAS objectives cannot be attained without external support from bilateral and multilateral sources. Some financial support has been realized, but there is little chance at present that the necessary foreign investment will steadily flow in for planned projects. Member states have not helped matters either by failing to be up-to-date in the payment of their financial contributions to ECOWAS. Outstanding contributions to the secretariat budget from member states from 1978 to 1984, for example, stood at $9.8 million of which $3.2 million was the arrears for the 1984 budget alone. This meant that only 50 percent of the total 1984 annual budget had been paid up. Similar problems have occurred over the last five years.[75] President Babangida of Nigeria was right when he described the delays by member states in paying their contributions as having "virtually crippled" the operations of the secretariat.[76]

Conclusion

The prospects for ECOWAS in the 1990s remain bright despite its limited achievements to date and the problems the community presently faces. From various standpoints, all sixteen member states have much to gain by creating the conditions that would facilitate effective operation of the community. They are consciously aware that integration will promote their collective development. It should be emphasized that industrial development and intercountry trade, which is its denominator, have hitherto been limited in ECOWAS, so that the contribution of economic integration to economic development has also been naturally limited.[77] Nigeria's presence in the community, contributing on average nearly 70 percent of the subregion's total gross national product, however, offers the prospect of greatly improved opportunities for import substitution and industrial development. The increasing emphasis on industrialization and economic growth by all member states will maximize the potential benefits of integration. The conversion of potential gains into actual gains will, however, require a true commitment on the part of each member state to the effective operation of the established framework for integration.

ECOWAS leaders are aware that disputes over the distribution of economic gains could destroy the organization, much as similar problems wrecked other integrative schemes. This awareness was one reason for ECOWAS's early emphasis on multilateral enterprises as the key to high levels of economic cooperation. The arrangements set out in the treaty, while not attempting to establish how acceptable distribution of industrial development within the community will be made, are initial steps to guard against more developed members benefiting at the expense of the less developed. Through various decisions made since 1979, the community has not only identified priority industrial areas and adopted a legal framework for granting community status to regionally oriented enterprises, but also has begun to undertake studies toward the identification of industrial projects that are to be given regional support.[78]   Such detailed studies of costs in alternative locations prior to industrial allocation will promote ECOWAS integration; failure to undertake background studies prior to the allocation of industries among the East African countries has been identified as one of the reasons for the initial failure of the EAC.[79]

Other signs, too, augur well for the potential success of ECOWAS.   The   common desire to wrest West Africa from external dependence, which initially brought the members together, is still burning.   That regional summits are still attended by high-level delegations from member states attests to the leaderships' acceptance that ECOWAS is of unquestionable benefit.   This has been maintained despite changes in government by democratic processes and coups d'etat in several member states.   Flight-Lieutenant Rawlings of Ghana was able to pay up arrears of millions of dollars in contributions in spite of his country's financial difficulties.   President Houphouët-Boigny of Côte d'Ivoire, one of the founders of CEAO, has acknowledged that the latter organization would one day have to disappear, thus providing encouragement to those who had doubted the "ECOWAS-mindedness" of CEAO members.   Successive Nigerian governments from the Gowon regime to the present have continued to demonstrate strong commitment to ECOWAS, the expulsions of illegal aliens not withstanding.   True to its ambitious drive for continental leadership, and endowed with relatively superior economic power vis-à-vis its subregional neighbors, Nigeria is ever ready to make payments.   Occasionally, it pays up the total yearly rent for the ECOWAS secretariat in Lagos.   Major-General Buhari's military government provided land at Abuja, deep inside Nigeria,   whence the federal capital is being moved, for the construction of permanent headquarters for the community; and its successor, President Babangida's government, provided $5 million toward the total cost of the project, estimated at some $15 million.[80]

The ECOWAS treaty clearly sets out the process of integration and institutionalizes a secretariat of more or less supranational officials to strike a balance on technical issues in the politics of national interest and disruptive bargaining that can impede integration.   Although regional policy-making is theoretically the monopoly of the authority, it has had to share this responsibility with the experts and regional bureaucrats of the secretariat, whose proposals, reports and recommendations on technical issues constitute significant inputs into decision-making.   The secretariat enjoys significant latitude in fund raising for community programs, execution of projects, and expending budgeted funds; it also invites tenders, awards contracts and supervises work in process. All these institution-building developments are the outgrowth of the harmonious political and cooperative atmosphere expressed in the ECOWAS treaty. It can be expected that stronger political will and support, coupled with institutional arrangements and reforms that may be introduced, could combine to generate the subregional cohesion necessary for maximizing ECOWAS economic and political goals in the 1990s.

Notes

1. The original fifteen members are Benin, Burkina Faso (formerly Upper Volta), Côte d'Ivoire, The Gambia, Ghana, Guinea, Guinea-Bissau, Liberia, Mali, Mauritania, Niger, Nigeria, Senegal, Sierra Leone and Togo. Cape Verde, the sixteenth state, joined in 1977.

2. Julius Emeka Okolo, "Integrative and Cooperative Regionalism: The Economic Community of West African States," *International Organization,* 39(1), Winter 1985, pp. 121-153.

3. On earlier efforts at West African economic integration, see Uka Ezenwe, *ECOWAS and the Economic Integration of West Africa* (Ibadan: West Book Publishers, 1984), Chapter 5; Adebayo Adedeji, "Prospects for Regional Economic Cooperation in West Africa," *Journal of Modern African Studies,* 8, July 1970; Nicolas G. Plessz, *Problems and Prospects of Economic Integration in West Africa* (Montreal: McGill University Press, 1968); Peter Robson, *Economic Integration in Africa* (Evanston: Northwestern University Press, 1968), Chapters 3 and 6; Arthur Hazlewood (ed.), *African Integration and Disintegration: Case Studies in Economic and Political Union* (London: Oxford University Press, 1967), especially Chapters 1, 4, and 9; and E.J. Usoro, "Past and Present Attempts at Economic Integration in West Africa" in E.C. Edozien and E. Osagie (eds.), *The Economic Integration of West Africa* (Ibadan: Ibadan University Press, 1982), pp. 38-58.

4. Ralph I. Onwuka, *Development and Integration in West Africa: The Case of the Economic Community of West African States (ECOWAS)* (Ile-Ife: University of Ife Press, 1982), pp. 53-55.

5. *Ibid.*, pp. 55-59.

6. In the present membership of ECOWAS, only Guinea-Bissau and Cape Verde, which were still under colonial rule, were excluded.

7. Louis B. Sohn (ed.), *Basic Documents of African Regional Organization*, volume 3 (Dubbs Ferry, N.Y.: Oceana, 1972), pp. 987-989. Benin, Côte d'Ivoire, Niger and Togo decided not to participate. See also Okolo, "Integrative and Cooperative Regionalism," pp. 124 and 128.

8. Adebayo Adedeji, *The Evolution of a West African Economic Community* (Lagos, undated), p. 8.

9. For a detailed analysis of the origins of ECOWAS and Nigeria's role in its creation, see Olatunde J.B. Ojo, "Nigeria and the Formation of ECOWAS," *International Organization*, 34(4), Autumn 1980, pp. 571-604.

10. *West Africa*, 12 May 1972, p. 605.

11. *West Africa*, 21 July 1972, p. 961.

12. See Table 3 in Okolo, "Integrative and Cooperative Regionalism," p. 127.

13. *Ibid.*, p. 134.

14. *Ibid.*, p. 124. The references are from Ernst B. Haas, "Turbulent Fields and the Theory of Regional Integration," *International Organization,* 30(2), Spring 1976, p. 1986; and Joseph S. Nye, Jr., "Central American Regional Integration," *International Conciliation*, 562, March 1967, pp. 50-57.

15. For a detailed analysis of Gowon's diplomatic maneuvers pursuant to the formation of ECOWAS, see Ojo, "Nigeria and the Formation of ECOWAS," pp. 579-600.

16. *Africa Diary*, 9-15 April 1973, p. 6425.

17. President Felix Houphouët-Boigny of Côte d'Ivoire personally attended the conference in Lagos at which the ECOWAS treaty was signed. This was significant since this was his first visit to Nigeria since the civil war. See *West Africa*, 2 June 1975, p. 644.

18. Similarly, successful negotiations between Liberia and Sierra Leone had led to the creation of the Mano River Union in October 1973, and the Republic of Guinea later joined the union in 1980.

19. Tamar K. Golan, "Nigeria's Shadow in Bamako," *West Africa*, 7 July 1972, p. 867.

20. *Africa Diary*, 8-14 January 1973, p. 6297.

21. Ojo has correctly noted that despite pressures from Gowon, President Diori of Niger not only initiated the CEAO draft treaty but went on to become the first chairman of the organization. It was not until after Diori's overthrow and replacement as head of state by Lt.Col. Seyni Kountché that Niger came out more firmly in support of ECOWAS. Ojo, "Nigeria and the Formation of ECOWAS," pp. 594-595. See also *Africa Diary*, 11-17 June 1973, p. 6505.

22. *West Africa*, 26 May 1975, p. 597.

23. "Five Years of Unity," *West Africa*, 19 May 1975, p. 558.

24. See Henry Fajemirokun, "The Role of the West African Chamber of Commerce in the Formation of ECOWAS," *Supplement: New Nigerian*, (Kaduna), 22 November 1976; Adedeji, *The Evolution of a West African Economic Community*.

25. *Africa Diary*, 3-9 December 1974, p. 7221.

26. ECOWAS, *Development of the Community; The First Five Years 1977-1981* (Lagos, 1981), p. 11.

27. *Treaty of the Economic Community of West African States*, article 2 (hereinafter referred to as the *ECOWAS Treaty*). Summaries of the treaty are found in Colin Legum (ed.), *Africa Contemporary Record 1976-77* (London: Rex Collins, 1977), pp. 196-199; and *West Africa*, 16 June 1975, p. 679 and 23 June 1975, p. 720.

28. These are: the Trade, Customs, Immigration, Monetary and Payments Commission; the Industry, Agriculture and Natural Resources Commission; the Transport, Telecommunications and Energy Commission; and the Social and Cultural Affairs Commission.

29. The two deputies are responsible for the two branches of the secretariat, administrative and economic matters, respectively. The deputy executive secretary for administration supervises four directors charged with the departments of Administration; Finance; Legal Affairs; and Social and Cultural Affairs. The deputy executive secretary for economic matters also supervises four directors who head the departments of Trade, Customs, Immigration, Monetary and Payments; Industry, Agriculture and Natural Resources; Transport, Telecommunications and Energy; and Economic Research and Statistics. ECOWAS, *Development of the Community*, pp. 12-15.

30. *ECOWAS Treaty*, article 8, section 7.

31. *Ibid.*, article 8, section 9.

32. Haas and Schmitter have identified decision-making style among the "process conditions" -- conditions prevailing after an integration agreement has been in force for a few years -- of integration. See Ernst B. Haas and Philippe C.

Schmitter, "Economic and Differential Patterns of Political Integration: Projections About Unity in Latin America" in *International Political Communities: An Anthology* (Garden City: Doubleday Publishing Company, 1966), pp. 268-272.

33. During the Lagos summit (1978), the authority designated Sierra Leone to nominate the external auditors and at the Dakar summit (1979), the appointment of R.A. Dillsworth and Company as the first external auditors was ratified. ECOWAS documents ECW/HSG/I/21, Rev. I and ECW/HSG/.II, 7REV. I.

34. ECOWAS, *Development of the Community*, pp. 12 and 15.

35. Arthur Davies, "Cost-Benefit Analysis within ECOWAS," *The World Today*, 39(5), May 1983, p. 171. See also Onwuka, *Development and Integration in West Africa, p. 75.*

36. *ECOWAS Treaty*, article 52.

37. Davies, "Cost-Benefit Analysis," p. 173.

38. Sam Olofin, "ECOWAS and Lomé Convention: An Experiment in Complementarity or Conflicting Customs Union Arrangements," *Journal of Common Market Studies*, 16, September 1977, p. 65. One conflict that embroiled the fund and the secretariat as regards the former's autonomy was resolved in 1979 with the executive secretary pronounced the head of the administrative structure of ECOWAS and the fund declared "the financial instrument of community policies." See *Official Journal of the Economic Community of West African States (ECOWAS)*, English ed., 1 June 1979, p. 13. See also *West Africa*, 25 February 1980, pp. 351-352.

39. E.C. Edozien and E. Osagie, "Intra-West African Trade in the Last Decade: Problems and Prospects" in Edozien and Osagie, *The Economic Integration of West Africa*, pp. 97-118.

40. *ECOWAS Treaty*, article 14.

41. *Official Journal of ECOWAS*, English ed., 2 June 1980, pp. 5-6. See also ECOWAS, *Development of the Community, 1977-81*, pp. 29-30.

42. *ECOWAS Treaty*, article 14.

43. In 1973, The Gambia reportedly had more than 50 percent of total government revenue originating from customs duties, Benin 49 percent, Burkina Faso 47 percent, Sierra Leone 37 percent, and Côte d'Ivoire 35 percent. See *West Africa*, 24 May 1982, p. 1371.

44. *ECOWAS Treaty*, article 27. For a detailed analysis of the protocol and some of its problems see Julius Emeka Okolo, "Free Movement of Persons in ECOWAS and Nigeria's Expulsion of Illegal Aliens," *The World Today*, 40(10), October 1984, pp. 428-436.

45. ECOWAS Document ECW/HSG/I/21/Rev. I.

46. Full text of the protocol is published in *Official Journal of ECOWAS*, English ed., 1 June 1979, pp. 3-5.

47. ECOWAS Document ECW/HSG/II.7 Rev. I. The first phase, the right to move freely, was at its adoption expected to last five years (i.e., until 1984).

48. *Official Journal of ECOWAS*, English ed., 4 June 1982, p. 56.

49. *West Africa*, 31 January 1983, pp. 243 and 245.

50. "ECOWAS: Phase Two Begins," *West Africa*, 7 July 1986, p. 1412.

51. *Ibid.*, 3 November 1986, p. 2333.

52. *ECOWAS Treaty*, article 32.

53. Davies, "Cost-Benefit Analysis," p. 174. See also P. Robson, *The Economics of International Integration* (London: Allen and Unwin, 1980), p. 116.

54. For details, see ECOWAS, *Development of the Community, 1977-81*, pp. 34-37.

55. Alex Rondos, "ECOWAS after Freetown," *West Africa*, 22 June 1981, pp. 1393-1395.

56. The industrially less developed states, besides the concession allowed in relation to contributions of member states to the ECOWAS budget and under the trade liberalization program, share 20 percent of contributions from more developed countries as compensation for loss of revenue over a period of five years, and they are paid special attention in the allocation of industries.

57. ECOWAS, *Development of the Community, 1977-81*, p. 26.

58. ECOWAS Document ECW/HSG/II.7 Rev. I, and *Official Journal of ECOWAS*, 1 June 1979, p. 13.

59. The Malian representative at the meeting believed that a defense pact would be a step toward the "colonial reconquest" of Africa, and would encourage a split of the continent into blocs dominated by outside powers. See *West Africa*, 9 June 1980, p. 1038.

60. *Ibid.*

61. Commenting on the defense pact, Radio Nigeria stated: "The significance of a defence protocol cannot be overemphasized, particularly at a time when almost every African country is becoming more vulnerable to external aggression. It is a fact that there cannot be any meaningful development without peace and adequate security. In fact both are necessary conditions for the welfare and prosperity of the citizens of any state, country or sub-region. And to the extent that this is the case for member countries of ECOWAS union, such a defence pact will be indispensable." Quoted in *Africa Research Bulletin* (Political), 15 July 1981, p. 6072.

62.   Document A/SP3/5/81, "Protocol relating to Mutual Assistance on Defence" in *Official Journal of ECOWAS*, 3 June 1981, pp. 9-13.

63.   *Ibid.*, articles 6 and 16.

64.   "Protocol relating to Mutual Assistance on Defence," articles 17 and 19.

65.   Document A/SP2/5/81, "Additional Protocol Amending Article 4 of the Treaty of the Economic Community of West African States relating to the Institutions of the Community" in *Official Journal of ECOWAS*, 3 June 1981, pp. 7-8.

66.   France has existing defense or military cooperation agreements with the ECOWAS states of Benin, Burkina Faso, Côte d'Ivoire, Mauritania, Nigeria, Senegal and Togo. See *The Military Balance, 1987-88* (London: International Institute for Strategic Studies, 1987). For a more detailed assessment of the defense pact, see Julius Emeka Okolo, "Securing West Africa: The ECOWAS Defence Pact," *The World Today*, 39, May 1983, pp. 177-184.

67.   See "Mali-Burkina Faso Border Flare-Up," *West Africa*, 6 January 1986, pp. 4-5; and "Togo Coup Attempt," *West Africa*, 6 October 1986, pp. 2084-2086.

68.   "Togo and ECOWAS Security," *West Africa*, 6 October 1986, p. 2083; and "Togo: The Affair Reverberates," *West Africa*, 13 October 1986, pp. 2147-2148.

69.   See, for instance, *Creation of a Single ECOWAS Monetary Zone*, Phase II Report (Lagos: ECOWAS, February 1986).

70.   For details see *Ten Years of ECOWAS, 1975-85* (Lagos: ECOWAS, 1985), especially pp. 81-88.

71.   For example, Niger alone belongs to twenty-five such organizations and institutions; *West Africa*, 30 June 1986, p. 1364.

72.   There has generally been a low rate of compliance with community decisions and many community policies and programs are not implemented. Member states also have a high default rate on ratification of protocols and conventions. This has been attributed not to member states' official policy or lack of desire to seek the necessary ratification, but to either the officials not being responsible enough and showing enough interest, or lack of political will on the part of the political leaders.

73.   On 18 June 1986, for instance, the Nigeria government announced that it had ratified the protocol and would allow citizens of ECOWAS member states to live and work in Nigeria without visas and work permits. But it quickly pointed out that only immigrants in six professional categories would be allowed, namely: doctors and health personnel; architects;

engineers; surveyors; teachers; and bilingual secretaries. Excluded were other professionals such as lawyers, accountants and journalists, as well as unskilled workers. Moreover, the certificates of the professionals in the six approved categories would be verified by government agencies, and such immigrants would be required to find employment within six months of arrival, failing which they would be expelled. See *West Africa*, 30 June 1986, pp. 1363-1364.

74. Okolo, "Integrative and Cooperative Regionalism," pp. 133-136.

75. See *West Africa*, 13-19 March and 20-26 March 1989.

76. *Ibid.*, 7 July 1986, p. 1412.

77. For details, see *Economic Profile Series no. 2: ECOWAS -- Industrial Sector -- External Trade and Balance of Payments* (Lagos: ECOWAS, 1982).

78. For details, see documents A/DEC.3/4/83 and A/DEC.4/5/83, "Decision Relating to Development Cooperation Policy" in *Official Journal of ECOWAS*, 5 June 1983, pp. 4-6.

79. Robson, *Economic Integration in Africa*, p. 233.

80. *West Africa*, 7 July 1986, p. 1412.

3

Francophone Regional Organizations and ECOWAS

Daniel C. Bach

Francophone regional organizations are among the oldest and most deeply rooted in sub-Saharan Africa. While regional links that existed during the colonial period between British colonies were severed before or soon after independence, in the case of the former French colonies, agreements signed with France at independence supported the continuation of numerous cooperation and integration arrangements: Air Afrique; the Union Africaine et Malgache des Postes et Télécommunications (UAMPT); the Union Monétaire de l'Ouest Africain (UMOA); the Union Douanière des Etats de l'Afrique de l'Ouest (UDEAO); the Banque Centrale des Etats de l'Afrique de l'Ouest (BCEAO).[1]

Until the signing of the first Lomé convention in 1975, gaullian policies, and also the association to the European Community (EC) of the former French and Belgian territories in Africa, encouraged contacts and the incorporation of the latter into francophone cooperation organizations. There is, however, little doubt that throughout these years francophone regionalism tended to remain a vector for close and exclusive links with France and, as a result of this, retained a high political profile. In the early 1970s, tensions developed as most francophone states demanded a renegotiation of their agreements with France. After Valéry Giscard d'Estaing's election in 1974, this was successfully completed and Franco-African relations gained a new impetus as a result of a broadening of the Franco-African summits and moves to improve trade relations with anglophone Africa.

In West Africa, francophone groupings, including the most recently established, the Communauté des Etats de l'Afrique de l'Ouest (CEAO), have contributed to the preservation of French influence in the subregion as much as to closer ties between the francophone countries themselves. Until the decision to institutionalize *francophonie* summits in 1986, francophone regionalism often constituted little more than a multilateral extension of bilateral links maintained with France.

In the following pages, we will first unravel the various layers of francophone regionalism in West Africa and assess their present-day significance. We will then proceed to discuss their effects on the adoption and implementation of the ECOWAS treaty. The chapter concludes by arguing that the difficulties encountered by both ECOWAS and CEAO basically result from the very fabric of the treaties and the inadequacy of the conceptions of economic cooperation which they aim to promote. Francophone regionalism cannot be held responsible for the disappointing achievements of the Economic Community of West African States (ECOWAS).

The Layers of Francophone Regionalism

The Conseil de l'Entente, founded in 1959, is the oldest existing francophone organization in West Africa. Besides Côte d'Ivoire, it includes Burkina Faso, Niger, Benin and, since 1966, Togo. The Council was initiated by President Houphouët-Boigny of Côte d'Ivoire to undermine the establishment of the Mali Federation. The Conseil de l'Entente soon formed the core of the Brazzaville group (1960), institutionalized as the Union Africaine et Malgache (UAM) in 1961 and superseded in 1965 by the Organisation Commune Africaine et Mauricienne (OCAM), designed as a *machine de guerre* against Nkrumah's and Nasser's radical Pan-Africanism. Seriously undermined by internal dissensions, OCAM did not survive the successive departures of Zaire, Congo, Cameroon, Chad, Madagascar and Gabon in the early 1970s. In 1978, the organization was transformed into a purely economic body, but this belated move did not succeed, and dissolution was formally pronounced in 1985. The only significant affiliated technical body which remains in operation is Air Afrique, currently undergoing severe financial difficulties.[2]

Until the early 1970s, the Conseil de l'Entente was a major instrument in the conduct of the regional diplomacy of Côte d'Ivoire as it helped to control its immediate environment. The council was viewed by Houphouët-Boigny as a tool in the implementation of his strategy of isolation of rival influence poles such as Ghana, Guinea, Nigeria and even Senegal.[3]

Within the Conseil de l'Entente, a Fonds de Solidarité was

initially introduced (1959-1963) to increase the political cohesion of the council to which Benin and Burkina Faso had only reluctantly agreed to belong. The solidarity fund operated a limited redistribution of the coastal states' customs and excise revenues, taking into account the respective wealth of member states. The system amounted in effect to an Ivorian subsidy to the budgets of other states. Despite pressure from the poorer states of the Conseil de l'Entente, Côte d'Ivoire resisted any development of economic cooperation throughout the 1960s. This was not surprising: in the mid-1950s Houphouët-Boigny had effectively lobbied for the dismantlement of the French West Africa Federation and he still considered that pursuing an independent economic policy was in the interest of richer Côte d'Ivoire.

An exception of significant importance resulted from Côte d'Ivoire's extensive appeal to labor from Burkina Faso.[4] In the course of a visit to Burkina Faso in December 1964, the president of Côte d'Ivoire suggested the creation of a *double nationalité* (common nationality) for the citizens of the two countries. The project would involve reciprocal rights which included access to land-ownership and employment (even in the civil service). The immediate advantage to be derived by Côte d'Ivoire from this consolidation of its informal links with Burkina Faso was the assurance of continued access to vital Burkinabe labor. After subsequent requests were made by Benin and Niger to participate, the convention on common nationality was signed on 30 December 1965 by all the members of the Conseil de l'Entente. Characteristically, hostility came from Côte d'Ivoire's single party, where it was feared that strong competition could arise for positions in the civil service. Opposition was so strong on this issue that a few weeks later Houphouët-Boigny publicly announced that the project would not be implemented. Thus came to an end the conseil's only attempt at promoting mechanisms of closer economic integration between member states.

Côte d'Ivoire's subsequent support to Biafra during the Nigerian civil war (1967-70) and, in 1971, its commitment to "dialogue" with South Africa severely damaged the political cohesion of the Conseil de l'Entente. Nonetheless, the conseil survived, thanks to its transformation into a loose, functionally based association henceforth of minor political significance. Council meetings are still held but tend to be at longer intervals, and relations between members remain confined to technical issues such as the activities of the Fonds d'Entraide et de Garantie des Emprunts. In existence since 1966, the fund is designed to promote economic cooperation within the council by stimulating the inflow of foreign private and public capital toward poorer members. Accordingly, financial guarantees and loans for special investment projects are provided, mostly by Côte d'Ivoire and western aid donors.

If the Conseil de l'Entente is the oldest existing francophone regional organization, the Union Monétaire de l'Ouest Africain (UMOA) is undoubtedly the most significant of all, as it provides the financial backbone to francophone regionalism. Indeed, UMOA includes all francophone West African states except Guinea and Mauritania. Since 1985, Equatorial Guinea has also been a member of the franc zone (through the Central African Monetary Union). To its members, the union provides free convertibility between the CFA franc and the French franc (1 French Franc = CFA 0.02) to which the former is pegged. Since 1973, UMOA's regional bank, the Banque Centrale des Etats de l'Afrique de l'Ouest (BCEAO), has been based in Dakar and the heads of states conference has become the highest authority in the union. The reform introduced wider autonomy of the UMOA vis-à-vis France, and compensation mechanisms when the French franc was devalued. For UMOA member states, relying on a regional central bank has meant that they could not compel the BCEAO to fund activities that they deemed essential to their development. The counterpart of the monetary orthodoxy imposed on the members of the union was the guarantee of the French treasury. As a result of being a convertible currency, the CFA was not undermined by black-market exchange rates.

Since 1980, new pressure on the BCEAO and the franc zone in general has arisen due to the deficit of the West African bank's current account. Until 1986, the problem was alleviated by the compensation offered by the Banque des Etats d'Afrique Centrale. Since then, the current account of the two monetary zones has shown a deficit, which in 1987 and 1988 represented for the French treasury a cost equivalent to 15.2 percent and 11.5 percent respectively of France's total public development aid for these years. Despite pressure from the International Monetary Fund for a devaluation of the CFA, such an alternative has so far been constantly rejected with equal unanimity by French and francophone monetary authorities. A devaluation would undoubtedly have serious social and political spill-over effects in the poorer member states of the monetary union.

Without the common financial basis provided by the UMOA, the establishment of the Communauté Economique de l'Afrique de l'Ouest (CEAO) (Côte d'Ivoire, Senegal, Mali, Niger, Burkina Faso, Mauritania and, since 1984, Benin) and its early spectacular progress would have been made considerably more difficult. The signing of the Abidjan treaty in April 1973 was a follow-up to three years of protracted negotiations over the transformation of the Union Douanière des Etats de l'Afrique de l'Ouest (UDEAO). UDEAO was initially established in 1959 as a tool for redistributing within the UMOA the customs duties collected by the coastal states on transit trade with their landlocked neighbors. The system never worked properly and was virtually abandoned when it came for renewal in 1970. Its reconstruction was ruled out from the outset by the landlocked members, which demanded that customs duties levied by the coastal states be effectively counterbalanced by redistribution mechanisms.

Following protracted discussions, concessions in this direction were agreed upon by Côte d'Ivoire and Senegal who could see the need to counterbalance Nigeria's potential economic influence in West Africa.[5] For this very reason, the CEAO treaty received open French support. Côte d'Ivoire and Senegal expected the CEAO to provide their industries with an opportunity to adapt, as a first stage, to a market of thirty-five million inhabitants. Industrial ventures established in the two countries were expected to realize within the community the economies of scale necessary for competing with Nigerian manufactured products within the West African region.

The CEAO treaty certainly presented the most elaborate prospects for francophone economic cooperation in West Africa since the short-lived Mali Federation (1959-60). A major difference, however, was that while the Mali Federation reflected a fundamental split within West Africa (Senegal versus Côte d'Ivoire), CEAO did not. CEAO was expected to evolve within thirteen years towards a customs union within which free trade would be counterbalanced by precise redistribution mechanisms meant to contribute to a reduction of inequalities between member states. The implementation of the treaty began early in 1976, and within two years its projected mechanisms were effectively in operation.

The Taxe de Coopération Régionale (TCR) was introduced to collect duties which previously were levied by individual states on manufactured imports from the members of the community. TCR agreements were negotiated on a product-by-product basis which conferred to the system a greater flexibility than ECOWAS's stage-by-stage approach. Agreed product status meant a simplification of customs formalities and a reduction of prices. In order to favor the poorer nations, different tax rates also applied to similar goods when they were produced by more than one country within the community. The establishment of the TCR system was to be a first step toward the total abolition of internal customs barriers and the adoption of a common external tariff by 1986. By 1980, 400 industrial items, mostly originating from Côte d'Ivoire and Senegal, were registered under TCR agreements. Transactions on these agreed products (*produits agrées*) remained, however, of modest importance: for 1981, they represented 28 percent of total intracommunity trade (1.92 billion FF) which amounted to 7.5 percent of the total of CEAO imports from nonmember countries.[6]

The revenues of the Fonds Communautaire de Développement (FCD) originated from the TCR. Two-thirds of them were redistributed as compensation for the losses of revenue incurred by poorer states as a result of trade liberalization.[7] For the remaining third, FCD funds were allocated to development projects within the community. These funds were considered insufficient by the landlocked countries, which still argued that Côte d'Ivoire and Senegal benefited most from the TCR system. For this reason, in 1977 CEAO heads of states had decided to fund a new structure, the Fonds de Solidarité et d'Intervention pour le Développement de la Communauté (FOSIDEC). FOSIDEC resembled very much ECOWAS's FCCD. It received in 1978 an initial endowment of 100 million FF essentially provided by Côte d'Ivoire (50 percent) and Senegal (30 percent), which both undertook to forego any right to draw on the fund during the first years of its existence. With the increased leverage that resulted from the inflow of substantial international aid, FOSIDEC began to encourage, through direct financial support or loan-backing, the establishment of regional projects designed to promote self-sufficiency in the fields of agriculture, rural hydraulics, transport and energy.[8]

Until 1980, CEAO progressed at a relatively satisfactory pace. In 1978, heads of state adopted a policy of freedom of movement and establishment of residence without limitation for nationals from the member states (compensation was even to be paid in the case of expulsions). A single nomenclature for statistical and customs purposes, adopted in 1976, contributed to a rapid increase in intracommunity trade. By 1980, 400 agreed industrial products were subjected to the TCR. Products from fishery, agriculture and forestry were entitled to free circulation. Five years later, however, the pace of registration under TCR agreements had come close to a halt. Only 428 products were registered. The asymmetrical nature of trade patterns within the community had not in any way been reduced. Senegal and Côte d'Ivoire still accounted for the bulk of the industrial products exchanged.

The limited complementarity between the CEAO economies has remained ever since a source of tensions which hamper progress in the direction of trade liberalization. Community spirit also suffered from the recession that followed the second oil boom: in 1980, Côte d'Ivoire and Senegal demanded a postponement of their contributions to the FCD (to which they owed a total of 100 million FF). This was a serious issue since trade liberalization within CEAO had developed only insofar as it related to mechanisms of compensation beneficial to poorer member states. The system itself began to face further difficulties and in February 1984, a substantial increase of existing TCR rates was favored by most member states. The following council of ministers meeting, however, decided to freeze any decision on the issue, aware that implementing such proposals would adversely affect the volume of intracommunity trade, subsequently FCD resources, and eventually the very fabric of the community. Since then, protectionist national policies have from time to time suddenly and unilaterally been applied (to non-industrial products) by landlocked members. Another problem has been whenever complementarity has existed between industrial productions within the community, cheaper or better quality supplies from nonmember states are often preferred.

In all respects, these difficulties of CEAO emphasized the limited potential of market integration between the West African economies concerned. Adding to this, CEAO activities suffered an unwanted psychological and financial setback as a result of the misappropriation of an estimated sum of 120 million FF, drawn by community officials from the FOSIDEC resources.[9]

Francophone Regionalism versus ECOWAS?

Is francophone regionalism an obstacle to the progress of West Africa's only fully subregional grouping, ECOWAS? My answer will be a qualified no.

When the charter of Abidjan was signed in April 1973, ECOWAS did not exist, but there was little ambiguity over the intention of countering the rival Togo-Nigerian sponsored initiative. The politics of the project were bluntly denounced by Benin, which argued that "since Ghana and Nigeria do not belong to the CEAO, Dahomey's membership of this organization would not have meant very much...[we] could not become a member of a Community from which Nigeria would be absent."[10]

Another important aspect of CEAO-ECOWAS relations relates to two preconditions that had to be met before the member states of CEAO agreed to participate in ECOWAS. The first concerned future relations with the European Community (EC). All the francophone West African states but Guinea belonged to the Etats Africains et Malgache Associés (EAMA) which, under the Yaoundé convention, received preferential treatment for their exports to EC countries as well as technical and financial support from the European Development Fund. In February 1975, the signing of the Lomé convention by the Commonwealth "associable" states, Guinea and the former EAMA, lifted a stumbling-block from the path of ECOWAS in that it unified the basis on which all independent West African states would pursue trade relations with EC countries. The successful completion of the negotiations and the signing of the Lomé convention in February 1975 were decisive for the establishment of ECOWAS. For the francophone states, the ECOWAS charter could no longer represent a potential threat to their access to the markets of Western Europe.[11]

The other precondition to signing the Lagos ECOWAS charter concerned its acknowledgment of the validity of agreements resulting from pre-existing groupings. Article 20(1) of the charter stated that "...in no case shall tariff concessions granted to a third country under an agreement with a Member State be more favourable than those applicable under this Treaty." The strength of this point was, however, considerably weakened by article 59(2) according to which: "The rights and obligations arising from agreements concluded [by member states] before the definitive entry into force of this Treaty...shall not be affected by the provisions of this Treaty."[12] This was of prime importance to the CEAO since its treaty was largely built along the same lines as the ECOWAS charter. In both cases, the elimination of customs duties between member states, the creation of a free-trade zone and the establishment of a common external tariff were to be achieved over relatively short periods (respectively thirteen and fifteen years). Differences lay in CEAO's more pragmatic product-by-product approach to trade liberalization and the inclusion in the CEAO treaty of specific provisions to meet the landlocked states' demands for compensation to their losses of customs revenues.

Partly for these reasons and partly because of the unifying monetary factor, regional cooperation within CEAO developed at a brisk pace until the early 1980s, which strongly contrasted with the much slower implementation of the ECOWAS charter. Throughout this period "the striking feature of the relationship between the two organisations was

CEAO's unexpressed aim of developing co-operation more quickly than ECOWAS so as to present a unified stance on the important issues to be tabled for discussion at summits of the larger Community."[13]

There were signs that CEAO-ECOWAS relations might improve when, in October 1980, Léopold Senghor, then president of CEAO, publicly advocated consultation between the secretariats of CEAO and ECOWAS. Indeed, concerted action successfully developed between the two organizations on various projects. In May 1983, however, the communique issued after the Conakry ECOWAS heads of states summit publicly held CEAO states responsible for the non-implementation of commonly agreed policies and invited them to take steps towards the harmonization of their customs tariffs with those of other ECOWAS members. The response came from Niamey where, a few months later, CEAO heads of states stated their concern for "preserving their francophone specificity."[14] Since then, the assumption that CEAO regionalism constitutes an impediment to ECOWAS has remained a convenient and popular explanation.

Limits to Regional Cooperation

Yet, ECOWAS's recent history clearly shows that it would be all too easy to hold CEAO countries solely responsible for the disappointing achievements recorded by ECOWAS during its first fifteen years of activity.

Since Oliver Knowles in Chapter 7 discusses these issues, I will briefly mention problems that arise from the absence of autonomy in secretariat decision-making (all issues having to be referred to the annual conference of the heads of states and government); poor language communication (very few functionaries are effectively bilingual, and there is a constant need to call on costly external translation services); bureaucratic hurdles (such as the long conflict between the administrative secretary and the director of the FCCD); a costly location in Lagos (in the late 1970s, two-thirds of the secretariat's budget was absorbed by accommodation costs). Besides these, as the "spirit of Lagos" rapidly dwindled after Gowon's eviction from power in 1975, member states (with the notable exceptions of Côte d'Ivoire and Nigeria) became increasingly erratic in the payment of their dues: as early as September 1978, the secretariat complained that it had only received one-third of member states' contributions. Since then, the situation has worsened considerably.

At another level, one cannot but notice the lack of implementation of decisions, despite the tight and ambitious schedule adopted. Here, as on financial issues, anglophone countries have not shown any greater community spirit than the francophone countries. When, in May 1983, ECOWAS heads of state and government met in Conakry, no member state had ratified the 1979 protocol on trade in unprocessed goods, handicrafts and industrial products. So far, besides a defense treaty which has little bearing on the economic objectives of the community, the only ECOWAS protocol of significance which is in operation is that on the free circulation of persons. It was adopted in 1979 as a first step (cancellation of visa requirements for a period under ninety days) towards the creation of a unified labor market. The adoption of the second phase of the protocol ran into difficulties when Nigeria suddenly expelled illegal (mostly West African) aliens in 1983 and again in 1985. The ECOWAS heads-of-states' summit then postponed for another year the implementation of the second phase of the protocol, which was eventually signed at the 1986 Abuja summit. A year later, when this author visited the Lagos secretariat, Senegal was the only country that had bothered ratifying it. With respect to technical work relating to the establishment of trade nomenclatures, work was far more advanced in francophone countries than in the anglophone member states of ECOWAS.

Fundamental difficulties are encountered by ECOWAS in relation to French-speaking countries and francophone groupings due to the inconvertibility of most non-francophone currencies in West Africa (the Liberian dollar is the exception). One cannot foresee how francophone countries could, in the current international economic situation, terminate their membership in UMOA and become members of a West African currency union offering convertibility to its members. However, were this possible, several francophone states would not wish to follow suit as they derive substantial advantage from the very coexistence of different monetary zones and customs duties.

Until the early 1980s, very substantial flows of unrecorded trade developed between Nigeria, Ghana and their francophone neighbors. Exchanges did not only develop to the benefit of the populations living across the frontiers but also to that of countries like Benin, Togo and, to a lesser extent, Niger. Consequently, one could appropriately refer to them as frontier states, as they derived more revenue from trade across their borders than from their own economic resource activity.

In Benin, re-exports to Nigeria of tobacco, textile products and alcohol represented between 35 percent and 80 percent of the turnover of commercial companies and individual traders according to various estimates.[15] When re-export trade suddenly decreased after 1983, a contraction of Beninois budget revenues followed and, for the first time since 1972, a French subsidy had to be requested to cover recurrent expenditure. Last but not least, if ECOWAS free-trade policy did reach the stage of implementation, it would be unthinkable to raise for discussion the issue of payment of compensation funds to the budgets of countries like Benin and Togo since "unrecorded" trade and financial (black-market) flows are officially deemed to be marginal and uncontrolled.

The experience of the CEAO and its difficulties make it possible to take the analysis one step further. Unlike ECOWAS, CEAO is supported by a common currency basis and a more pragmatic (product-by-product) approach to trade liberalization, which involves payment of compensation to the least developed member states. In spite of this, CEAO has encountered difficulties and appears to be in a stalemate since the early 1980s due to the limited complementarity between richer coastal and poorer landlocked member states. Customs revenues represent a decisive source of income for the budgets of countries like Benin, Niger, Burkina Faso or Mali. As a result of this, compensation paid for the implementation of a common external tariff policy must constitute a significant source of income, the burden of which coastal states have become more and more reluctant to bear. The relative stagnation of CEAO intracommunity trade gives an idea of the difficulties which ECOWAS would meet were it able to push further the implementation of its treaty. What is at stake is the very fabric of the treaties and their inadequate view of the limited complementarity between the West African economies of richer Côte d'Ivoire or Nigeria and the least developed states, which account for the majority of members of each of the organizations.

Conclusion

Like the Conseil de l' Entente, the CEAO and, to a lesser extent, ECOWAS have, with fair success, funnelled foreign aid and investment towards regional projects relating to technical training, transnational infrastructures, communications and industry. This is perhaps the only area where regional economic cooperation can be considered a success. If this is to become the rationale for their continuation, one should ask why costly bureaucracies and their various ramifications are needed in view of the experience of such other organizations as the Southern African Development Coordination Conference (SADCC), which does not share the ambitions of ECOWAS and operates on a lower cost basis through a sectoral allocation of responsibilities between the various member states: Zimbabwe is in charge of coordination in the field of agriculture, Angola deals with energy, Mozambique with transport, etc. In Gaberone, the SADCC secretariat operates with a senior staff of half a dozen, as opposed to more than 100 for the Lagos ECOWAS secretariat.

In the West African case, regional economic cooperation organizations have often had more to do with subregional politics than economics. How else can one understand that Togo and Benin were among the strongest supporters of ECOWAS in the 1970s while having no interest in its implementation owing to the income they derived from the smuggling of currency and commercial goods? The time has clearly come for a reappraisal of the operations of the two organizations and the best means for them to encourage truly regional projects.

Notes

1. For a comprehensive list of the various organizations, see F. Wodie, *Les institutions internationales régionales en Afrique occidentale et centrale* (Paris: LGDJ, 1970). For a discussion of francophone Africa in general, see Patrick Manning, *Francophone Sub-Saharan Africa, 1880-1985* (Cambridge: Cambridge University Press, 1988).

2. Zaire's decision to withdraw (1972) was followed by Cameroon, Chad, Congo and Madagascar in 1973. OCAM only survived by laying increasing emphasis on economic cooperation between its members, a trend explicitly endorsed by the 1974 heads-of-states' summit in Bangui. See R.A. Fredland, "OCAM: One Scene in the Drama of West African Development" in Domenico Mazzeo (ed.), *African Regional*

Organisations (Cambridge: Cambridge University Press, 1984), pp. 103-130.

3. Daniel C. Bach, "L'insertion de la Côte d'Ivoire dans les rapports internationaux" in Y.-A. Faure and J.-F. Medard (eds.), *Etat et Bourgeoisie en Côte d'Ivoire* (Paris: Karthala, 1982), pp. 89-124.

4. By 1965, Côte d'Ivoire employed about 300,000 Mossi from Burkina Faso on a regular basis and several thousand more for seasonal work on the plantations.

5. Detailed analysis in Daniel C. Bach, "The Politics of West African Economic Co-operation: CEAO and ECOWAS," *Journal of Modern African Studies*, 21(4), 1983, pp. 605-623.

6. CEAO, *Rapport Annuel 1983-84*, Ouagadougou.

7. In 1977, Côte d'Ivoire contributed 61.5 percent of the FCD's total income and received in return 26.6 percent of compensation, while Senegal paid 33.1 percent and received 8.3 percent. On the other hand, Burkina Faso, Mali, Niger and Mauritania paid in 3.5 percent, 1.3 percent, 0.5 percent and 0.1 percent respectively, but received compensation up to ten times higher.

8. For a list of projects see *Bulletin d'Afrique Noire* (Paris), 12 November 1980, pp. 20528-20529. See also CEAO, *Rapport Annuel 1983-84*, Ouagadougou.

9. *Jeune Afrique*, 25 November 1984, pp. 36-40. The funds had not been recovered when in 1986 three former officials of the community were sentenced to fifteen years imprisonment.

10. Michel Alladaye, Benin's minister of foreign affairs, in *Daho-Express*, 19 April 1973.

11. Unlike the Yaoundé agreements, the Lomé convention earmarked specific funds to encourage ACP regional projects. Daniel C. Bach, "La Coopération régionale dans les Conventions de Lomé," *Revue du Marché Commun*, 296, April 1986, pp. 236-239.

12. "Treaty of the Economic Community of West African States" in *Nigeria: Bulletin on Foreign Affairs* (Lagos), 5(1-2), 1975, p. 119 ff.

13. Daniel C. Bach, "The Politics of West African Economic Co-operation," p. 617.

14. *Le Monde*, 2 November 1983.

15. See John Igue, "Le Nigeria et ses périphéries frontalières" in Daniel C. Bach, J. Egg and J. Phillippe (eds.), *Nigeria: un pouvoir en puissance* (Paris: Karthala, 1988), pp. 219-239.

4

Obstacles to Intraunion Trade in the Mano River Union

Amadu Sesay

The world oil crisis of the 1970s had an unprecedented adverse effect on the world economy in general, and African economies in particular. Although the continent of Africa was never the main target of the oil embargo, it nonetheless was the most hard hit by the crisis due to its overdependence on western countries, the main target of the boycott by the Arabs, for their crude as well as refined oil needs. That crisis, more than anything else, impressed upon African leaders the urgent need to pool their resources at the subregional and continental levels to achieve economic self-sufficiency.

Although Liberia and Sierra Leone had been toying for many years with the idea of an economic union between them, the oil crisis seemed to give that desire added momentum. Thus, on 3 October 1973, the former presidents of Sierra Leone and Liberia, Siaka Stevens and William Tolbert respectively, met at the border town of Malema to sign the Mano River Declaration which ushered in the Mano River Union.[1] The goals of the union (of which Guinea became a member in 1980) were spelt out in the declaration as follows:

> (i) To expand trade among the members through the elimination of all barriers to mutual trade, and through cooperation in the expansion of mutual productive capacity, including the progressive development of a common protective tariff,
> (ii) To secure a fair distribution of the economic benefits of cooperation among the members and finally,
> (iii) To establish a customs union.

The creation of the customs union was to be carried out in two main stages. Under phase one, from 1973 to 1977, it was expected that the members would harmonize their customs nomenclature, harmonize customs law, customs regulations, and their external tariffs. The second phase was to start in 1978 during which intraunion trade would be introduced between the members thus formally creating the customs union. It was, however, difficult to keep to the official timetable. For instance, the first phase did not end until 1978, a year behind schedule. However, by 1979 when the second phase was in progress, the members had made so much headway with the harmonization of their marketing policies that they felt confident enough to set a date for the introduction of intraunion trade, 1 July 1980. But again, it was not possible to adhere to the timetable because of the unexpected and violent death of Tolbert in April 1980, in the aftermath of the bloody coup of the then Master Sergeant Samuel Doe.

The Benefits Expected from Intraunion Trade

Intraunion trade was expected to bring a number of benefits to the partner states: (a) accelerate the development of trade by dismantling all obstacles to free trade within the union, (b) provide goods of local origin with a much bigger and protected market, (c) induce industrialization in the partner states and (d) stimulate economic growth. To achieve these objectives, the union secretariat, located in Freetown, undertook a number of measures including: (i) the introduction of a payments mechanism to facilitate speedy settlement of intraunion trade transactions and (ii) the introduction of guidelines and regulations governing the administration of trade in "goods of local origin."[2] A detailed examination of these measures is outside the scope of this chapter. Suffice it to say here that it was principally designed to increase the volume of trade between the members of the union and so reduce their external dependence. However, since 1981 when intraunion trade was formally encouraged, not much trade has taken place between the two countries, or the third member, Guinea. Indeed, intraunion trade has been bedeviled by numerous problems, many of which are of a nontariff nature.

The major objective of this chapter is two-fold. First, to examine some of the obstacles to intraunion trade in the MRU free trade regime, and second, to suggest ways and means of minimizing those obstacles in the future. The organization of the rest of the chapter reflects this twin-objective. The first section identifies and discusses the obstacles to intraunion trade while the conclusion offers suggestions which, if implemented, would improve intraunion trade among the partner states in the 1990s.

Obstacles to Intraunion Trade

It is noteworthy that most of the obstacles to the free flow of intraunion trade in the MRU are of a nontariff nature. We can identify at least seven barriers to intraunion trade. These are: (a) the nature of the economies of the member states, (b) the nature of their political systems, (c) the presence of multiple national currencies within the union, most of which are not readily convertible, (d) the commercial banking systems, (e) the absence of adequate transport and telecommunications facilities and infrastructure, (f) the numerous security and nonsecurity roadblocks and checkpoints along their interstate roads, and finally, (g) administrative procedures and/or bottlenecks. Each of these obstacles will be examined in detail.

The Economies of the Member States

Guinea, Liberia and Sierra Leone are small states even by African standards. Their combined land area is approximately 429,000 sq. kms. More significantly, Sierra Leone and Liberia are respectively the fifth and sixth smallest countries on the African continent. In addition, the total union population is also small, 12.6 million. Out of this total, Guinea, which was slow to participate fully in intraunion trade, accounts for approximately half, 6.5 million. The three states have been characterized by the Economic Community of West African States (ECOWAS) of which they are members, as "less developed." Indeed, Guinea and Sierra Leone are among countries designated by the United Nations as the "least developed" in the world. Although Liberia was classified in the 1970s as a "middle income" country, it successfully applied to the United Nations in 1982 to be reclassified as a "least developed" country because of its acute economic problems.[3]

Guinea, Liberia and Sierra Leone, then, are all underdeveloped, both economically and technologically. They are overwhelmingly agrarian societies. This is reflected in their gross national products per capita: $300, $450 and $320 respectively for Sierra Leone, Liberia and Guinea.[4] All three countries were also heavily indebted to external creditors in the West by the late-1980s; Guinea $1.78 billion, Sierra Leone $660 million and Liberia $1.62 billion.[5] Besides that, all the partner states are heavily dependent on exports of minerals and agricultural resources to the developed countries in the North for foreign exchange to pay for their imports from the same sources. Their major foreign exchange earners are: Liberia -- iron ore, timber and rubber; Sierra Leone -- diamonds, gold, bauxite, coffee and iron ore; and Guinea -- iron ore, bauxite and pineapples. The economies of the MRU states are thus competitive, rather than complementary. Consequently, the propensity for trade among them is very low indeed. They literally have no need for each other's major exports.

This situation has served to reinforce trading links with their erstwhile colonial masters at the expense of intraunion trade. For instance, there is no effective domestic demand for Sierra Leone's major export, diamonds, in Liberia. They have to be exported to Europe, America and Israel where they are processed and then re-exported back to the union in the form of jewelry. It should be stressed that all three countries send almost all their exports to the West: 94 percent in the case of Liberia, while only 5 percent represents trade with other developing countries; 66 percent of Sierra Leone's trade is with the West, while 34 percent is with other developing nations. Finally, Guinea has 89 percent of its export trade with the West, and only 11 percent with other countries.

Since the early 1970s, the world price of the major exports of the partner states has been falling relative to the prices of their imports. Although this is a common phenomenon among most Third World countries, it has nonetheless led to very acute balance of payments problems as well as severe shortages of foreign exchange in the union, but perhaps more so in Guinea and Sierra Leone for reasons we shall examine later. What is important for now is that their bid to conserve their paltry foreign exchange earnings led directly and indirectly to a strangulation of intraunion trade.

The Political Systems

Another important nontariff barrier to intraunion trade relates to the different political systems in the member states. Guinea before the coup of 1984 operated a socialist system, Sierra Leone practices a one party system, while Liberia is under a civilianized military regime. All three regimes are, however, autocratic. The diverse political systems, at least up to the untimely death of President Sékou Touré, were also reflected in the national economies of the members; Guinea operated a centrally planned economy, whereas Liberia and Sierra Leone have mixed capitalist economies. The effect of all this on intraunion trade has been negative.

First, even if we assume for the moment that Guinea had no foreign exchange problems, its centrally planned economic system under the late Sékou Touré was nonetheless a hindrance to intraunion trade for several reasons. Unlike Liberia and Sierra Leone, the import and export trade of Guinea was done either directly by the government or by state-owned parastatals. There were no independent manufacturers, importers or exporters. On the other hand, the agents of intraunion trade in both Sierra Leone and Liberia are private individuals and companies. Consequently, businesspersons in both countries did not have counterparts in Guinea with whom they could transact their business. Since its economy was centrally planned, Guinea was not very enthusiastic about intraunion trade, which it found ideologically unacceptable. They were reluctant to accept arrangements whereby thousands or even millions of dollars would go into the hands of private individuals in Liberia and Sierra Leone as a result of intraunion trade. Indeed, such transactions were seen in Conakry as "imperialistic" and "exploitative."

In short, Guinea under Sékou Touré preferred to deal directly with either the national governments of Liberia and Sierra Leone or their parastatals. That way, Conakry believed that money accruing to the governments and parastatals as a result of intraunion trade would go straight into government coffers and not to private business. Such a situation would seem more psychologically acceptable to the then ideologically conscious Guineans. This is because they believed that money that is given to both national governments would subsequently be used in the "larger interest" of the peoples of the governments concerned. Of course, whether this is done in actual practice is a moot point. What is salient to note though, is that such political-cum-ideological problems and differences among the partner states of the union explain in large measure Guinea's slow response to intraunion trade.

Another political problem relates to what we can call the overwhelming and largely unrestrained power that all three leaders of the union then possessed. Again, this phenomenon is an outgrowth of the political systems in the three countries. Consequently, their domestic and foreign policies were heavily influenced by the whims and idiosyncrasies of all their leaders. A couple of examples from Sierra Leone and Liberia will suffice here.

First, in 1980 when Tolbert was killed in the coup led by Doe, Siaka Stevens of Sierra Leone shunned the new Liberian head of state completely for over a year because Tolbert was his (Stevens's) personal friend. Together with President Shehu Shagari of Nigeria and President Felix Houphouët-Boigny of Côte d'Ivoire, Stevens spearheaded a campaign of ostracism which led to the exclusion of the Liberian delegation to the special Organization of African Unity (OAU) economic summit in Nigeria in April 1980. The following month, Stevens was again among West African leaders who successfully prevented Doe from attending the annual ECOWAS summit in Lomé, Togo, although the Liberian head of state was in the Togolese capital for the meeting.[6] The strained relations between the two members delayed the commencement of intraunion trade for over a year.

Our second example is from Liberia. In February 1983, the Liberian leader, Samuel Doe, abruptly closed the Liberia-Sierra Leone border in protest against an article in one of the independent dailies of Sierra Leone, which claimed that Doe had shot and killed his wife.[7] The Liberian leader demanded an official apology from the government in Freetown as the condition for reopening the common border -- a demand that was flatly rejected by Siaka Stevens because he considered it political blackmail. So the border remained closed. Obviously, while it remained closed, no legal trade could have taken place across the border. What has become clear in the actions of these founding members since 1973 is that they were both willing to subordinate the interests of the union to political exigencies. This conclusion reinforces the perception of the union's secretariat that political leaders give the union attention only when it is seen as enhancing their own political careers and stature both at home and abroad.

Inconvertible Currencies and Scarcity of Foreign Exchange

The existence of three national currencies within the MRU -- the Syli in Guinea until 1985,[8] the U.S. dollar in Liberia and the Leone in Sierra Leone -- has been a serious obstacle to intraunion trade expansion. Two of the currencies, the Syli and the Leone, are inconvertible, while the Liberian dollar is universally convertible and acceptable when it is available. The implication of this situation is that while Guinean and Sierra Leonean exporters to Liberia encounter no serious problems in getting payments for their wares, the same is not true for Liberian exporters to the two countries. Liberian traders are usually reluctant to accept what they consider "useless currencies"-- the Syli and the Leone -- from their business counterparts in Guinea and Sierra Leone. Consequently, importers in Guinea and Sierra Leone have had to go through their central banks for the necessary clearance to obtain foreign currency to pay for their imports from Liberia. However, the chronic shortage of foreign currency in both countries usually makes it very difficult for importers to get the foreign exchange approval.

The two governments have very stiff foreign exchange regulations, which invariably lead to long delays in settling payments for intraunion trade. Although intraunion trade arrangements have built-in provisions for preferential treatment to be given to requests for foreign exchange for payments in respect of intraunion trade, it has not been possible for the central banks of Guinea and Sierra Leone to honor such arrangements because of their need to conserve their meager foreign currencies. In fact, in the case of Guinea, foreign exchange allocations were made by the central bank "strictly in accordance with government priorities,"[9] which, in this case, did not include the promotion of intraunion trade. The union secretariat was forced to intervene on several occasions to ensure that payments due to Liberian exporters were sent to them from Sierra Leone.

Apart from directly holding back the development of intraunion trade, the scarcity of foreign exchange in the partner states also created suspicion in Liberian exporters. They were reluctant to sell their products to Sierra Leone because of fear that the proceeds would be "tied-up" in Freetown for long periods of time. Besides that, Liberians-- government officials as well as businesspersons -- believed that their country was being unduly "exploited" by Guinea and Sierra Leone. In general, Liberians see intraunion trade as an unnecessary drain on their country's treasury. Such essentially antiunion feelings became much more pronounced against the background of intraunion trade statistics, which were heavily in favor of Sierra Leone. However, the continuing economic crisis, coupled with the foreign exchange squeeze in the three countries, have had serious negative effects on the growth of intraunion trade. Liberia is no longer as attractive to investors in Guinea and Sierra Leone as it used to be in the late 1970s and early 1980s because of the acute shortage of American dollars in Liberia. Businesspersons in Sierra Leone and Guinea are reluctant to accept "Doe dollars," which the Liberian government has put into circulation to ease the foreign exchange crunch, because they are not readily convertible to U.S. dollars, even in Liberia.

The Commercial Banking Systems

A payments related problem is the commercial banking systems in the member states. The banking systems are of course a colonial inheritance in all three countries.[10] During the colonial era, commercial banks were set up mainly to promote trade between the colonies and the metropolitan capitals in Europe and America. However, after independence the commercial banks still maintained very close banking ties with their parents in Europe and America. To be sure, some of the banks have been nationalized while others have opened their doors to African shareholders. Nevertheless, few changes have taken place in terms of their banking links. In fact, commercial banks in the union still depend on their foreign parents for foreign exchange transactions including the issuance of traveler's checks. Not surprisingly, it is faster and much easier for importers in Sierra Leone, for example, to transact business with their partners in Paris, London or New York, than it is with those in Monrovia or Conakry.

In the first place, intraunion trade transactions have to be routed via the metropolitan capital cities of the parent banks before they eventually get to their destinations in Freetown, Monrovia or Conakry as the case may be. Second, the system is rather expensive for the small businessperson in terms of the fees that local commercial banks charge for acting as intermediaries. Third, the commercial banking systems drain the meager foreign exchange earnings of the partner states. This is especially important given the reluctance of businesses to go through the West African Clearing House (WACH), which was set up purposely to minimize the use of foreign exchange in intra-West African trade, including trade within the MRU. Although the secretariat has embarked upon a campaign aimed at getting businesses to patronize WACH, the results so far have not been encouraging. However, until most businesses can channel their payments through the clearing house, the present banking systems in the union will continue to strangle intraunion trade.

Inadequate Transportation and
Telecommunications Infrastructure

The absence of good transport and telecommunications linkages between the partner states does not facilitate the rapid growth and expansion of intraunion trade. In order to appreciate the seriousness of the problem, we shall divide this section into two subsections, namely transport and telecommunications. Under the former, we shall also examine air and sea transportation facilities between the partner states and evaluate their impact on intraunion trade.

Transport Infrastructure. There is a glaring absence of good all-weather trunk roads between the capital cities of the Mano River Union. The lack of good roads affects the free flow of goods within the union all year round. In the rainy season (for about six months) the muddy roads are slippery and sometimes they are even not motorable for days. The dry season (the other six months) does not bring relief either, because the roads are usually very dusty and bumpy. Plying interstate roads in both seasons not only causes a lot of delay -- because of the need to go slowly -- but can also be expensive in terms of wear and tear on vehicles and fatigue to drivers, which can increase the risk of accidents on the roads. In these circumstances, it is risky for manufacturers of breakable products to embark upon intraunion trade all year round. Besides, although the distances between capital cities are relatively short -- 380 miles between Freetown and Monrovia, 400 miles between Monrovia and Conakry and 197 miles between Conakry and Freetown -- it normally takes a truck load of goods over twelve hours to ply the Freetown-Monrovia road. Clearly, such a slow pace does not encourage trade in perishable goods among the union's members. There are currently plans to upgrade the roads and work has been done on the Freetown-Monrovia road. However, progress has been painfully slow.

If the roads are a hindrance to intraunion trade, sea transport facilities have not been of much help either, although all three member states of the union have access to the Atlantic Ocean. (Freetown has the finest natural harbor on the west coast of Africa while Liberia operates a free port in Monrovia. However, such potential has not been harnessed by the union in the interest of intraunion trade.) At the moment, the MRU states rely almost exclusively on foreign merchant ships to bring in their imports and take out their exports. So far, there has been no talk of setting up a union shipping line that could bridge the transportation gap in the union. Sea transportation is of course cheap and, if well planned and developed, could neutralize many of the barriers which the poor road transport networks have imposed on intraunion trade.

Air transport facilities between the MRU states are equally poor and underdeveloped. There is a complete lack of air freight/cargo services between the member states.[11] There are passenger flights between union states, but only on certain days of the week. And even then, such flights have been provided by either Nigeria Airways or Ghana Airways -- both of which are not MRU members. Nigeria Airways was forced to cut most of its West African routes in 1988 because of high debts, thus causing further problems to the MRU. There is also a total absence of air transport agreements between the partner states. Although all three states have what we can loosely call "international airports," they have remained underutilized for various reasons such as the lack of adequate aviation equipment at the airports, and the chronic shortage of aircraft both for passengers and freight. In fact, a significant proportion of the aircraft used by MRU states are on wet-lease. In 1982, for example, almost a decade after the union was established, partner states had a combined total of just fifteen aircraft.

The impact of the poor air transportation links in the MRU on intraunion trade has been serious. Importers have not been able to take advantage of the speed provided by an efficient air transport system in sending their wares to the various capital cities in the union. In addition, businesspersons in each of the three capitals find it rather difficult to travel within the union by air. A good example of this problem occurred back in 1982 when Nigeria and Ghana Airways changed their flight schedules. According to the MRU secretariat, the impact of the changes was particularly "felt on the sectors Freetown/Conakry/Freetown (1 hour's flight time), where there is no flight northbound (i.e. Freetown/Conakry)."[12] The situation was at one time so bad that "Liberian delegates attending a meeting of the Union in Conakry have to travel to Freetown by air and there join the Sierra Leone delegates to proceed to Conakry by road (sic)."[13] Besides, staff of the diplomatic missions of the partner states have been "forced to use circuitous routes, e.g. Guinea Embassy staff in Monrovia wishing to travel to Conakry have to go via Abidjan (Côte d'Ivoire) and Dakar (Senegal) at extra cost."[14] In short, the air transport facilities in the member states then and now do not "further a principal objective of the Mano River Union -- namely to further intra-union trade."[15]

Although there are moves to set up a union airline, it would take some time before this multilateral venture could be realized. African states are notoriously slow in working out interstate cooperation agreements: they guard their brittle sovereignty rather jealously and are reluctant to pool their resources with others. Besides, national airlines are status symbols for many African countries, including the MRU states. That being so, they are not likely to dismantle them overnight in favor of a multilateral airline. Thus, in 1982 for instance, Sierra Leone decided to set up an independent international airline, thereby abrogating the arrangement with British Caledonia Airways (now British Airways), which had served the country's needs rather well for many years. One of the reasons for the move was that Siaka Stevens was "tired of asking his colleagues for 'rides'" whenever there were important international conferences for him to attend in Africa and abroad.[16] The satisfaction of such purely personal needs did not, however, take into consideration the perilous state of the nation's economy and the acute shortage of foreign exchange to pay for the two B727s, which were wet-leased from Air Jordan, and their foreign pilots. Similar problems occurred in the late 1980s, exacerbated by the chronic economic condition of the states. Until all three set aside such parochial nationalism and "prestige" projects in the interest of a more viable subregional airline, intraunion trade will continue to be adversely affected.

Telecommunications. The dearth of good telecommunications links, i.e. telephones and telegraphs, within the MRU is a colonial legacy. During the colonial era, telecommunication links were established vertically, that is, they ran from the metropole to the colonial capital city. There was no serious attempt to link colonial capitals with the interior towns by phones, nor did the colonial masters try to establish telephone and telegraphic linkages between colonial capital cities. This policy, part of the popular "divide and rule" strategy, served the colonial masters very well.

At independence, African states found themselves almost completely cut off from one another. Thus, it is much easier for businesses in Sierra Leone to phone partners in Paris, London or New York, than it is for them to contact partners in Monrovia or Conakry. The implications of this situation for intraunion trade are clear. Businesses in the union experience a lot of delays in trying to contact their counterparts within the union by phone or telegraph. Sometimes the telephones do not work for days. Apart from that, domestic postal systems are not reliable. It is highly risky to post valuable items within the union. Not only are the postal systems slow -- especially those in Liberia and Guinea -- but valuables are sometimes stolen at post offices while in transit. Intraunion trade, then, is at the moment a delicate venture for producers and manufacturers, who need to learn the ropes of export marketing within the region as they do for exports abroad. Intraunion trade poses more risks to local businesspersons than trade with overseas partners. In the case of the latter, at least an anxious exporter/importer in Monrovia or Freetown can pick up a telephone and get in touch with the partner in London or New York without much delay. Alternatively, one could catch any of the many international flights to Europe and America to see partners personally without much ado. The net result of this anomaly has been the strengthening of postindependence trade links between Africa and its erstwhile colonial masters at the expense of intra-African trade.

Roadblocks

Roadblocks are a reflection of political and economic problems in the partner states and constitute very real barriers to the growth of intraunion trade. Roadblocks are erected along interstate roads for a variety of reasons, among which are security considerations and the need to curtail smuggling, especially of diamonds and produce, across the Sierra Leone-Liberia border. But as we pointed out earlier, all three partner states are autocratic. As a result, there is a lot of pent-up opposition and discontent among their peoples. This problem has been reinforced by the endemic ethnic rivalries in all three states, which have led to violence and political instability within union members.[17] Consequently, the leaders of the union are hypersensitive to what we can call threats to the integrity of their regimes as well as threats to the integrity of their persons.

Roadblocks are particularly noticeable along the Sierra Leone end of the Freetown/Monrovia road. In the early 1980s, for instance, there were eleven road checkpoints on the Freetown side alone.[18] They were controlled at various points by either customs officials, immigration officials, the police, local party vigilantes or officers from the Special Security Division (SSD), the heaviest armed and most undisciplined security unit in Sierra Leone during the time of the late Siaka Stevens. At each roadblock, traders and their vehicles would be stopped and thoroughly "searched" by the various "officials" on duty. The "officials" would ask for "donations" from the businesspersons, irrespective of the legality or otherwise of their business, before they would be allowed to continue their journey. The average person would be subjected to much intimidation and extortion before arriving in Monrovia or Freetown to deliver the goods. As a report commissioned by the union noted:

> ...even if bold enough to face the interrogation and search (the businessman) could not afford the fees and contributions all along the way. For larger scale operators, on the other hand, time is money, and the eleven checks could easily double the time required to take a truck load of goods from one capital city to the other. The borders are difficult to cross in any fashion, even by air. Customs and immigration procedures between these two "united" countries (Liberia and Sierra Leone) are more cumbersome and time consuming than those at the frontiers of countries which have no system of economic integration whatsoever, such as the United States and Mexico or Switzerland and France.[19]

There is no doubt, then, that the continuing use of roadblocks constitutes a serious hindrance to the development of intraunion trade. For traders dealing with perishable goods, for instance, the time spent on the 380-mile-long road from Freetown to Monrovia could mean the difference between profit and total loss. Although under the intraunion trade regulations "goods of local origin" are not taxable if consigned straight from one member to the other, small producers would nonetheless "prefer to be taxed 'officially' and save precious time and money on the road if that would do away with the eleven 'gates' which they have to scale before they finally arrive at their destination."[20] The member governments are not unaware of the numerous roadblocks along intercity roads. However, political exigencies, usually more potent than economic considerations and often translated into ill-defined and all-embracing "national interest" or "security needs," have not allowed the politicians to take effective measures to eliminate the roadblocks.

Administrative and Legal Obstacles

Our final barrier to intraunion trade is what we can loosely call administrative/legal problems. These relate to some of the administrative, legal and indeed institutional arrangements within the union which have impeded the development of trade among the partner states. One such problem relates to the regulations dealing with the registration of "goods of local origin." Manufacturers must first of all apply to the secretariat in writing, stating that they want their products to be placed on the list of "goods of local origin." However, this is exactly where the problem starts. The application form requires detailed information that the small trader cannot supply. For instance, the prospective exporters are required to supply the following details, among others, about their products and activities:

(a) description of the goods for which the application is made;
(b) common external tariff classification of the goods, i.e. the tariff item number and subheading in the external tariff;
(c) most recent ex-factory price of goods per unit of production;
(d) number of units produced during the period;
(e) materials used, both local and imported, during the production of the goods, and finally,
(f) expected volume of exports to the other states of the union during the next twelve months.[21]

It is clear from this brief examination of some of the procedures for registration of "goods of local origin" that the system does not encourage small, local businesses to take advantage of intraunion trade. This situation explains the domination of intraunion trade so far by Levantines and Orientals. But even for these relatively large-scale manufacturers, there are still some problems: they must also produce other documents after registration before they can start the export business proper. Among the many documents required are the following:

(a) five copies of the Mano River Union Movement Certificate;
(b) export and import licenses and permits for the export of consignments valued at over $500. These forms are obtainable from the Ministry of Trade and Industry

in the respective Partner States;
(c)   customs export/import entry forms -- obtainable from the Customs and Excise in the Member States;
(d)   foreign exchange form CD2 for exports from Sierra Leone only, and
(e)   Health Certificates for the importation of live animals, fish and related products.   The certificate can be obtained from the Chief Fisheries Officer in the Ministry of Natural Resources in the Member States.[22]

Trying to obtain the above forms/documents can be time consuming and even costly in monetary terms. First, some of the documents may not be readily available from the relevant ministries at all times. Second, even if they are always available, officials may deliberately "sit" on them so as to extort money from the prospective exporter/importer. This point is worth emphasizing because at a time of economic recession and austerity measures in all the partner states, civil servants, even the most highly placed, do ask for "tips" or "kickbacks" in return for their "favors," particularly in Sierra Leone and Liberia. Third, as far as foreign exchange form CD2 in respect of exports from Sierra Leone is concerned, it is doubtful whether the central bank of Sierra Leone would treat any request for such a form with enthusiasm, given the persistent acute shortage of foreign exchange in the country. Central bank officials could deliberately hold onto the form while they wait for instructions from the government. All the above problems, then, point to the inevitable conclusion that intraunion trade in the MRU will continue to face many nontariff barriers into the 1990s. In that regard, it will be a long time before the major objective of intraunion trade is realized, that is, the increase of trade among the partner states.

Conclusion: Policy Changes

This chapter has tried to demonstrate that although intraunion trade came into effect in the Mano River Union many years ago, it has not succeeded in expanding trade between the members. We have also identified what we consider to be the most potent obstacles to intraunion trade in the union. Of course, the union's secretariat is aware of some, if not all, of the barriers we have identified in the chapter. In fact, it has tried through position papers to find lasting solutions to some of the problems. For instance, back in August 1983 the secretariat prepared a paper which it presented to the union's Working Group on Banking and Finance at its third meeting in Freetown in the same month.[23] The working group made a number of far-reaching recommendations, whose main objective was to rejuvenate intraunion trade. Three of the recommendations remain particularly relevant to our discussion. They are:

(a) that the secretariat should set up a bureau which would monitor and follow up intraunion trade payments in the respective member countries;
(b) that member states should set aside $100,000 each in their foreign exchange budgets specifically to facilitate payments in respect of intraunion trade, and
(c) that members should relax their foreign exchange control regulations in favour of intraunion trade.[24]

Although the working group did not categorically say so, it is plausible to believe that it wanted the national governments to give priority to all applications for foreign exchange in respect of intraunion trade.

The recommendations are undoubtedly in the right direction, but the working group seemed to have ignored the prominent role that political considerations and decisions have played, and can play, in promoting and/or retarding intraunion trade. Thus, any recommendations aimed at improving trade among the partner states should first of all start by appealing to the heads of state to develop the political will that would enable them to make political and indeed economic sacrifices in the superior interest of the union. Once political leaders are prepared to make the necessary sacrifices, a lot of the current, or for that matter future, problems of the union would be reduced if not eliminated entirely. For instance, politicians must try to minimize, if not eliminate, nontariff barriers such as roadblocks. In peacetime, only customs officials and the police should be allowed to supervise roadchecks. The SSD, the soldiers and party vigilantes should be asked to go back to their "legitimate" jobs.

Again, given the right political will and "political climate," the frequent border closures would also be reduced to the barest minimum in peacetime. Finally, the MRU leaders should not allow personal friendships and considerations to transcend the larger interest of the union's survival, as has often been the case since Tolbert's death a decade ago.

Vigorous and regular public relations campaigns must be undertaken by the secretariat to educate the people in the partner states on the advantages of intraunion trade and how they can participate in it. This is very important in a community where the majority of the citizens are illiterate. Literacy rates in 1988 were 29 percent each for Sierra Leone and Guinea and 35 percent for Liberia. Regular public relations exercises will not only bring the union's activities closer to the people, but will also remind the national governments of the existence of the union. Closely allied to this point is the need for the union to set up intraunion trade committees, which will keep a register of all businesspersons and manufacturers who are engaged in intraunion trade. The committees should also liaise closely with manufacturers and traders in order to monitor their problems and progress in the conduct of intraunion trade. The committees could also work closely with the three national governments to ensure that arrangements made by them to facilitate intraunion trade are strictly adhered to. Governments that do not abide by agreed arrangements to enhance intraunion trade could be "reported" to the secretariat for necessary action. Such action could be a visit to the appropriate government ministry/officials or even to the heads of state, to find out why they have not honored their commitments to the union.

However, for intraunion trade to improve significantly or for the union itself to survive in the 1990s, it must be seen by the partner states as promoting their individual or collective national interests. This calls for dedication and impartiality on the part of the union's international civil servants. They should put aside narrow nationalism in the interest of the greater welfare of all the peoples of the partner states. Union staff must, in that regard, see themselves as international civil servants and not mere representatives of their national governments in the secretariat. That way, both the interests of the union and those of the member governments would be harmonized and protected.

Intraunion trade should not be seen by the secretariat staff or, for that matter, government officials as benefiting only a particular member state, as has been the case. Rather, the union should embark upon measures to redress the present trade imbalance, which favors Sierra Leone. There are various ways in which this could be done. First, what is needed in the union is an expansion of productive capacity as well as measures to reduce costs. This would make it possible for the member states to expand their exports within the union. The present situation whereby intraunion products are competitive rather than complementary does not augur well for the growth of intraunion trade.[25] Second, and closely related to the last point, is that the union must as a matter of priority embark upon union industries. Such a move would take care of some of the obstacles to intraunion trade examined in this chapter. As union industries, they would belong to all the partner states and not just to an individual or one national government. Besides, union industries would also be much more efficient because they would be able to take advantage of economies of scale.

Finally, intraunion trade could be improved if large-scale manufacturers are encouraged to set up subsidiaries in the other member states. Such subsidiaries would help to reduce the current high demand for foreign exchange in intraunion trade transactions. For instance, a Sierra Leonean company with a Liberian subsidiary could export directly to Liberia through the subsidiary. The money from the transaction would be retained in Liberia and used to expand the business of the subsidiary in that country. Likewise, a Liberian company with a subsidiary in Freetown could export directly to that subsidiary. More importantly, the money realized from the transaction would be in Leones, which are inconvertible. The Leones would be retained in Sierra Leone and used to expand the activities of the Liberian subsidiary in the country. Such arrangements would no doubt enhance intraunion trade. They would also reduce the present high demand for scarce foreign exchange within the union and speed up payments in respect of intraunion trade. Such an arrangement would eliminate the feeling among Liberians that their country is being "exploited" by Sierra Leone. If some of these recommendations are implemented, there should be an appreciable increase in intraunion trade in the Mano River Union.

Notes

1. Guinea, the third member, joined in 1980. It is still slowly adjusting to operations within the union, so the analysis here leans heavily on Liberia and Sierra Leone.

2. For a definition of "goods of local origin" see *MRU/E/TRA/2 Information Guide to Intra-Union Trade in the Mano River Union*, 9 March 1981, p. 2.

3. For details on the Mano River Union's progress since 1973, see Amadu Sesay, "The Mano River Union: Politics of Survival or Dependence?" in Ralph I. Onwuka and Amadu Sesay (eds.), *The Future of Regionalism in Africa* (London: Macmillan, 1984); and also F.B.L. Mansaray, "The Growth of the Mano River Union" in *Regional Cooperation in Africa: Problems and Prospects* (Addis Ababa: The African Association for Public Administration and Management, 1977), pp. 61-67.

4. *World Development Report 1989* (New York: Oxford University Press/World Bank, 1989).

5. UN Africa Recovery Programme, *Briefing Paper*, 1, June 1989, p. 2.

6. For details, see Amadu Sesay, "Le coup d'etat au Liberia: Facteurs internes et effets regionaux," *Politique Africaine*, 7, September 1982, pp. 91-106.

7. For details on the incident and Sierra Leone's and Liberia's reactions, see *West Africa*, 7 March 1983, pp. 598-599, and 14 March 1983, pp. 699-700. Sierra Leone and Liberia did not in fact mend their relations until September 1983 when Doe visited Freetown. See *West Africa*, 12 September 1983, pp. 2097-2098.

8. Guinea returned to the CFA franc zone in 1985 after the coup following Sékou Touré's death in April 1984. With the growing scarcity of U.S. dollars in Liberia, it is conceivable that investors will begin to turn their attention to Guinea for investment opportunities, now that the country has abandoned its socialist policies.

9. *MRU Doc. DP/Banking/WGLL/2, Proposals for the Effective Payments Arrangements in Respect of Intraunion Trade in Mano River Union* (Note by the Secretariat), 4 April 1983, p. 7.

10. Liberia, unlike Sierra Leone and Guinea, was not colonized by a European power but by freed American slaves known popularly as Americo-Liberians. Everything in the country is patterned along American lines. All the banks are subsidiaries of American banks.

11. See *MRU. DOC.E/ALC/TC/SUB/1; Report of the Sub-Committee Appointed by the Technical Committee on Airline Cooperation*, 22 September 1982, for details on the air transport facilities within the union.

12. *MRU. DOC. E/ALC/TC. 1/2, Joint Airline Cooperation*, pp. 2-3.

13. *Ibid.*, p. 3.

14. *Ibid.*

15. *Ibid.*

16. Discussions with officials in Freetown. The writer was in Freetown in October 1984 and witnessed a situation whereby passengers on one of the international flights by Sierra Leone Airways had to be sent home because Siaka Stevens wanted to use "their plane" to attend a conference abroad. At the time of writing (1990), Sierra Leone Airlines does not have an external service since the withdrawal of Jordanian Air in 1988, due to non-payment by Sierra Leone of wet-lease fees for its two aircraft.

17. See Amadu Sesay, "Societal Inequalities, Ethnic Heterogeneity and Political Instability: The Case of Liberia," *Plural Societies*, 11(3), Autumn 1980, pp. 15-30. The December 1989 invasion of Nimba County in Liberia by the forces of the former Liberian minister, Charles Taylor, is the most recent case in point. It has led to sour relations with Côte d'Ivoire, where there are some 50,000 Liberian refugees from the fighting. There are also some 11,000 refugees in Guinea. For details, see *West Africa*, 8-14 January 1990, pp. 3-4; and 22-28 January 1990, p. 93.

18. Commonwealth Fund for Technical Cooperation, *The Mano River Union: An Assessment of Past Performance and Some Guidelines for the Future* (Freetown: MRU Secretariat, 1981), p. 129.

19. *Ibid.*

20. *Ibid.*

21. *MRU/TRA/5*, pinnex 111, pp. 1-3.

22. *MRU. DOC.DP/Banking/WG111/2*, p. 10.

23. *Ibid.*

24. *Ibid.*

25. For more details on orthodox arguments about the utility of customs union arrangements among developing countries, see Sidney Dell, *A Latin American Common Market* (London: Oxford University Press, 1966); R.G. Lipsey, "The Theory of Customs Unions: A General Survey" in *The Economic Journal*, 70(279), September 1960; C.A. Cooper and B.F. Massell, "Towards a General Theory of Customs Union for Developing Countries," *Journal of Political Economy*, 73(5), October 1965; B.W.T. Mutharika, *Toward Multinational Economic Cooperation in Africa* (New York: Praeger, 1972); and Felipe Pazos, "Regional Integration of Trade among Less Developed Countries," *World Development*, 1(7), July 1973, pp. 1-3.

5

ECOWAS, the First Decade: Towards Collective Self-Reliance, or Maintenance of the Status Quo?

Phoebe Kornfeld

Since 1975, the greatest common denominator of the sixteen countries belonging to the Economic Community of West African States (ECOWAS) has been precisely that: their membership in ECOWAS. Prior to the formation of ECOWAS, the most distinctive mutual attribute of these countries was their peripheral status in the world economy and the concomitant limitations to independent socioeconomic growth.

These latter features are, of course, still prevalent. The reliance upon the export of primary commodities for foreign exchange earnings to pay for the import of manufactured goods is a fact of life for every West African economy. This remains as characteristic of each of the ECOWAS member states as it is of other countries in the Third World, which have been caught in the vicious circle of dependence since the days of colonialism.[1]

With ECOWAS has been created the potential for its members to break out of that cycle, but if its ascendancy is to be assured, ECOWAS must demonstrate the ability to counteract and overcome those ever-present negative commonalities. The purpose of this chapter is to explore the extent to which ECOWAS appears to have met its potentialities during its first decade of existence between 1975 and 1985.[2]

Who Needs Collective Self-Reliance?

Theoretically, ECOWAS presents its members with an alternative to the neo-imperialistic status quo: collective self-reliance. That this is a recognized, though not necessarily paramount, goal of the organization is clear from the agreement of all of the participants to article 32 in the ECOWAS treaty. There it states that:

> In the implementation of the aims of the Community, the
> Council of Ministers shall recommend measures designed
> to promote the industrial development of Member States
> and shall take steps to reduce gradually the Community's
> economic dependence on the outside world and strengthen
> economic relations among themselves.[3]

Within this statement is to be found a call for the two
essential elements of the concept of collective self-
reliance, namely the weakening of the limiting external
nexus, and the concurrent improvement of the regional
exchange network.

That the signatories were willing to allow this
declaration to be burrowed away in the middle of the ECOWAS
treaty indicates their unwillingness to focus attention on
the concept of collective self-reliance. In the preamble of
the ECOWAS treaty a brief mention is made of the need for "a
determined and concerted policy of self-reliance."[4] Yet this
pales in significance when compared with article 2, the "Aims
of the Community," which is an extensive elaboration of the
incremental measures that the community would be striving to
implement.

This emphasis on incrementalism is typical of the
established approach to regional integration, of which the
European Community and its predecessor organizations are
considered to provide optimal examples. Ernst B. Haas, one
of the outstanding theorists in the field, goes so far as to
say that "Most theories of regional integration have been
anchored on the notion of incrementalism..."[5] Much of the
early program initiated by ECOWAS maintained this tradition,
and there can be little doubt that ECOWAS's declared plans
in the agricultural and industrial sectors, as well as those
for transport and energy, are important contributions to
regional cooperation.[6] However, excessive concentration on
this path to regional integration, a path which Haas himself
has identified as being obsolete,[7] will condemn ECOWAS to
die the same death that many regional organizations have
already experienced.

Taking his analysis a step further, Haas is able to
isolate one of the major weaknesses in conventional regional
integration theory. He writes that:

> mistakes are made in not properly identifying the
> *spatial* focus of the process: efforts at regional
> integration prove to be far more susceptible to
> influences exogenous to the system created by the
> participants than has been allowed.[8]

Given Africa's colonial and neocolonial past and its present precarious situation on the edge of the world economy, exogenous influences can indeed be said to have been important, as do they continue to be. It is to collective self-reliance, therefore, that these countries must turn, for its aims of reduced external dependence and increased intraregional cooperation precisely fit their needs.

The importance of collective self-reliance for the Third World has been widely acknowledged in international forums ranging from the sixth and seventh Special Sessions of the UN General Assembly to the economic summits of the Organization of African Unity held in 1981 and 1986.[9] However, to espouse the rhetoric of identifying collective self-reliance as a worthwhile and essential goal is a much simpler procedure than to ensure its achievement. It is for this reason that it is necessary to concentrate here on an evaluation of ECOWAS in terms of the organization's progress towards collective self-reliance.

Trade Figures as an Evaluative Tool

The intent here is to examine the trade patterns within ECOWAS, and between ECOWAS and the exogenous influences which provided the indirect impetus behind the formation of the regional organization. This should lead at least to some general conclusions concerning the direction in which ECOWAS headed during its first decade.[10]

By juxtaposing the trade data for 1975, 1980 and 1985, much can be determined about the extent of regional interaction in those years following the signing of the ECOWAS treaty. At the subsystemic, or regional, level of analysis, it can be shown that trade between ECOWAS nations remained of minor significance relative to their total trade volume. Nigeria's status as the regional economic giant can also be explored, as can be the possible sources of conflicts of interest with other regional groupings. In addition, it must be taken into consideration that the Communauté Economique de l'Afrique de l'Ouest (CEAO) and the franc zone represent possible rival associations, and ones whose cohesiveness has been determined primarily by a common colonial heritage. Whether or not ECOWAS can supersede their influence is a true test of its ability to accomplish half of the task of collective self-reliance -- that of increasing regional cooperation and interaction.

Possible ECOWAS-inspired advances in decreasing external dependence can be evaluated by turning to trade patterns at the systemic level. Looking at ECOWAS trade with the industrialized countries and with the former colonial powers, much can be learned about the ECOWAS countries' reliance on these extraregional elements.

It is clear that such an analysis is not a sufficient basis from which to draw absolute conclusions as to the degree of success of this organization during its first decade. Aggregate data can serve only as a general indicator, for there is much that they do not reveal about the policies of the constituent governments or about the activities of individuals within and between those countries. Probably the best example of such an omission is the illicit cross-border trade that continues to flourish fifteen years after the formation of ECOWAS.[11]

On the other hand, there is a certain amount of utility in the exercise of examining aggregate data. Firstly, it is a necessary component of any broader evaluation of ECOWAS; and secondly, it will contribute to the process of deducing the all-important level of commitment of the ECOWAS countries to the concept of regional cooperation and collective self-reliance. One of the leading practitioners in the field of the international economics of Africa notes that:

> The real constraint to the realization of African multinational enterprises is the lack of political goodwill. Total commitment to the cause of African economic integration is still more of an ideal than a practice; too often individual African leaders regard economic cooperation as a threat to their political sovereignty.[12]

Although the political variable in regional organizations of a primarily economic nature is difficult to quantify, its broad influence is, all the same, generally conceded, and the analysis which follows will show that this political variable is the key to a productive future for ECOWAS.[13]

The Depth and Breadth of Regional Cooperation

As has already been mentioned, intra-ECOWAS trade from 1975 to 1985 was of minor significance when compared with the total volume of trade of the ECOWAS countries.[14] Little enlightenment is provided by repeating this, given that ECOWAS was so young and that trade levels between Third World countries are often appallingly low. It must also be recognized that in absolute terms the economies of these countries are in general quite small and in not the healthiest of conditions. One author points out that "Except for the Ivory Coast, Nigeria, Ghana, Senegal, and Liberia, the remaining 11 [countries of West Africa] have been classified by the World Bank as belonging to the 36 low-income developing countries of the world with an income per capita of $370 or less in 1979."[15]

To harp on these facts would only be counterproductive, especially since ECOWAS is supposed to provide the means to the end of rectifying this situation. A little more revealing is to call attention to a temporal comparison of the trading habits of the ECOWAS members. For example, between 1975 and 1980, intra-ECOWAS exports as a percentage of the total exports of the group fell from an already low 4.1 percent to a disparaging 2.8 percent.[16] This figure fell despite the doubling of intra-ECOWAS exports between 1975 and 1980, because of the tripling of ECOWAS countries' world exports during those years. (See Table 5.1) By 1985, intra-ECOWAS exports had inched up to 3.5 percent of the group's total world exports, even though 1985 intra-ECOWAS exports were 22 percent lower than they had been in 1980. If one is looking for signs of an increased depth of interaction between these sixteen West African countries, this perspective over time is a discouraging comment on the early state of affairs.

Table 5.1
Basic ECOWAS Indicators

	Total ECOWAS Exports To World (Million US$)	Intra-ECOWAS Exports (Million US$)	Intra-ECOWAS Exports As Share Of Group's Total Exports (%)
1975	11,706	477	4.1
1980	33,091	919	2.8
1985	20,732	717	3.5

Source: Calculated from data in *Direction of Trade Statistics*. Yearbook 1986 (Washington, D.C.: International Monetary Fund, 1986).

Another simple indicator of the predilection of these
countries to trade with one another is that of the possible
increase or decrease in the number of fellow ECOWAS members
being dealt with. One would look to find that ECOWAS had
facilitated an overall increase in the breadth of the
regional exchange. This was not the case between 1975 and
1980 when each ECOWAS country was trading with a constant
average of six fellow member states.[17] However, by 1985,
each ECOWAS country was trading with an average of nine other
member states.[18] Thus, despite the decline in the absolute
value of intra-ECOWAS exports, there was a slight broadening
of the network of trade between ECOWAS members.

If the analysis of the extent of intra-ECOWAS trade is
broken down further, one finds that despite some evidence of
ECOWAS-inspired extension of economic interrelationships,
there is no sign of a decrease in intracommunity trade
disparities. Table 5.2 shows each country's percentage share
of intra-ECOWAS exports and imports for 1975, 1980 and 1985.
Ten years after the signing of the ECOWAS treaty, the same
three countries, Nigeria, Côte d'Ivoire and Senegal,
dominated the intra-ECOWAS export market. By 1980, their
combined exports represented 87.4 percent of the intra-ECOWAS
total, and in 1985 that figure stood at 85.4 percent. On the
other hand, their combined imports from ECOWAS members for
1985 was only 34.1 percent of the intracommunity total, down
from 38.1 percent in 1975.

It would appear that those countries struggling to stay
afloat in the world economy face a similar dilemma within
ECOWAS. A glance at the intra-ECOWAS balance of trade
figures reconfirms this tendency. In both 1975 and 1980,
Nigeria, Côte d'Ivoire and Senegal headed the short list of
countries with an intra-ECOWAS balance of trade surplus.
Gambia joined the club in 1985. The four countries had an
intra-ECOWAS balance of trade surplus of $340 million in
1985. At the same time, Ghana, Burkina Faso, Mali and
Nigeria were dealing with a combined intra-ECOWAS trade
deficit of $353 million. The ECOWAS parallel to the
predicament of countries hard hit by natural and world
economic disruptions is well illustrated by the case of
Niger, which went from an intra-ECOWAS surplus of $17.1
million in 1975 to a deficit of $37.74 million in 1980, and
to a greater deficit of $51.5 million in 1985.[19]

The similarities between ECOWAS configurations and those
of the world economy do not stop with the plight of the least
developed of the ECOWAS countries. It can also be shown
that in many respects, Nigeria was becoming the core of this
peripheral grouping. Within West Africa, Nigeria has far

Table 5.2
Intra-ECOWAS Trade (%)

	Share of Intra-ECOWAS Exports		
	1975	1980	1985
Nigeria	31.9	48.7	39.7
Côte d'Ivoire	31.5	28.6	32.1
Senegal	14.7	10.1	13.5
Burkina Faso	4.7	.3	1.9
Niger	4.2	.8	4.3
Mali	3.6	2.0	1.1
Ghana	3.4	4.4	.5
Benin	2.2	.5	.8
Togo	1.5	2.7	.6
Liberia	1.0	1.1	.7
Sierra Leone	.7	0.	.3
Gambia	.3	.7	2.3
Guinea-Bissau	.2	.2	.1
Guinea	.1	.2	.7
Mauritania	.1	.01	1.3
Cape Verde	0.	0.	.1

	Share of Intra-ECOWAS Imports		
Côte d'Ivoire	19.4	15.6	19.9
Ghana	16.4	26.4	20.5
Senegal	12.5	8.4	10.9
Sierra Leone	11.3	5.9	3.4
Mali	11.2	10.9	10.8
Burkina Faso	8.0	10.2	7.8
Mauritania	7.4	.3	3.5
Nigeria	6.2	9.1	3.4
Benin	3.1	3.3	3.5
Togo	2.0	2.2	1.5
Gambia	.8	.6	.6
Niger	.7	4.9	9.9
Liberia	.7	1.4	2.5
Guinea	.5	.4	1.5
Guinea-Bissau	.2	.3	.2
Cape Verde	.1	.04	.06

Source: Calculated from data in *Direction of Trade Statistics*. Yearbook 1986 (Washington, D.C.: International Monetary Fund, 1986). The columns do not add up to 100 percent because of rounding-off of the figures.

and away the single largest economy as a base from which to work. In 1978, the Nigerian GDP represented 64 percent of the total ECOWAS GDP, and by 1981 that figure had reached 74 percent. Despite the economic and political difficulties of the mid-1980s, in 1986 the Nigerian GDP was still 69 percent of the total ECOWAS GDP.[20]

The single commodity of oil allowed Nigeria to be one of the few ECOWAS countries to prosper between 1975 and 1980. During that time, the Nigerian proportion of total ECOWAS exports to the world increased from 68 percent to 76 percent, and this increase of 8 percent is more than matched by the climb in Nigeria's share of intra-ECOWAS exports from 32 percent to 49 percent.[21] Even in 1985, Nigeria still accounted for 68 percent of total ECOWAS exports to the world, and Nigeria's share of intra-ECOWAS exports was 40 percent.[22] However, this initially positive evaluation of Nigeria's performance is marred if one applies a relative perspective to Nigeria's activities. First of all, compared with the jump in Nigerian intra-ECOWAS exports between 1975 and 1980, Nigeria's share of intra-ECOWAS imports rose only minimally from 6 percent to 9 percent, and by 1985 Nigeria's share of intra-ECOWAS imports was only 3.4 percent.[23] Secondly, whereas Nigeria's contribution to the expansion of intra-ECOWAS exchange appears significant when compared with that of its smaller regional neighbors, in fact, only approximately 2 percent of Nigeria's total exports went to ECOWAS countries in 1980 and 1985, and imports from fellow ECOWAS member states represented only 0.5 percent of Nigeria's total imports for 1980, and just 0.4 percent for 1985.[24]

In short, it would appear that during the first decade of ECOWAS, Nigeria had as yet done little to protect itself from becoming the regional core country with all of the associated imperialistic implications. Nigeria's disproportionate size and wealth contribute to a possible setting of a vertical division within ECOWAS to parallel that found in the world economy as a whole. If the member states are serious about striving towards a goal of collective self-reliance, ECOWAS does provide the potential to counter this tendency. One author who has thoroughly studied the causes and ramifications of imperialism in its variety of forms views national and collective self-reliance as alternatives to the syndrome of dependency. He writes that:

> the key to the politics of self-reliance is to regain control over resources -- over capital, raw materials, labor, and the most precious of them all -- human

creativity. The whole theory of self-reliance hinges
on one fundamental hypothesis: that together these
resources constitute a reservoir, now partly drained
away, partly misdirected, and largely underutilized...[25]

In the late 1980s there were few signs that this is the way
Nigeria perceives of ECOWAS. Not only does the economic data
belie any such notion, but the expulsion of foreign labor
from Nigeria in the spring of 1983 and again in 1985 can
hardly be viewed as constructive utilization of an ECOWAS-
wide "reservoir" of resources.[26] While Nigeria was within
its legal rights to proceed as it did, such an action
undermines that difficult to quantify variable of political
commitment to the goals of ECOWAS, without which the
community has little chance of making a substantial
contribution in the 1990s.

Latent Interorganizational Conflicts of Interest

The last of the subsystemic aspects of collective self-
reliance which can be explored through the trade data being
used here is the issue of possible conflicts of interest
between ECOWAS and other local regional organizations. That
this has always been a point of concern to ECOWAS members is
made clear by the inclusion towards the end of the ECOWAS
treaty of article 59, which allows for the participation of
the member states in other regional organizations, "provided
that their membership of such associations does not derogate
from the provisions of this Treaty."[27] While there is a wide
range of regional and subregional associations which the
ECOWAS signatories had in mind, the two strongest rivals for
ECOWAS members' commitment, the CEAO and the regional group
of franc zone participants, are the ones which will be
discussed here.

Once again, it must not be forgotten that between 1975
and 1985 ECOWAS was still in its first decade, and the
flexibility which the treaty provides with regard to
overlapping membership in other organizations was important
during these initial years of institutional consolidation.
At the same time, however, the question must be raised as to
whether or not this one truly umbrella organization in West
Africa can withstand the pressures from within which are
engendered by its coexistence with other fairly broad-based
subregional groupings.

It had been recognized since the planning phases of the
ECOWAS formation that there existed the possibility of

interorganizational dissonance in the region. This concern over internecine rivalry was especially directed toward the six-member CEAO which had been formed in 1973, and all of whose participants became signatories to the ECOWAS treaty two years later.[28] The very similar aims of ECOWAS and the CEAO would make it seem likely that the smaller CEAO would eventually merge into the more comprehensive of the two organizations. Indeed, during a moment of optimism about the strength and future of ECOWAS, one of the founders and linchpin contributors to the development of the CEAO, President Houphouët-Boigny of Côte d'Ivoire, is reported to have "acknowledged that the CEAO would one day have to disappear."[29] That this merger has not yet occurred further denotes that commitment to, and perhaps even confidence in, ECOWAS are not all that they should be.

The endurance of the CEAO is also an indication that the task which has been set for ECOWAS, namely to cross and overcome historically created boundaries within the region, is not an easy one. For ECOWAS is an anomaly in its attempt to unite functionally and philosophically countries with such diverse colonial backgrounds. The postindependence period in the West African region is widely characterized by continued strong relations between the newly independent nations and their respective former colonial power, and consequently between the nations with the same colonial heritage.[30] In terms of practical interrelationships, this was even more the case for most of the former French colonies in the region due to the maintenance of the link between the francophone-African and French currency and banking systems.

In order to best adjudge any progress ECOWAS might have made in dissipating these colonial ties, it is necessary to examine not just a distinctive entity of continued colonial cohesiveness such as the CEAO; it is equally as important to consider the role of organizationally less formal intra-ECOWAS groupings as possible sources of friction, or stumbling blocks to further ECOWAS-wide cooperation. This purpose would seem to be served by a comparison of the trade patterns of ECOWAS, the CEAO, the ECOWAS franc zone, and Anglo-ECOWAS.[31] If there is a significant internal source of ECOWAS inconstancy related to more than just the political whims of any one member state, such a comparison would most likely reveal it.

Table 5.3 presents a compilation of the key data for an analysis of the intraregional trade patterns for the four groupings of West African countries being dealt with. Line one gives an idea of the importance to each group's members of intragroup exports relative to each group's total exports.

It can be seen from line one that the CEAO and the ECOWAS franc zone have been consistently more cohesive units than either Anglo-ECOWAS or ECOWAS has been. In 1985, intragroup exports for the CEAO and the ECOWAS franc zone, respectively, represented 6.32 and 6.27 percent of the group's total exports. During that same year, intragroup exports for ECOWAS and Anglo-ECOWAS, respectively, were only 3.46 and 0.98 percent of the group's total exports. Nonetheless, it should be noted that despite the continued greater reliance of the CEAO and the ECOWAS franc zone on intragroup trade relative to the behavior of ECOWAS and Anglo-ECOWAS, intragroup exports as a percentage of the group's total exports have declined considerably over time for both the CEAO and the ECOWAS franc zone. Perhaps the ties of history have in fact been somewhat weakened, and if that is so, ECOWAS must do all it can to take up the slack.

Although the distinction between lines two and three in Table 5.3 might initially be unclear, it should not be overlooked. Briefly, they provide, respectively, depth and breadth indicators for each of the groups relative to ECOWAS. Line two denotes the intensity or depth of each group's relations within the realm of the totality of ECOWAS members' trade with one another. The greatest magnitude in both 1980 and 1985 lay with the intra-ECOWAS franc zone trade, its intragroup exports representing 37.49 (1980) and 37.69 (1985) percent of total intra-ECOWAS exports. By 1985, intra-CEAO exports had reached 37.26 percent of total intra-ECOWAS exports, thereby putting the CEAO on par with the ECOWAS franc zone with regard to its strength as a subgroup within ECOWAS. From line two of Table 5.3, it appears that between 1980 and 1985, the only intragroup exports to decline as a percentage of total intra-ECOWAS exports were those of Anglo-ECOWAS. That result is directly attributable to the fact that exports to the other Anglo-ECOWAS states had been nearly cut in half between 1980 and 1985.

Perhaps the most telling sign of change in the dynamics of the postcolonial fraternities appears in line three of Table 5.3. By looking at what percentage intragroup trade represented vis-à-vis the exports to ECOWAS, an indicator is provided of the extent of the group's regional interaction beyond the group's own boundaries. The CEAO, the ECOWAS franc zone, and Anglo-ECOWAS all appear to have expanded horizontally within ECOWAS, as can be seen from the drop in percentage that intragroup exports represented relative to each group's total exports to ECOWAS. Despite increased insularity of the ECOWAS franc zone and Anglo-ECOWAS between 1975 and 1980, by 1985 each of those group's intragroup

Table 5.3
West African Intraregional Trade

	ECOWAS	CEAO	ECOWAS Franc Zone	Anglo- ECOWAS
1. Intra- group exports as a per- centage of group's total exports				
1975	4.1	11.02	11.27	.91
1980	2.78	6.96	7.71	.98
1985	3.46	6.32	6.27	.98
2. Intra- group exports as a per- centage of total intra- ECOWAS trade				
1975	100.	46.69	46.78	17.11
1980	100.	32.23	37.49	28.5
1985	100.	37.26	37.69	20.23
3. Intra- group exports as a per- centage of group's exports to ECOWAS				
1975	100.	79.48	75.09	47.3
1980	100.	77.34	83.71	53.13
1985	100.	69.37	69.40	47.22

Source: Calculated from data in *Direction of Trade Statistics*. 1986 Yearbook (Washington, D.C.: International Monetary Fund, 1986).

Table 5.4
Intergroup Trade in West Africa

	Total (Million US$)	As Share Of Intra-ECOWAS Exports (%)
ECOWAS franc zone exports to Anglo-ECOWAS:		
1975	42.73	8.96
1980	57.8	6.29
1985	65.84	9.18
CEAO exports to Anglo-ECOWAS:		
1975	35.42	7.43
1980	48.96	5.33
1985	63.88	8.9
Anglo-ECOWAS exports to ECOWAS franc zone:		
1975	87.47	18.34
1980	223.09	24.28
1985	156.94	21.88
Anglo-ECOWAS exports to CEAO:		
1975	80.87	16.95
1980	156.89	17.07
1985	150.56	20.99

Source: Calculated from data in *Direction of Trade Statistics*. Yearbook 1981 (Washington, D.C.: International Monetary Fund, 1981).

exports as a percentage of the group's exports to ECOWAS were at or below the 1975 level.

One other set of calculations, as provided in Table 5.4, can be used to help assess the validity of these inferences. There it is possible to see the scope of intergroup exchanges in West Africa, and its variation between 1975, 1980 and 1985. Between 1975 and 1980, exports to Anglo-ECOWAS from both the ECOWAS franc zone and the CEAO decreased as a percentage of intra-ECOWAS exports. This is in contrast to an increased percentage of intra-ECOWAS exports being accounted for by Anglo-ECOWAS exports to the CEAO, and especially to the ECOWAS franc zone. A closer look at possible reasons for the greater increase in Anglo-ECOWAS exports to the ECOWAS franc zone as compared with those to the CEAO must focus on the one country which is a participant in the former and not in the latter group. To be sure, it turns out that in 1980 Togo was the recipient of just over one-quarter of the goods exported by Anglo-ECOWAS to the ECOWAS franc zone, and the vast majority of those goods ($59 million worth) originated in Nigeria. Once more, the disproportionate role which Nigeria can play in the region comes to the fore.

By 1985, however, it is possible to discern some stabilization of the West African intergroup trade patterns over the decade since the establishment of ECOWAS. Nigeria's exports to Togo were no longer so extensive as to skew the figures for Anglo-ECOWAS exports to the ECOWAS franc zone. Across the board in West Africa, intergroup trade constituted a greater percentage of intra-ECOWAS trade in 1985 than it had in 1975. If that pattern remains constant, ECOWAS states may be able to claim that headway has indeed been made in overcoming historical differences to the benefit of the broader regional organization.

The conclusions which have been drawn from the above information on intraregional cooperation in West Africa are varied. While using the data as a means of absolute prediction would be inappropriate, they do form a reasonable basis for an appraisal of the framework within which ECOWAS has proceeded in an effort to determine whether the region is on a path towards collective self-reliance in the 1990s.

On the whole, it would seem that the espoused commitment to the development of intraregional cooperation has been difficult to put into practice. The weakness of indications of an increased depth or breadth of regional interaction stems in part from the competitive rather than complementary nature of the economies of the ECOWAS member states.[32] This is a hurdle which can only be overcome through a concerted regional planning effort such as ECOWAS has been working to implement in the 1980s. That work must proceed as quickly as possible.

Nigeria's domination of the regional exchange patterns must also be of concern to the ECOWAS members, and particularly to Nigeria itself. ECOWAS is in need of a reliable network of protracted interchange built on a foundation of mutual confidence. It does not need the specter of a regional imperial power waxing and waning according to the whims of the oil market. Nigeria, too, stands to profit from stable interaction with other West African economies.

Lastly, the concern over intergroup conflicts of interest continues to have some validity for the region. However, it was not just the formal institution of the CEAO, but also the informal groupings which posed a challenge, although not necessarily a threat, to ECOWAS. The ties of a common anglophone or francophone colonial past, while showing slight signs of weakening, were still acting as a bond, one reinforced by the ease of currency convertibility and the strength of French backing for members of the ECOWAS franc zone.[33] A common currency throughout ECOWAS, although not an item for an immediate agenda, should certainly be on the table in the future, especially as doubts arise over the future of the CFA franc after full European integration in 1992. Such a common currency is a direct action which can be taken at the subsystemic level to solidify the intention to maintain a system of collective self-reliance.

ECOWAS and Exogenous Influences

While it has thus far been possible to identify characteristics of divided loyalties at the subsystemic level within the ECOWAS region, this last section of the analysis will be concerned with the role of systemic dynamics in the shaping of ECOWAS. In this way it can be estimated how effectively ECOWAS has been able to deal with the second component of collective self-reliance, that of working towards a disengagement from the enervative external nexus. To this end, the ECOWAS members' relations with industrial nations and the former colonial powers will be examined, and then they will be compared with the same extra-ECOWAS relations of other intraregional groupings.

The scenario presented in Table 5.5 is one which is typical for economies of the Third World. Trade with the

Table 5.5
ECOWAS Members' Extra-ECOWAS Trade

| | Trade with Industrial Countries as a Percentage of Country's Total | | | | | | Trade with Former Colonial Power* as a Percentage of Country's Total | | | | | |
| | Exports | | | Imports | | | Exports | | | Imports | | |
	1975	1980	1985	1975	1980	1985	1975	1980	1985	1975	1980	1985
Benin	55.3	86.7	84.4	74.7	83.3	68.3	27.2	18.0	10.4	28.6	24.4	19.0
Burkina Faso	40.3	72.0	56.2	67.7	60.9	64.4	18.8	16.9	29.0	43.4	37.7	33.4
Cape Verde	4.3	51.7	30.2	15.0	53.1	57.6	91.3	41.4	30.2	62.9	35.3	26.7
Côte d'Ivoire	74.1	90.1	74.2	74.3	78.4	70.5	27.2	24.8	17.2	39.3	43.8	33.1
Gambia	87.1	72.5	51.9	57.4	61.8	64.9	49.8	16.0	8.0	26.5	27.9	13.5
Ghana	73.8	69.1	79.7	70.6	54.9	57.3	14.5	16.2	20.6	15.0	17.2	20.2
Guinea	74.5	79.7	88.1	74.6	86.9	79.7	7.8	9.3	8.7	26.9	28.6	30.5
Guinea-Bissau	9.2	35.1	26.2	24.2	50.5	54.9	70.2	29.5	12.4	43.6	29.2	20.1
Liberia	94.5	90.1	75.1	77.9	55.1	52.6	22.0	11.1	12.1	31.5	6.2	3.7
Mali	26.3	68.4	73.1	52.3	55.6	68.5	9.8	19.3	18.2	34.0	34.9	32.0
Mauritania	96.9	94.3	93.7	77.2	81.2	77.0	22.0	29.0	14.7	47.8	41.4	30.6
Niger	70.0	96.3	83.3	61.3	72.6	62.3	63.7	73.5	75.5	30.4	44.8	29.8
Nigeria	82.3	94.3	80.2	88.5	83.4	70.5	14.1	1.3	5.3	23.3	22.8	17.9
Senegal	66.5	69.6	46.3	67.0	71.2	65.7	48.3	40.5	25.4	41.4	40.0	30.2
Sierra Leone	91.8	100.0	72.6	53.9	70.0	57.2	56.1	51.3	11.4	21.4	23.9	15.8
Togo	92.2	68.0	70.9	80.8	86.7	76.7	39.2	16.1	21.4	35.0	34.2	31.1

*With regard to Liberia, the figures represent trade with the United States.
Source: Calculated from data in Direction of Trade Statistics. 1986 Yearbook (Washington, D.C.: International Monetary Fund, 1986).

industrialized countries constitutes the mainstay of their
existence and generally parallels the highs and lows of the
world economy as a whole. As a percentage of their total
exports, exports to industrialized countries were up between
1975 and 1980 for ten of the sixteen ECOWAS members. As the
world economy slowed down, however, so too did exports to
industrialized countries for eleven of the ECOWAS states. At
the same time, imports from industrialized countries as a
share of each country's total imports were up in twelve
cases. A little additional figuring shows that on average,
the ECOWAS economies were dependent on the industrialized
countries as a market for 75 percent of their exports and as
a source of 74 percent of their imports in 1980, up from 1975
levels of 65 and 64 percent, respectively. By 1985, ECOWAS
economies had shifted back to just about their 1975
positions, relying on average on industrialized countries as
markets for 68 percent of their exports and as a source of 66
percent of their imports. Once again, Nigeria stands out,
both relative to the group as a whole and when compared with
the few other moderately strong economies in the region. The
bond between Nigeria and the industrialized countries can be
seen to be well above average in strength. Gavin Williams,
author of a study of the Nigerian political economy, remarks
of this phenomenon, that "Decolonisation thus paved the way
for capitalist development in Nigeria. But the development
of capitalism consolidated rather than undermined foreign
economic domination."[34] The question remains as to whether
or not ECOWAS will be afforded the opportunity to contribute
to the rectification of this situation.

Another comment made by Williams about the neocolonial
economy of Nigeria is also worth noting here. He states that
"Markets and sources of investment and technology have been
diversified among different metropolitan countries, or, to
put a different slant on the same thing, foreign exploitation
has been multilateralised."[35] The information provided in
the second half of Table 5.5 makes it clear that this
statement holds true not only for Nigeria, but for many of
the other West African nations as well. In contrast to the
overall high level of reliance on the external markets
evidenced in the left hand columns of Table 5.5, the right
side points to decreased dependence of the ECOWAS countries
on the specific markets of the former colonial power.
Nigeria is a prime example, with only 1.3 percent of its
exports going to Great Britain in 1980 and just 22.8 percent
of its imports originating there. By 1985, Nigeria's exports
to Great Britain had increased slightly as a percentage of

Nigeria's total exports, but its reliance on Great Britain
for imports had continued to decline. The mean for the
ECOWAS members' trade also corroborates this tendency. In
1985, the average percentage of exports going to each
country's former colonial power was 20 percent, and the
latter was the source of an average of 24 percent of each
country's imports. These figures are close to one-third of
those cited above regarding the level of significance of
ECOWAS trade with the industrialized countries in general.
It would seem that Williams's reference to the
"multilateralisation of foreign exploitation" is markedly
appropriate.

Whether or not one can differentiate between dependency
patterns of the ECOWAS participants according to which was
their colonial task-master, can most easily be determined
for most of the countries by returning to a comparison of
the aggregate information on intra-ECOWAS groups.[36] Hence
the provision of Table 5.6, which begins in lines one and
two with a reminder of the prevailing insignificance of
intra-ECOWAS trade for the Anglo-ECOWAS group. At the same
time, the extent of their relative economic potential is
highlighted once again in line three, which shows that Anglo-
ECOWAS's world exports have consistently accounted for more
than 70 percent of total ECOWAS world exports.

Lines four and five of Table 5.6 reconfirm that the
general trend between 1975 and 1980 towards an increased
reliance on the industrialized countries as a market for
ECOWAS members' exports and as a source of imports was
reversed between 1980 and 1985. Nonetheless, Anglo-ECOWAS as
a group still shows a greater degree of reliance on
industrialized countries as trading partners than do any of
the other regional subgroups. It is a pity that the
reciprocal appropriateness is lacking which would allow the
Anglo-ECOWAS exports to be rerouted to become the francophone
imports.

The last two lines of Table 5.6 are an indication of a
greater dependency of the francophone ECOWAS countries on
France relative to the anglophone members' ties with Great
Britain. At the same time, however, lines six and seven of
Table 5.6 confirm that there has been a steady decrease in
the level of reliance by francophone ECOWAS countries on
trade with France. The systemic trading patterns of the
ECOWAS nations do indeed seem to extend beyond the confines
of traditional colonial partisanship well into the realms of
diversified external dependence.

Table 5.6 (part 1)
Extraregional Trade of ECOWAS and Regional Subgroups

	ECOWAS	CEAO	ECOWAS Franc Zone	Anglo-ECOWAS
1. Group's exports to ECOWAS as a percentage of group's total exports (%):				
1975	4.1	13.9	15.0	1.9
1980	2.8	9.0	9.2	1.9
1985	3.5	9.1	9.0	2.1
2. Group's imports from ECOWAS as a percentage of group's total imports (%):				
1975	4.6	10.3	9.3	2.0
1980	3.4	8.1	7.8	2.1
1985	5.2	13.5	12.3	2.7
3. Group's world exports as a percentage of ECOWAS world imports (%):				
1975	100.	17.3	16.9	76.7
1980	100.	12.8	13.5	80.8
1985	100.	20.6	20.8	71.7

(continued)

Table 5.6 (part 2)
Extraregional Trade of ECOWAS and Regional Subgroups

	ECOWAS	CEAO	ECOWAS Franc Zone	Anglo-ECOWAS
4. Share of group's exports going to industrialized countries (%):				
1975	80.5	72.8	71.3	81.7
1980	91.0	81.3	79.2	93.1
1985	78.3	72.2	68.5	80.0
5. Share of group's imports coming from industrialized countries (%):				
1975	80.6	70.1	70.5	85.2
1980	77.5	73.8	75.4	80.8
1985	69.1	68.5	68.5	73.0
6. Share of group's exports going to former colonial power (%):				
1975	18.5	32.6	34.0	15.0
1980	6.9	31.5	30.0	2.6
1985	9.6	21.3	21.4	5.9

(continued)

Table 5.6 (part 3)
Extraregional Trade of ECOWAS and Regional Subgroups

	ECOWAS	CEAO	ECOWAS Franc Zone	Anglo-ECOWAS
7. Share of group's imports coming from former colonial power (%):				
1975	27.2	41.5	38.2	22.1
1980	23.4	40.1	39.7	19.1
1985	20.1	31.8	30.4	18.0

Source: Calculated from data in *Direction of Trade Statistics. 1986 Yearbook* (Washington, D.C.: International Monetary Fund, 1986).

Conclusion

On the whole, it would seem that the obstacles in the path of ECOWAS towards collective self-reliance are many, and are of both internal and external derivation. Barring an unmitigated awareness of the restraints and a fixed determination to overcome them, ECOWAS will not be able to pull the region out of the stagnant mire of the 1975 status quo.

Within ECOWAS, the distinction between the have and the have nots is all too clear and should not be exaggerated by arbitrary political maneuvers by individual member states. The role of historically-based proclivities in the region is revealed by the increased intra-Anglo-ECOWAS interaction during the period of capricious prosperity for Nigeria. The strength of intra-ECOWAS franc zone exchange indicates that the historical tendencies receive reinforcement from an accommodating monetary and financial arrangement with France.

While the absolute value of intra-ECOWAS trade remained low, by 1985 intra-ECOWAS trade had begun to take on slighly greater significance for the member nations' economies than had previously been the case. At this point in time it would be difficult to establish any causal link between the formation of ECOWAS in 1975 and the indications that over the decade leading to 1985 there was some slight permeation of historical trade boundaries in West Africa. Any debate over causation should not be allowed to detract attention from the fundamental issue of whether or not ECOWAS can build on whatever progress may have been made during its first decade.

The generally constrictive size of the manufacturing sector within ECOWAS members' economies is partially responsible for the continuing low level of intraregional trade. ECOWAS industrial programs to improve this avenue of interchange are of great importance. Without them the vertical integration of West Africa into the world economy will surely continue, and with it the static peripheral positioning of the region within the system. After reviewing the prospects for Africa in the 1980s, Steve Langdon and Lynn Mytelka pessimistically concluded that without the benefit of regional industrial planning:

> Export manufacturing, in Africa, then, will undoubtedly increase.... But this manufacturing is likely to be largely under the direction of foreign enterprises and integrated into the structure of internationalized production. In consequence, the linkage, employment, and income effects of such manufacturing will be fairly

limited within Africa -- and probably will be enjoyed mainly by those local elites who will extend their import-substitution symbiosis to the export sector.[37]

All of the evidence examined here indicates that this would indeed be the fate of the ECOWAS members should the economic rationality of a strong regional organization not be accepted and implemented.

However, the success of ECOWAS is dependent on far more than positive results from regular evaluations of economic variables. As great as, if not greater than, the economic constraints to collective self-reliance in West Africa are the political obstacles which hamper progress towards that goal.[38] The data examined here indicate that this was true during the first decade of ECOWAS. Yet in 1986, more than a decade after the formation of the organization, Nigeria's head of state was still expounding that "The hallmark of integration has been inaction and cosmetic commitment."[39] At some point, the African leaders need to look beyond the limiting tenets of nation-building if they are going to shape a strong future for their people. If ECOWAS is not to be doomed to failure, national self-interests must be replaced by regional priorities.

Notes

1. For a theoretical elaboration of these characteristics and their origins, see Samir Amin, *Unequal Development*, trans. by Brian Pearce (Sussex, England: Harvester Press, 1976), especially Chapter 4, pp. 198-292. A more detailed analysis of the current socioeconomic standing of Africa vis-à-vis the rest of the world can be found in Adebayo Adedeji, "Development and Economic Growth in Africa to the Year 2000: Alternative Projections and Policies" in Timothy M. Shaw (ed.), *Alternative Futures for Africa* (Boulder: Westview Press, 1982). Many of the other essays in this volume are also of relevance to this subject.

2. It will of course be interesting to update the analysis for 1990 as soon as satisfactorily reliable trade figures are published.

3. Ralph Uwechue (ed.), *Africa Today* (London: Africa Journal, 1981), "Treaty of the Economic Community of West African States (ECOWAS), 29 May 1975, article 32.

4. *Ibid.*, preamble.

5. Ernst B. Haas, *The Obsolescence of Regional Integration Theory* (Berkeley: Institute of International Studies, 1975), p. 12. For a further discussion of the development of regional integration theory, see Donald J. Puchala, "Integration Theory and the Study of International Relations" in Richard L. Merritt and Bruce M. Russett (eds.), *From National Development to Global Community* (London: George Allen & Unwin, 1981).

6. These and other programs are reviewed in "Economic Community of West Africa -- ECOWAS," ECOWAS Executive Secretariat, *West Africa*, 25 May 1981.

7. Haas, *Obsolescence*, especially Chapter 1, "Obsolescent: Where and Why?"

8. *Ibid.*, p. 5.

9. See John P. Renninger, "The Future of Economic Cooperation Schemes in Africa, with Special Reference to ECOWAS" in Timothy M. Shaw (ed.), *Alternative Futures for Africa*, pp. 154-155.

10. A similar use of trade data to evaluate ECOWAS's progress through 1981 has been made by C.E. Enuenwosu, "Trade Liberalisation and Finance -- The Ecowas Experience" in Akinola A. Owosekua (ed.), *Towards an African Economic Community* (Ibadan: Nigerian Institute of Social and Economic Research, 1986).

11. The development of this illicit cross-border activity is traced in O.J. Igue, "L'officiel, le parallèle et le clandestin," *Politique Africaine*, 9, March 1983. It is, of course, ironic that smuggling should be such a profitable business within an economic community meant to facilitate the free-market exchange of goods.

12. Adebayo Adedeji (ed.), *Indigenization of African Economies* (London: Hutchinson University Library for Africa, 1981), p. 388.

13. It is a general submission to the essentially unpredictable political nature of growth in regional organizations, and recognition of its relative neglect in the correspondent theory, which causes Haas to declare that theory obsolete. See Haas, *Obsolescence*, especially chapter 5, "Integration or Interdependence?"

14. A succinct recounting of the historical development of West African trade patterns can be found in chapter 4, "External Trade" in Douglas Rimmer, *The Economies of West Africa* (London: Weidenfeld and Nicolson, 1984).

15. Uka Ezenwe, "Trade and Growth in West Africa in the 1980s," *Journal of Modern African Studies*, 20 (2), 1982, p. 313.

16. Calculated from *Direction of Trade Statistics*. Yearbook (Washington, D.C.: International Monetary Fund. 1981, 1986). The errors inherent to just about all foreign trade statistics are fully recognized by this author. Given, however, that the basic issues involved here are of a relative nature, it would seem that the extrapolations, if not entirely precise, are at least consistent in their margin of error.

17. *Ibid.*

18. *Ibid.*

19. *Ibid.*

20. Calculated from data in *Statistical Yearbook 1979-80* (New York: United Nations, 1981); *Survey of Economic and Social Conditions in Africa, 1985-86* (New York: United Nations, 1988); and *Survey of Economic and Social Conditions in Africa, 1986-87* (New York: United Nations, 1988).

21. *Ibid.*

22. *Ibid.*

23. *Ibid.*

24. *Ibid.*

25. Johan Galtung, "The Politics of Self-Reliance" in Heraldo Munoz (ed.), *From Dependency to Development: Strategies to Overcome Underdevelopment and Inequality* (Boulder: Westview Press, 1981), p. 175.

26. For discussions of the effect of Nigeria's expulsion of illegal immigrants on ECOWAS's progress, see Margaret A. Novicki, "West Africa After the Exodus," *Africa Report*, 30(4), 1985; and Gladson I. Nwanna, "ECOWAS and Labor Migration in West Africa," *The Journal of Social, Political and Economic Studies*, 11(2), 1986.

27. "Treaty of the Economic Community of West African States," article 59.

28. The members of the CEAO are: Burkina Faso, Côte d'Ivoire, Mali, Mauritania, Niger and Senegal.

29. "ECOWAS poised to advance," *West Africa*, 7 June 1982, p. 1492.

30. The extent of the influence of the actual process of decolonization on the postindependence continuation of bonds between former colony and former imperial power remains to be fully determined. See, for example, Tony Smith, "A

Comparative Study of French and British Decolonization,"
Comparative Studies in Society and History, 20(1), January
1978.

31.   By ECOWAS franc zone is meant here those members of
ECOWAS whose currency remains linked to the French franc.
This would include: Benin, Burkina Faso, Côte d'Ivoire, Mali,
Niger, Senegal and Togo.   Anglo-ECOWAS refers to the four
ECOWAS countries of Gambia, Ghana, Nigeria and Sierra Leone,
for whom Great Britain is the former colonial power.

32.   Reliance on the export of primary commodities for
income is an ECOWAS-wide characteristic.   In 1979, two to
four primary commodities accounted for at least 70 percent
of each ECOWAS country's total exports.   In 1978, the average
share of manufacturing in the GDP of the ECOWAS countries was
just 8.5 percent.   Calculated from data in *Statistical
Yearbook 1979-80*.

33.   For a detailed analysis of the economic relations
between France and the franc zone in Africa, see P. Hugon,
"L'Afrique noire francophone: L'enjeu economique pour la
France," *Politique Africaine*, 2(5), February 1982.

34.   Gavin Williams. "Nigeria: The Neo-Colonial Political
Economy" in Dennis L. Cohen and John Daniel (eds.), *Political
Economy of Africa* (Harlow, Essex: Longman, 1981), p. 47.

35.   *Ibid.*, p. 45.

36.   This method excludes analysis of the two former
Portuguese colonies and Liberia.   However, since their
combined world exports in 1980 represent less than 4 percent
of total ECOWAS world exports, it does seem that
generalizations can indeed be made without them.   It would,
of course, be interesting to take a microscope to the intra-
and extra-ECOWAS patterns of trade of the more recently
independent Guinea-Bissau and Cape Verde for the sake of
comparison with the other countries which received their
independence earlier and under considerably less blatantly
confrontative circumstances.   But that is a research topic
unto itself.

37.   Steven Langdon and Lynn K. Mytelka, "Africa in the
Changing World Economy" in Colin Legum, I. William Zartman,
Steven Langdon and Lynn K. Mytelka, *Africa in the 1980s* (New
York: McGraw-Hill, 1979), p. 204.

38.   Another author who emphasizes the exigency of
political cooperation if ECOWAS is to have a long and strong
future is Julius Emeka Okolo, "Integrative and Cooperative
Regionalism: The Economic Community of West African States,"
International Organization, 39(1), 1985; and in Chapter 2 of
this volume.

39. President Babangida at the ninth summit conference of ECOWAS states, as cited in *Africa Research Bulletin, Economic,* 23(6), 31 July 1986, p. 8264.

6

Regionalism and the African Crisis: Towards a Political Economy of ECOWAS and SADCC

Timothy M. Shaw

Regional cooperation is not new in Africa. In fact the myriad regional and subregional organizations testify to the intensive efforts made to harness regional cooperation to the task of African development... Yet, as elsewhere, the results have not been impressive. While this record has caused disenchantment among integration theorists, (my) thesis...is that for Africa the realities still point to the imperative of regional cooperation.

-Shridath S. Ramphal[1]

There is no doubt that in spite of all the difficulties and all the constraints, there has been some remarkable progress in laying the foundation for meaningful economic cooperation in Africa. Although there has been no breakthrough yet, there is cause for hope, if not for optimism. The balkanisation of Africa is one of the major constraints to the economic transformation of the continent...it is imperative that African countries should strengthen their solidarity in all fields and stress the factors that unite rather than those that divide them.

-Adebayo Adedeji[2]

The continuing continental crisis of underdevelopment highlights the distance between rhetoric and reality in African regionalism. It also draws attention to the distinction between "old" and "new" regionalisms: i.e., between formal and comprehensive declarations on the one hand and informal and specific arrangements on the other. If the crisis led to reevaluations of development direction -- the Lagos Plan of Action (LPA) and self-reliance[3] -- it also generated reconsiderations of regionalist doctrine -- from free trade areas and common services to sectoral and infrastructural agreements. In short, the future of Africa's development policies in general and regional proposals in particular has led over the last difficult decade to a redefinition of both in which national and collective self-reliance are taken to be the criteria of development. Regionalism remains an imperative, but it has been largely restated to fit current needs, experiences and contexts in the 1990s as indicated at the end of this chapter. As Sam Asante lamented:

By 1980 -- when the LPA was adopted -- almost all the economic cooperation schemes optimistically launched in the 1960s -- the halcyon years of African integration -- had become largely moribund.[4]

Regionalism in Africa

Since the beginning of the 1980s marked a conjuncture in continental affairs -- the post-Bretton Woods and post-oil shocks -- economic (dis)order finally caught up with Africa. The Sahel famine was merely symptomatic of a larger failure, not of rain but of development. Fortuitously, a few more enlightened African leaders had anticipated such a collapse by gathering in Monrovia in 1979 where they designed a collective strategy subsequently embodied in the LPA. The pair of continental economic summits -- in 1981 in Lagos and 1986 in Addis Ababa -- mark a turning point in African affairs: from a preoccupation with short-term, political rhetoric towards longer-term economic reform. The LPA and Addis Ababa Declaration, prepared for the Special General Assembly of mid-1986, signify a cluster of forces and factors:

(a) Africa's reluctant recognition that contemporary rates of development were either unsatisfactory or negative;
(b) a belated appreciation that global recovery would not necessarily help Africa and that many external agencies had only a temporary interest in continental

development;
(c)   international recommendations were not always
appropriate, so Africa had to design its own strategy;
(d)   continental balkanisation had to be overcome to
provide the basis for sustained recovery;
(e)   indigenous interests, exchange and policies should
be primary so that both South-South and South-North
negotiations could proceed from a position of cohesion
rather than division; so
(f)   Africa needs self-confidence as well as -reliance
and -sustainment to advance towards redevelopment,
redirection and a continental community by the end of
the century.[5]

The failure of national economies, regional integration,
South-South relations and South-North redistribution combined
with inflation, recession (often with regression),
desertification, regional conflicts and debt reschedulings[6]
meant that Africa had to reevaluate its development
directions rapidly and critically. With the encouragement
of the UN Economic Commission for Africa (ECA) this process
had resulted in a new framework for regional endeavors if
not yet unequivocal regional benefits.   According to the
major animateur, Adebayo Adedeji, the LPA and related
declarations and documents made   collective   cooperation
and   self-reliance an all-pervasive issue with the ultimate
goal of an African Economic Community by the year 2000,
approached in a series of stages:

> Thus, it calls, during the 1980s, for the strengthening
> of existing regional economic communities and for
> establishing new ones so as to cover the continent as a
> whole; for the strengthening of sectoral integration at
> the continental level; and for promoting coordination
> and harmonization among existing and future economic
> groupings. And during the decade of the 1980s, it calls
> for sectoral integration.[7]

Adedeji proceeded to identify a trio of novel regional
groupings as indicative of such stages of integration,
pointing to the ECA-sponsored Preferential Trade Area (PTA)
(for Eastern and Southern Africa) rather than the Frontline
States (FLS) - supported Southern African Development
Coordination Conference (SADCC):

> Excessive openness and external dependence of African
> economies are inimical to the achievement not only of

national but also of collective self-reliance so that progressive inter-African economic penetration is a *sine qua non* for the achievement of national and collective self-reliance. There is no doubt that the developments of the past few years have heralded the emergence of a sound foundation for achieving this objective. ECOWAS, PTA and ECCAS constitute the main instrumentalities for achieving this goal. Among them, these three institutions cover the entire area of sub-Saharan Africa. Therefore, we need urgently to put them into the position of helping direct African economic policy.[8]

But these institutional developments take place in a continent characterized not only by cyclical droughts but also by exponential declines and inequalities and in a world system preoccupied by a new international division of labor rather than a new international economic order. In short, the national, continental and global galaxies of forces are hardly in a propitious orbit.[9] To advance development, let alone cooperation, substantial changes need to take place in the character of production, contradictions and institutions within and between African political economies. And such changes are a function of history as well as of ideology and diplomacy. Together these determine whether the continent can advance from old to new forms of regionalism, from extroversion to self-reliance, and from orthodox to radical analysis and *praxis*.[10]

Africa is not only the largest regional subsystem in terms of territorial size and number of states;[11] it is also the least industrialized and the one characterized by the most inequality. Its colonial inheritance -- "dualistic" economies, authoritarian regimes and high levels of ethnic and racial consciousness -- is not an advantageous one and if current projections materialize with regard to both its continued inability to meet Basic Human Needs (BHN) and the incidence and impact of growing inequalities, its prospects in the 1990s are rather gloomy.[12] Nevertheless, despite its unfortunate inheritance and mixed performance, Africa has emerged as an important actor in the contemporary arena of world politics.

Ambiguities and contradictions in the past and present characterize the political economy of Africa; in addition it is a Southern continent in a global system still dominated essentially by the interests and actions of the North. The discontinuities and dilemmas of "economic" dependence and "political" interdependence are revealed most poignantly in the very tenuous and vulnerable form of "independence" presently achieved by African countries. The uneven rates and results of development -- with its interrelated political, economic, social and strategic components -- have served to exacerbate inequalities and tensions both within and between the states of Africa as well as between continental and global actors.[13]

The position and prospects of Africa in an unequal world order pose problems for both analysis and action, perception and prediction. This chapter is concerned, therefore, not only with the comparative study of the Economic Community of West African States (ECOWAS) as a regional subsystem, but also with alternative approaches to analysis as well as alternative development strategies. In particular, it will consider and contrast both the more "orthodox" and "radical" modes of analysis and modes of production, taking into account the interrelationship between theory and policy. The paradoxes and dilemmas of Africa's role in the world system are relevant to the comparative analysis of regionalism, to comparative explanations of integration and to comparative policy choices. They also inform contrasts between ECOWAS and SADCC as case studies.

Alternative Modes of Analysis and Advocacy

The revival of ideology in Africa is one aspect of a broader trend towards divergent political economies caused by the highly uneven impact of incorporation into the world system. The myth of equality dies hard among scholars as well as statesmen, and the emergence of a few leading powers on the continent is forcing a reassessment in both perception and policy. Nevertheless, the orthodox school sticks doggedly to the assumption that the continental system consists of essentially equal and similar actors, while the radical approach attempts to relate novel concepts -- such as that of "subimperialism"[14] -- to changes in Africa's position in the world order. Both modes of analysis retain their currency in a global system characterized by a return to realpolitik and power politics. Nevertheless, I. William Zartman continues to assert that it is simply not possible to understand the relations of the continental system through a study of the few states which, through a combination of such elements of national strength as location, area, population, GNP and foreign policy interests, might be counted as the powerful of the continent.[15]

Nonetheless, the orthodox approach has moved some way towards recognition of the growing inequalities on the continent, conceiving of them, however, as changeable and unstable phenomena rather than as reflections of a gradual evolution in Africa's substructure. Instead of treating Africa's new group of "middle powers" as indicative of changes in the international division of labor, Zartman views them merely as centers of momentary conflicts and coalitions. According to him the three major features of the leading African states are:

> temporary initiatives on the regional level, delicate positions of predominance within a subregion, and limited arrays of resources available as a power base even for the strongest...in short, African states have little with which to threaten and little to share, and they are not in a position to win or enforce long-term commitments.. At best, they can command temporary advantages, since most African states' resources are meager.[16]

By contrast, the radical mode sees regional powers as being less transitional, not restricted to strategic issues alone and more structurally defined. From this viewpoint, the emergence of subimperialism on the continent is related to the evolving international division of labor in which some limited forms of industrialism can take place, albeit under the auspices of the multinational corporation, in the "semi-periphery".[17] Production is restructured within corporations and center states so certain countries may advance from the periphery into the semi-periphery, but technological, financial and administrative controls are largely retained in the center.

Internationalization of production does not mean internationalization of control. Rather, the center is able to secure favorable terms and attitudes by offering some limited degree of semi-industrialization to cooperative regimes or countries with particularly valuable natural or organizational resources. According to Immanuel Wallerstein's world system framework, a few African states, either by invitation or by accident, will come to enjoy upward mobility in the international hierarchy, while the majority will continue to stagnate and remain underdeveloped in the periphery.[18] The possibility or prospect of advancing into the semi-periphery serves to reinforce confidence in orthodox development theory as well as to encourage quiescence in established spheres of influence. In turn, a few semi-industrial states dominate their own regions of the continent partially on behalf of center interests.

In the mid-term future, semi-industrialism in the semi-periphery may reinforce confidence in orthodox development strategies and in the continent's ability to maintain order. However, in the longer term as Steven Langdon and Lynn Mytelka suggest, the subimperial "solution" may generate its own contradictions and demise because of its association with the established capitalist international division of labor:

> Export manufacturing in Africa, then, will undoubtedly increase -- as the signs of change in such countries as the Ivory Coast, Senegal, Ghana and Kenya suggest. But this manufacturing is likely to be largely under the direction of foreign enterprises and integrated into the structure of internationalized production. In consequence, the linkage, employment, and income effects of such manufacturing will be fairly limited within Africa -- and probably will be enjoyed mainly by those local elites who will extend their import substitution symbiosis to the export sector. Significant restructuring of African economies, with wide dynamic advantages for African majorities, cannot be expected to emerge from this export-manufacturing growth.[19]

The emergence of inequalities and regional powers on the continent may, paradoxically, serve to increase the level of interaction in Africa, at least in the short-run and among the group of emergent middle powers. To date, the proportion of intra- versus extra-continental exchange has been very limited, because of Africa's dependent status within the world system. Economic interaction and military relations have been concentrated at the subregional level, increasingly under the dominance of a few regional centers and cities -- such as Abidjan, Cairo, Dakar, Harare, Lagos and Nairobi -- that serve as intermediaries between metropolises and peripheries.

Interdependences based on integration in Africa remain largely an aspiration rather than a reality. Despite declarations and diplomacy, integration as measured in terms of economic, communications and social transactions remains at a stubbornly low level. The orthodox view of this situation is that integration takes time and that, given Africa's colonial inheritance, its postindependence performance is quite promising. By contrast, the radical perspective sees extra-continental economic dependence as an essential characteristic of the capitalist world system; it does not expect high levels of continental integration while Africa remains incorporated within global networks. These divergent perspectives have informed alternative current policies, as indicated below.

So, whereas the orthodox approach sees no necessary incompatibility between global, continental and regional integration, the radical school considers continental and regional self-reliance to be incompatible with global and transnational integration. Regional exchange has a rather mixed record, with inter-African trade rising less slowly than extra-African trade; i.e., inter-African exchange continues to fall as a percentage of total African trade. Moreover, most of this trade is either transit of non-African goods to landlocked states, or the export of manufactures by multinational branches located in regional centers such as Abidjan, Harare, Lagos and Nairobi.

Intra-African trade is unlikely to increase much until the continent escapes from its colonial heritage of North-South links and produces goods with markets on the continent as well as outside. A regional industrialization policy is necessary to maximize compatibility and exchange; yet this cannot be designed or realized until decisions made by foreign countries and corporations are transcended.[20] This, in turn, requires a degree of autonomy that can only be achieved through collective action. Hence, the vicious circle of exogenous rather than endogenous growth, of a highly open rather than relatively closed continental system. The elusiveness of intra-African exchange is reflected in the underdeveloped state of the continental infrastructure. Communications by land, sea, air and telex are improving but still by no means balance extra-African connections.

Political Economy and Foreign Policy

The established African response to colonialism and underdevelopment has been advocacy of nationalism at the state level; all these reactions call for a redistribution of authority and resources without involving a real transformation in Africa's world position. These three clusters of values have constituted the core of Africa's collective foreign policy and have led to current demands for a new international economic order (NIEO).[21] However, with the emergence of inequalities on the continent and the reappearance of ideological cleavages, common international positions have tended to fragment. The espousal of "alternative" development strategies, such as the "noncapitalist path" and various forms of socialism, inspired by Marxist-Leninist rather than traditional thought, have undermined the continent's ideological consensus and have led to a variety of foreign policy orientations and emphases.[22]

The orthodox approach, recognizing Africa's common heritage and transition, still emphasizes commonalities in the continent's foreign policies; the radical approach, reflecting changes in the political economy of parts of the continent, accepts and examines contradictions in the foreign relations of participating state and nonstate institutions. The orthodox perspective, based on certain sociological, cultural and psychological affinities conceives of Africa's foreign policy as being singular and consensual. It appreciates the imperative of unity if Africa's voice is to be heard. Under the impact of various associations, however, it has begun to accept that there may be different foreign policy emphases or nuances, particularly based on membership of, say, the Commonwealth, francophonie, Arab League or Islamic States:

> The recognition of overlapping systems in interpreting foreign policy alternatives and possibilities for states with dual membership is both a more helpful and more realistic way of looking at foreign policies than is the attempt to force such states exclusively into one area or the other.[23]

While African states may belong to a variety of international institutions, their foreign policy choices may be quite limited, particularly by their selection of a development strategy. The comparative study of foreign policy in Africa remains rather embryonic, although a few frameworks for analysis now exist.[24] One major factor in foreign policy-making is, of course, choice of development strategy which, given Africa's dependence and openness, means essentially how to respond to external pressures and opportunities. Donald Rothchild and Robert Curry have proposed a trilateral typology of such responses that may also serve as a framework for comparative foreign policy analysis. They identify three policy options -- accommodation, reorganization and transformation[25] -- which span the spectrum from acquiescence to resistance, respectively. But, in agreement with the general tenor of the orthodox school, they treat these as mere policy responses rather than as political strategies that reflect underlying structural contradictions.

By contrast, the radical perspective concentrates on development alternatives rather than on foreign policy, and attempts to relate these to modes of production and incorporation rather than to international associations and ideologies. More radical African scholars such as Micah Tsomondo and Teti Kofi argue in this genre that Pan-Africanism is representative of "bourgeois" interests and needs to be transcended both in analysis and practice by a more "scientific" variety of socialism. Moreover, they see the adoption of socialism at the continental level as a prerequisite for effective unity based on an appreciation of class politics and the adoption of a continental industrial strategy. In other words, they conceive of socialism as a response to fragmentation and functionalism on the one hand, and to dependence and underdevelopment on the other hand.[26]

The orthodox approach, however, still sees Pan-Africanism as a reaction to colonialism and does not go much beyond the re-Africanization of the continent as an objective. It still has faith in orthodox theories of convergence and "trickledown" development, and extroverted strategies of growth. By contrast, the radical approach has largely abandoned the assumptions and remedies of the orthodox perspective in favor of an approach that is more introverted and self-reliant, based on an appreciation of the international division of labor as it affects Africa.[27]

Old and New Regionalisms

The orthodox approach has analyzed attempts at regional integration in Africa as part of a diplomatic strategy to improve the balance of forces between the continent and the rest of the global system. This approach conceives of regionalism, not so much as a development strategy or an attempt to restructure the international division of labor, so much as a diplomatic tactic designed to enhance Africa's visibility and autonomy -- a collective form of decolonization. Its focus has been on regional constitutions and institutions -- the form rather than the relationship-- and on mediation and liberation rather than structural transformation. From this perspective, the process is as important as, if not more than, the results. And although one motive of the Pan-African movement has been to reduce balkanization and to transcend nationalism, in fact the record of the Organization of African Unity (OAU) to date has served to reinforce fragmentation and to reify the state:

From the start the existence of the OAU has been far more important to African statesmen and politicians than any functional role it may perform in promoting economic cooperation or even the alignment of foreign policies...By merely being there, the OAU does indeed perform one vital role in African diplomacy -- it bestows legitimacy on its members and on the movements and causes which they chose to recognize...It has always been the OAU's main task to set the seal of legitimacy on both the distribution of power within African states and on those liberation movements, mainly in Southern Africa, which were contesting power with colonial or minority regimes.[28]

By contrast to the orthodox school's focus on diplomacy and legitimacy, the radical approach considers the developmental and economic impact of nationalism. And whereas the orthodox school tends to produce relatively positive evaluations, the radical approach leads to essentially negative conclusions. The OAU network may have served to stabilize the continental system in terms of decolonization, mediation and consultation, but the ECA and its "subregional" associates have not yet begun to escape from a position of economic dependence on the world system.

The OAU has shown a remarkable resilience over its first twenty-five years in its ability to weather the storms of "dialogue" and "detente" with South Africa, of conflict in Shaba, Sudan, Chad and Western Sahara, and of OPEC and Afro-Arab divisions.[29] But these rather ephemeral, "diplomatic crises" are seen by the radical school as merely reflections of fundamental contradictions that the OAU-ECA system has yet to confront seriously. Despite a growing range of proposals and scenarios, regional interactions did not lead to significant advances at least until the 1980s.

The radical school suggests that the reason for this condition is the continued integration of Africa into the world system.[30] Whereas at the level of diplomacy and ideology, the OAU can score pyrrhic victories, at the level of exchange and capital and the continental political economy, it cannot, with profound implications for both metropolitan and African elite interests. Given the close transnational links between the new elite and foreign countries, corporations and classes, such a prospect is unlikely to continue, unless and until global and national conditions change. In an attempt to make Africa's powerlessness and assertiveness compatible with each other, Zartman has recognized the discontinuity between continental dependences and demands while ignoring the structural contradictions that generated such ambiguity:

In a world where Africa does not have the power to protect itself and promote its own goals, it proposes a new system of international relations that emphasizes its rights and deemphasizes the classical means to attain them. The inherent contradiction, sharpened by the fact that the faster developing states in Africa do in fact seek to increase their power and use it in classical ways, is typical of an idealistic view of international relations.[31]

If the orthodox approach, with its emphasis on the new diplomacy, is "idealistic" in tone then the radical perspective, with its emphasis on the old dependence, is "realistic" in orientation. This analytic and existential dichotomy is reflected in patterns of contemporary regional cooperation and conflict -- i.e., ECOWAS versus SADCC -- which are themselves but aspects of contemporary contradictions within and around the continent. These extend to continued advocacy of extracontinental regionalism -- EurAfrica -- as well as intracontinental, despite repeated nationalist critiques of dominance and dependence.

Revisionism, Regionalism and the
Continental Crisis

Contemporary contradictions between regionalisms within and around Africa take place in a world system characterized by recession, inflation and transition. The demise of the post-war Bretton Woods order of relative expansion and diffusion has resulted in a more anarchic, unyielding world of general contraction and highly uneven patterns of growth and decline, from the resilience of South Korea and Singapore to the stagnation of Senegal and Zambia, and the decay of Ghana and Tanzania, i.e., the new division between Newly Industrializing Countries (NICs)[32] and Least Developed Countries (LLDCs), between "Third" and "Fourth" Worlds. The last decade, then, has seen a relatively homogeneous continent become considerably more heterogeneous, with myriad implications for cohesion and regionalism. It has also witnessed a growing tension between the political and the economic, as well as an emerging set of contradictory responses symbolized by the OAU's Lagos Plan of Action, on the one hand, and the World Bank's Agenda for Action on the other.[33] If the latter advocates extroverted growth, compatible with EurAfricanism, then the former advances

African self-reliance, compatible with continental regionalism.

In short, the present conjuncture of global and continental crises has stimulated a variety of responses at the levels of politics and economics on the one hand and of EurAfrican and continental regionalism on the other hand. Given the new diversity of political economies on the continent, these alternative, and not necessarily compatible, policies and preferences are advocated by different states, classes and fractions. The myth of Pan-Africanism is thus under attack from both extra- and intra-African forces of either disinterest, division or dominance. Regionalism is a controversial ideology and policy because of a multiplicity of interpretations, interests and implications. Its tendency to manipulation and ambiguity is a reflection of the range of contradictions generated by the current crisis and the intensity of competition for scarce resources in a period of no growth. Regionalism becomes more problematic and antagonistic as growth is elusive and projections are unpromising. Hence the willingness of diverse interests to define it in different ways to maximize their prospects of renewed growth, if not development.

Therefore, regionalism has had a rather checkered history in Africa; yet, despite many cautionary tales, optimism abounds over regionalism in the continent. In many ways a "second-generation" institution, ECOWAS is both bigger and more ambitious than most previous experiments in either Africa or elsewhere. Nevertheless, its prospects remain problematic, and its aspirations remain ambiguous. Its tenuous situation and support lead to a set of questions about its future that are posed in the concluding section, although the turbulent future of southern Africa -- the conjuncture of racism and repression, destabilization and disengagement -- may yet spill over to affect ECOWAS.

Regional development and unity are likely to remain elusive in Africa in the mid-term future because of changes in the global political economy as well as because of related shifts in the continental system. If regionalism was difficult in previous decades, it is likely to be even more so in the 1990s because of interrelated changes in the global and continental divisions of labor and economic priorities. Until the mid-1970s, international growth was sufficiently large for the marginal redistribution of surplus and opportunity from the center to the periphery to be neither impossible nor controversial. However, in the less benign and more calculating world of the early-1990s -- a world of recession and inflation still trying to live with fluctuating

exchange and interest rates and higher prices for energy --
Third World regional development at the expense of
metropolitan growth is most unlikely. International
economics are once again zero- rather than mixed-sum; the
environment of regionalism is no longer tolerant, let alone
supportive.

If ECOWAS fails, the causes may well be extra- rather than
intra-African; and, if it succeeds, the benefits may well
flow outside rather than inside the region. Yet, despite the
problems of regionalism in Africa over the last twenty-five
years, many of which arose in less difficult times than
today, West African leaders retain the faith that ECOWAS will
be exceptional. Given the lack of visible, viable options,
such faith may be the lack of any alternative: regionalism
and self-reliance by default.

The rest of this chapter attempts to explain and evaluate
the elusiveness of regionalism in Africa by contrast to the
seeming resilience of EurAfricanism, by situating it in the
context of the changing global political economy. The
prospects for unity and development on the continent in the
1990s will be profoundly affected by pressures on the
international division of labor elsewhere. Likewise, any
projections for regionalism in Africa in general and West
Africa in particular, cannot exclude world trends and
forecasts: the ambiguity of dominance, especially of
EurAfrica.[34]

International capitalism has evolved considerably in the
three decades that Africa has been formally independent.
This evolution -- from liberalism to protectionism, from
American hegemony to "trilateralism," and from growth to
recession -- has important implications for the African
continent. If most African states failed to grow before the
mid-1970s, their prospects have since deteriorated. And any
improvement that has occurred -- before but especially after
the mid-1970s -- has been unevenly generated and distributed,
both between and within countries.

Growing inequalities in Africa have important implications
for unity as well as for development. In response to the
elusiveness of growth, the "development strategies" of states
have diverged away from a consensual form of "African
socialism" and towards various types of "state capitalism"
or "state corporatism."[35] And these alternatives tend to be
related to differences in international position and
potential. Uneven development in terms of both empirical and
ideological orientation is not new to Africa. However, the
emergence of a small group of "middle powers" is unlikely to
be a transitory phenomenon. Rather, their position at the

"semi-periphery" -- by contrast to the peripheral position of most African states -- is structural, not just political or ephemeral, encouraged by continued EurAfrican relationships. Independence did not bring development for all but it did facilitate growth for some.

African unity has always been something of a myth. But its mythical qualities have multiplied as the continent has become more unequal. In particular, the uneven impact of recession and inflation in the mid-1970s exacerbated inequalities: a minority of "Third World" states weathered the storm, whereas the majority of "Fourth World" states were further depressed and impoverished economically. The Third World of Newly Industrializing/Influential Countries (NICs) includes the major centers of manufacturing and communications -- Algeria, Egypt, Côte d'Ivoire, Kenya, Nigeria and Zimbabwe -- whereas the Fourth World of the real periphery, including the majority of ECOWAS states, is increasingly marginalized. The latter, most seriously affected states, can hardly afford to import enough food, let alone capital, so that their economic prospects continue to dim, rather than brighten. By contrast, the NICs have adjusted to OPEC more readily and positively and they have captured most of the (inadequate) increase in the regional product that has been generated in the last decade. In Africa the "middling rich" get somewhat richer, while the poor get even poorer. And European Community (EC) interests concentrate on the former at the expense of the latter, disclaimers of North-South dialogue notwithstanding.

Development and Regionalism in the 1990s

Dependence or Self-Reliance?

African unity is becoming more tenuous because African states have increasingly divergent positions within the world system; a divergence which Lomé conventions do not transcend and may even exacerbate. The majority of primary commodity producers has suffered declining terms of trade as the prices of manufactures and petroleum have increased; over the last fifteen years the LLDCs have hardly grown at all, with several enduring negative growth rates. By contrast, the would-be NICs initially grew at an almost exponential rate, especially those that are also OPEC members (e.g. Algeria and Nigeria) until the bursting of the oil bubble in the early 1980s. Africa is, therefore, an increasingly unequal continent in which growth, industrialization and optimism are concentrated in a few NICs, while the majority of countries and peoples suffers minimal growth, continued marginalization and a pessimistic outlook. In these circumstances, development strategies diverge, as do growth rates, despite collective economic policies in the OAU, Lomé and Group of Seventy-Seven arrangements.

In general, the LLDCs have looked inward, while NICs looked outward; poorer African states advocate self-reliance, while the richer favor further incorporation. These "back-to-back" developmental orientations have important implications for regional as well as continental cooperation. The LLDCs tend to favor collective as well as national self-reliance, but the prospects for autonomy through regionalism are reduced when the "core" of each potential region is more extroverted in policy and in practice: African and EurAfrican regionalisms become contradictory at such junctions. The periphery cannot effectively turn around regional institutions towards disengagement, when the semi-periphery seeks to play an intermediary role, involving continued association with metropolitan countries and corporations. In other words, regional integration in Africa is now jeopardized because regional leaders are either disinterested or diverted: successive Lomé arrangements provide alternative avenues for pressure and position.

The logic of the semi-periphery has negative implications for successful integration within the periphery except as an extension of ubiquitous EurAfrican connections. Regional powers grow not only because of their relatively large extractive, manufacturing or service sectors, but also because they have come to dominate regional relations, diplomatic as well as economic. In an era of relative superpower withdrawal, they have had their intermediary role recognized and expanded. So they play effectively the role of regional leader-catalyst and core -- but their connections with metropolitan countries and corporations make them linkages in the center-periphery chain. In other words, their interest in regionalism as the semi-periphery -- dominance and growth -- may be quite different from that of the periphery -- development and self-reliance. The conception of regionalisms within Africa and EurAfrica are quite distinctive and may be dialectical.

This also means that the semi-periphery has an orientation quite different from that of the other major continental organization -- the ECA. Yet, in an era when the Pan-African *political* consensus within the OAU has become elusive -- see disputes over Angola, Chad, Western Sahara, Shaba, Somalia, etc. -- the apparent Pan-African *economic* consensus within the ECA has become broader and more solid. Given projections of increased inequalities, dependence and underdevelopment, the ECA has called for a collective response outside of the EC-ACP (African, Caribbean and Pacific) nexus to head-off an unpromising future.[36] At a time when the definition and implementation of (political) nonalignment and Pan-Africanism have become diluted, advocacy of (economic) self-reliance has become relatively commonplace. The ECA, in suggesting designs for national and collective self-reliance, is taking the part of the majority of peripheral, Fourth World states rather than advancing the interests of the minority in the semi-periphery. Instead of being permissive about Africa's inheritance of integration within the world system, especially within EurAfrica, the ECA has called for a reconsideration of unequal exchange, a reevaluation of international economic relations:

> Their significance lies in the role they play in facilitating or inhibiting (a) the establishment of self-reliance, i.e., the substitution of domestic for foreign factor imports, and (b) the promotion of self sustainment, i.e., the substitution of internally generated forces determining the speed and direction of economic growth...[37]

From EurAfrica to Pan-Africa? From ECOWAS to SADCC?

The site of the first economic summit, Lagos, was also the center of ACP strategy in the negotiations for Lomé I prior to 1975, and is now the headquarters of ECOWAS. Despite the problems of effective collective self-reliance at the regional level in Africa since independence, optimism persists that this largest-ever grouping can succeed[38] and so become one of the foundations for the proposed continental common market. This scenario of regionalism paving the way for continentalism serves to resolve the historic debates over the primacy of regionalism or continentalism, functionalism or federalism that have bedeviled previous attempts at development through integration. Yet the contradiction between Pan-African integration remains despite increasing disinterest in Europe and growing diversity in Africa.

Paradoxically, ECOWAS was being discussed and designed at the same time as on the other coast the East African Community (EAC) was in a state of disorder and decay. Some ECOWAS institutions were structured with the failure of EAC in mind, but there are limits to which West African political economies can be pushed to avoid a similar tragedy on the west coast. The interests of dominant regional forces -- those of indigenous and international capitalisms and of the semi-periphery -- cannot be easily disregarded unless regionalism is defined in more radical terms than collective self-reliance. But, given the central role of elements within incumbent ruling classes[39] in espousing regionalist causes, any such redefinition in practice is quite unlikely, unless more regimes go beyond the constraints of state capitalism and state socialism towards more genuine forms of socialism, regionalism may still serve established national and transnational class interests rather than advancing the BHN of the poor countries and communities. Despite frequent claims to the contrary, the continuing popularity of Pan-African regionalism may lie in its compatibility with dominant interests. And it is these very interests which are still attracted to EurAfrica too, recognizing that some fractions are more Pan-African and others more EurAfrican in orientation.

Thus John Renninger is skeptical about the formulation and implementation of the ECOWAS treaty.[40] He concludes that it is unlikely to overcome either dependence or underdevelopment because of diverse economic and political interest within the region clustered around the competing EurAfrican nexus: transnational class linkages and uneven development work against a more fundamental definition or interpretation of regional integration. "Thus, although ECOWAS can undoubtedly contribute to the achievement of collective self-reliance in West African sub-regions, it will not, by itself, lead to collective self-reliance."[41] More basic issues of political economy would have to be addressed for such regional plans to be designed and effected. But the postcolonial ruling class has little interest in going beyond reform towards a more radical definition of regionalism, especially the ruling classes within regional centers like Côte d'Ivoire, Nigeria and Senegal with their EurAfrican connections.

ECOWAS is essentially an orthodox common market with some developmental content, but its structural intent is quite limited: it seeks free trade in goods and peoples rather than the creation of a more self-reliant regional political economy, the rhetoric of collective self-reliance notwithstanding. Although the diversity of interests and resources -- and learning from the demise of EAC -- was reflected in the creation of a Fund for Cooperation, Compensation and Development, this fund is not central to

ECOWAS's structure or success. Moreover, its novel "collective defense" potential reflective as it is of the centrality of "security" issues as prerequisites for regionalism is an adjunct to its central purpose rather than integral to its design; it may also raise questions about the compatibility of ECOWAS with the OAU, given the latter's off-on interest in an African high command. However, the basic issue confronting regionalism in Africa is not compatibility with either the EC or the OAU, although these remain important issues; rather, it is compatibility with established political economies and ruling classes. And, when these are outward-oriented towards extracontinental integration, intracontinental connections remain undeveloped and unimportant.

In a critical vein, James Sackey has raised concern about regional organizations, notably their external support and their regional consequences. On extra-African advocates, he laments that "the role of class interest and the transnational domination through peripheral organizations, such as the local merchants, in shaping the ultimate destiny of ECOWAS appears not to be recognized by authors in the area."[42] And on regional class solidarity -- as expressed in plans for regional collective security -- he warns that regionalism may constrain experimentation in political economy:

> The presence of class interest and political opportunism in the formation of ECOWAS would, as in the case of CARICOM, mean the endorsement of a developmental ideology which favor capitalism as the only solution to the poverty of the region. This, in turn, would create a favorable atmosphere for the development and consolidation of the class interests of the rapidly rising national bourgeoisies and petty bourgeoisies within the region.[43]

With remarkable foresight -- he wrote before the Rawlings and Doe coups and before the anti-Pereira *putsch* in Guinea-Bissau and the abortive uprising in Gambia -- Sackey warned progressive forces in West Africa about collective conservatism rather than collective self-reliance or socialism:

> This might take several forms, such as a military coup in Guinea or support for further state capitalist development in Guinea-Bissau. The ultimate of these developments is the entrenchment of an authoritarian

central state, at the service of capitalism.[44]

In which case, regionalism would not only fail to advance either development or disengagement, it would also serve to limit the range of choice of African states: regional political order may be achieved at the cost of regional economic development. This, after all, is the function of regional powers -- to maintain regional order. The felt need for this "interventive" role may grow, as semi-periphery and periphery diverge in the future. Moreover, protectionist pressures in the world system may make development ever more elusive, generating more contradictions and antagonisms.

In short, the prospects for regionalism advancing either development or self-reliance in Africa would appear to be less promising for the final ten-year period of the century than in the previous thirty years, a period characterized by exceptional growth in the global economy. Neomercantilism in the North may reinforce the regional dominance of the semi-periphery and serve to marginalize the periphery further. In which case, Pan-African regionalism may seek to contain increased contradictions rather than advance self-reliance. Yet, even the maintenance of the status quo is problematic, given divisive external pressures, especially those within the EurAfrican regionalist nexus. In sum, for different fractions, different forms of regionalism may come to represent control and connections rather than autonomy and development.

The stand-off between the EC-supported SADCC and the ECA-supported PTA illustrates these differences.[45] SADCC as an institutional development of the FLS -- from rather exclusive diplomatic to a more inclusive economic grouping -- is concerned about two forms of dependence: first, on South Africa, and second, on the industrialized states. It is a reaction to the achievements of and constraints on African liberation given the intransigence and interference of the white regime: authoritarianism at home and destabilization in the region. Despite SADCC's assistance from the EC and other western states and its primary goal of transcending South Africa's dominance through infrastructural projects, it is also determined to increase its collective self-reliance in relation to the advanced capitalist states.[46] By contrast, the PTA as a broader and more orthodox free trade association has proposed distinctive rules of origin for intra-African trade. As in the short-lived Andean Pact, local products require local control of companies.[47]

By comparison, ECOWAS lacks the focus on the indigenous

capitalism of PTA and on the development projects of SADCC, in part because it lacks the immediate threat, economic and strategic, posed to the region by South Africa. Moreover, somewhat akin to Zimbabwe's role in SADCC and those of Zimbabwe and Kenya in PTA, in ECOWAS, the subimperial powers are internal -- Côte d'Ivoire, Nigeria and Senegal -- as South Africa will be after apartheid. But in emphasizing the structural bases of regionalism, namely infrastructure and ownership respectively, SADCC and PTA go beyond orthodox formulations. To this extent, they are suggestive of the degree to which liberation rather than nationalist struggles in the region have made a difference to policies on development and integration. ECOWAS may be in danger of merely rationalizing the periphery on behalf of extra-African capital. Both SADCC and PTA in different ways represent a challenge to South African and western capitalisms and so constitute a redefinition of African regionalism reflective of innovative responses a) to world crises and conditions and b) to revisionist analyses and insights.

Unity and Development: Beyond EurAfrica

Given a) changes in the global and regional political economies and b) ambiguities in the design and direction of regionalisms in Africa, predictive scenarios are rather problematic. However, the distinction in the literature between orthodox and radical investigations and prescriptions can be extended into the mid-term future. This would at least provide a framework for evaluating the prospects for, and progress of, ECOWAS. Nevertheless, such a task remains hazardous, as unforeseen eventualities can arise (e.g., dramatic increases in the prices of energy or money) and social relations are not readily predictable (e.g. the expansion, contraction and reaction of the indigenous proletariat). Quite clearly, however, linkages among the center, semi-periphery and periphery are not static, while the impact of regionalist schemes on them is likely to be rather marginal. Nevertheless, the outcome of the dialectic between semi-periphery and periphery is of considerable importance to the definition and orientation of regional communities like ECOWAS.

At least five central questions can be raised about the intention and direction of regional integration in Africa before the year 2000, the answers to which will depend on whether a more orthodox or a more radical mode of analysis is applied. In turn, any projections will be informed by the different positions and perceptions of these divergent approaches. All need to be situated in the context of prevailing and pervasive security and economic structures.

First, who are the major advocates of regionalism? They may be located outside or inside the region (e.g., transnational corporations and international organizations versus national bourgeois fractions or the labor aristocracy within the proletariat). Which of these social formations is dominant in designing and establishing regional institutions will be reflected in regional priorities and processes. In general, the more national the bourgeois forces and the more proletarian the advocates, the greater the prospects for African self-reliance, even if not necessarily for socialism. Conversely, the more comprador the bourgeois fraction and "aristocratic" the labor, the greater the prospects for EurAfrican connections.

Second, and related to the first point, does regionalism seek to reform or refine the international division of labor? If on the one hand its concern is with increased self-reliance rather than with increased trade, it would seek to reform or transform the regional and global division of labor away from the "peripheral capitalism" of extraction and towards a greater degree of industrialization. If, on the other hand, its concern is with increased exchange, as in EurAfrica, it will attempt to refine but not reform its position: producing more and selling higher, but not altering its place in the global hierarchy. Clearly some regionalists (inside and outside West Africa) would prefer reform -- Pan-African regionalism -- while others would support just refinement in the region's place in the international division of labor -- EurAfrican regionalism.

Third, depending on which transnational coalition of regionalists prevails and the degree of reform thereby advanced, regional cooperation may be concentrated in different sectors: trade, industry, agriculture, service or labor. Orthodox functionalists tend to concentrate on trade creation and diversion, whereas neofunctionalists emphasize industrialization, technology and capital-formation. Few regionalists advocate agricultural growth because of assumed lack of complementarity, although in fact regional food production is becoming an imperative. A balanced range of regional sectors may be desirable but that would have to be premised on a balanced set of regional advocates and resources, an unlikely situation. In general, regional schemes lay down a political framework and physical infrastructures for cooperation: who benefits depends on who can best exploit these facilities.

Fourth, the purposes of regionalism can differ from development to dominance. The peripheral participants would tend to favor the former orientation; semi-peripheral and core actors (state and nonstate) the latter, despite their relative disinterest in regionalism because of the global reach of their interests. Clearly, the direction of any regional institution depends on which advocates, functions and sectors are dominant. In the ECOWAS case, is regionalism a) to help the majority of poor states and citizens to develop, and/or b) to help the minority of middling rich (e.g. state and nonstate interests in Cote d'Ivoire and Nigeria) to grow, and/or c) to advance the interests of metropolitan countries and corporations (e.g., those most closely associated with EurAfrica, a collective and contemporary form of "neocolonialism" in an essentially post-neocolonial world)?

And finally, fifth, what results might be expected from these alternative variants of regionalism? An orthodox, semi-peripheral perspective would favor the development of underdevelopment, because its advocates can benefit thereby. However, a more radical, peripheral position would prefer the reduction of dependence and the encouragement of development through collective self-reliance. But, because the latter position threatens established metropolitan and semi-peripheral interests, its prospects are circumscribed. On the other hand, if protectionism on a world scale leads to trade wars, then regions as well as states may be forced to look inwards rather than outwards, as noted in the final paragraph below.

In any event, the outcome of the orthodox versus radical competition overlaps with the periphery versus semi-periphery tension as well as with Pan- versus Eur-African conception. Both of these respective modes of analysis and modes of production are preferred by antagonist national, regional and global social formations, with their respective transnational coalitions. The future of ECOWAS depends essentially on the outcome of these complex confrontations which, in turn, are functions of changes in "national" political economies within the world system.

The environment for regionalism in Africa depends not only on regional, continental and global conditions in general but also on the outcome of the struggle in southern Africa in particular. Will uneventful (reformist) or eventful (revolutionary) scenarios materialize there? For just as political and economic relations among regions have affected the character and potential of ECOWAS (i.e., North-South linkages with EC and South-South linkages with ASEAN,

138

CARICOM, etc.), so the prospects for regionalism in southern Africa constitute, on the one hand, an intriguing model for West Africa and, on the other hand, a potential resource base.

In the past, African continental unity has been facilitated by collective opposition to colonialism and racism in southern Africa. In the future, African regional unity may, as suggested above, be encouraged by the model and resources of southern Africa, with implications for the ability to resist EurAfrican pressures. The "pariah" middle power of that region -- South Africa -- has made a series of largely unsuccessful attempts since World War Two to widen patterns of regional cooperation in the southern part of the continent to enhance its own economic growth and military security. However, the execution of successful wars of liberation in Angola, Mozambique, Zimbabwe and now Namibia has not only increased opposition to South Africa's schemes but has provided the foundation for counter-dominance institutions like SADCC and PTA, despite the latter's relentless pressure for bilateral strategic understandings.

If SADCC or PTA regionalism works, it will constitute a challenge not only to South African "subimperialism" but also to more orthodox patterns of regionalism elsewhere on the continent. The appearance of more radical regimes in southern Africa because of the protracted liberation struggle there has already upset the continental dominance of more conservative (often semi-peripheral) states. The further transformation of these state socialist regimes into a viable, radical, regional political economy would pose another challenge to more benign forms of regionalism as in ECOWAS, as well as to prevailing axes of EurAfricanism.

Consequently, by both example and resources, southern Africa might come to affect the orthodox versus radical political and analytical balances in West Africa. In turn, this would serve to reinforce the pressures towards more progressive and self-reliant Pan-African strategies already apparent because of the protectionist mood in the advanced industrialized states. The international division of labor between center, semi-periphery and periphery would be further undermined as mercantilism in the North and disengagement in southern Africa came to produce alternative patterns of exchange and accumulation. Langdon and Mytelka have put such change in southern Africa into the context of shifts within global and continental political economies:

> Armed conflict in Southern Africa, though, is likely to be no more than the most dramatic form of confrontation

between dependence and self-reliance in the 1980s. We expect the contradictions of periphery capitalism in Africa to become more acute in countries on the continent in the next decade, and we expect the struggles for change in such countries to become more bitter as a result. We are confident, however, that out of such conflict can come more equitable and self-reliant development strategies that benefit the great majority of Africans.[48]

In which case, the future for unity and development at continental and regional levels in Africa may be rather brighter but no less certain than already suggested.

ECOWAS, and other Pan-African regionalist designs on the continent, can only be explained and projected in the context of such pressures -- national, regional, continental and global -- in the international division of labor. Hence the continuing dialectic with EurAfrican conceptions, unless protectionism and recession so undermine extroverted fractions among Europe's bourgeoisies that the EC comes to pull away from the ACP rather than vice versa. In a post-neocolonial world, ACP advocates of Lomé may yet be abandoned by a combination of a) introversion and isolation in Europe[49] and b) Africa's Fourth World, leaving the semi-periphery fractionless between a protectionist center and a self-reliant periphery. In which case, Pan-African conceptions of regionalism would no longer have to compete with residual EurAfrican definitions, and Pan-Africanism could reestablish its primacy over EurAfricanism, a prerequisite for the redefinition of regionalism as self-reliance. In this as in other ways, economic as well as political liberation in Africa could yet start in the southern African revolution. As Sonny Ramphal has argued already, "The SADCC approach has made a contribution to the rethinking on regional integration movements among developing countries by its radical departures from both the common market and the integrated community approaches."[50]

Postscriptum

Regionalism in Africa at the start of the 1990s is both constrained and necessitated by two profound, interrelated shifts in policy and practice. First, within the continent, *structural adjustment* has emerged as the dominant policy framework or context, insisted upon not only by the World Bank and International Monetary Fund, but also necessitated by the new international division of labor. And second, outside the continent, *superpower detente* has served to cool African and other regional conflicts. The global trend toward privatization and (cross)conditionalities has affected African as well as East European policies and possibilities: reduced prospects for either socialism in the North or self-reliance in the South, unless both are redefined taking into account transformations in national and global political economies.

The long-standing dialectic between the World Bank and ECA -- Berg Report and LPA, respectively -- was updated in 1989 by the almost simultaneous appearances of their divergent prescriptions for the 1990s: *Crisis to Sustainable Growth*[51] and *African Alternative Framework*,[52] respectively. These reports reflect informed but distinct analyses and preferences, based on more orthodox and more radical assumptions, respectively. While these have been modified for the 1990s -- the jargon and data are novel -- the Bank's report is essentially based on modernization, while the ECA's focuses upon dependency. The initial, rhetorical "pamphlet" published in March 1989 from the World Bank (with the UNDP) was on *Africa's Adjustment and Growth in the 1980s*.[53] It was severely criticized the following month by the ECA on methodological and political grounds in *Statistics and Policies: ECA preliminary observations on the World Bank Report "Africa's Adjustment and Growth in the 1980s."*[54]

But the two major restatements and reconsiderations, both of which had been under parallel consideration for months even years, appeared in the second half of 1989. Both of these *revisionist* statements emphasized the long-term human dimensions of development despite any shorter-term disruptions of adjustment, from human needs to rights. And the World Bank's report rediscovered regionalism, while the ECA's advocated participation. Both advanced liberalization of and support for ubiquitous informal sectors, although neither recognized their regionalist potentials: from exchange and labor, and from currencies to drugs. And both unrealistically expected significant augmentation of limited extra-continental resources for redevelopment.

Nevertheless, the new international division of labor, especially the rise of the NICs, even before the transformation of Eastern Europe, served to encourage national and regional self-reliance. And dramatic shifts in the global balance of power likewise demand that Africa attends to its own developmental needs. Even the EC is preoccupied in the early 1990s not so much by Lomé IV or 1992, as by trans-European continental cohesion. So despite the claims for massive aid flows and debt forgiveness, if *conditionalities* are satisfied, self-reliance is likely to become more essential than ever in the 1990s and beyond. If such a direction, based on radical rather than orthodox conceptions, is to be effective, then democratic development is a related imperative: participation and accountability for women as well as men. Hence the revisionist mood about such externally-imposed reforms, given their problematic impacts, with profound implications for regionalism on the continent into the twenty-first century.

Notes

*Earlier and shorter versions of this chapter appeared as "Towards a Political Economy for Regionalism in Africa" in Ralph Onwuka and Amadu Sesay (eds.), *The Future of Regionalism in Africa* (London: Macmillan, 1985), pp. 8-21 and "The Dialectics of Regionalism: EurAfrica and West Africa" in Amadu Sesay (ed.), *Africa and Europe: From Partition to Interdependence or Dependence?* (London: Croom Helm, 1986), pp. 222-245; and in the *Jerusalem Journal of International Relations*, 11(4), 1989.

1. Shridath S. Ramphal, "Economic Cooperation and Collective Self-Reliance in Africa: Retrospect and Prospect" in Bernard Chidzero and Altaf Gauhar (eds.), *Linking the South: The Route to Economic Cooperation* (London: Third World Foundation, 1986), p. 3.

2. Adebayo Adedeji, "Inter-African Economic Cooperation in Light of the Final Act of Lagos" in Adebayo Adedeji and Timothy M. Shaw (eds.), *Economic Crisis in Africa: African Perspectives on Development Problems and Potentials* (Boulder: Lynne Rienner, 1985), p. 77.

3. See David Fashole Luke and Timothy M. Shaw (eds.), *Continental Crisis: The Lagos Plan of Action and Africa's Future* (Washington: University Press of America, 1984).

4. S.K.B. Asante, "Development and Regional Integration since 1980" in Adedeji and Shaw (eds.), *Economic Crisis in Africa*, p. 82.

142

5. See Timothy M. Shaw, *Towards a Political Economy for Africa: The Dialectics of Dependence* (London: Macmillan, 1985); and Richard Sandbrook, *The Politics of Africa's Economic Stagnation* (Cambridge: Cambridge University Press, 1985).

6. For invaluable insights into debt in Africa see Alwyn B. Taylor, "The Changing International Financial Environment and Africa's External Indebtedness" and Philip Ndegwa, "The Deteriorating Debt Problem in Africa" in Chidzero and Gauhar (eds.), *Linking the South*, pp. 39-104.

7. Adedeji, "Inter-African Economic Cooperation" in Adedeji and Shaw (eds.), *Economic Crisis in Africa*, p. 66.

8. *Ibid.*, pp. 74-75.

9. See John Ravenhill (ed.), *Africa in Economic Crisis* (London: Macmillan, 1986); and Robert J. Berg and Jennifer Seymour Whitacker (eds.), *Strategies for African Development* (Los Angeles: University of California Press, 1986), pp. 127-147.

10. See Timothy M. Shaw, "Towards a Political Economy of the African Crisis: Diplomacy, Debates and Dialectics" in Michael H. Glantz (ed.), *Drought and Hunger in Africa: Denying Famine a Future* (Cambridge: Cambridge University Press, 1986), pp. 127-147.

11. See Leon Gordenker, "The OAU and the UN: Can They Live Together?" in Ali A. Mazrui and Hasu H. Patel (eds.), *Africa in World Affairs: The Next Thirty Years* (New York: Third Press, 1973), pp. 105-119.

12. See Timothy M. Shaw (ed.), *Alternative Futures for Africa* (Boulder: Westview Press, 1982); and, with Olajide Aluko (eds.), *Africa Projected: From Recession to Renaissance by the Year 2000* (London: Macmillan, 1985).

13. For an introduction to these see Timothy M. Shaw, "Discontinuities and Inequalities in African International Politics," *International Journal*, 30(3), Summer 1975, pp. 369-390.

14. See Timothy M. Shaw, "Inequalities and Interdependence in Africa and Latin America: Sub-imperialism and semi-industrialism in the semi-periphery," *Cultures et Développement*, 10(2), 1978, pp. 231-263.

15. I. William Zartman, "Africa as a Subordinate State in International Relations," *International Organization*, 2(3), Summer 1967, p. 571.

16. *Ibid.*, p. 574.

17. See, for instance, Timothy M. Shaw, "Kenya and South Africa: Sub-imperialist States," *Orbis*, 21(2), Summer 1977, pp. 375-394; and "International Stratification in Africa:

Sub-imperialism in Eastern and Southern Africa," *Journal of Southern African Affairs*, 2(2), April 1977, pp. 145-165.

18. See Immanuel Wallerstein, "Dependence in an Interdependent World: The Limited Possibilities of Transformation within the Capitalist World Economy," *African Studies Review*, 17(1), April 1974, pp. 1-26.

19. Steven Langdon and Lynn K. Mytelka, "Africa in the Changing World Economy" in Colin Legum *et al.*, *Africa in the 1980s: A Continent in Crisis* (New York: McGraw-Hill, 1979; Council on Foreign Relations, 1980s Project), p. 204.

20. See ECA, OAU and UNIDO, *A Program for the Industrial Development Decade for Africa* (New York, 1982); and George M. Kimani, "Industry in Africa: Continental Cooperation and the Industrial Development Decade" and D. Babatunde Thomas, "Technology and Industrial Development in Africa" in Adedeji and Shaw (eds.), *Economic Crisis in Africa*, pp. 219-265.

21. See Craig Murphy, *The Emergence of the NIEO Ideology* (Boulder: Westview Press, 1984).

22. See Timothy M. Shaw and Olajide Aluko (eds.), *The Political Economy of African Foreign Policies: Comparative Analysis* (New York: St. Martin's, 1984), especially pp. 1-24.

23. Zartman, "Africa as a Subordinate State," p. 581.

24. For a review of these, see Timothy M. Shaw, "Peripheral Social Formations in the New International Division of Labour: African States in the mid-1980s," *Journal of Modern African Studies*, 24(3), September 1986, pp. 489-508; and Bahgat Korany, "The Take-Off of Third World Studies: The Case of Foreign Policy," *World Politics*, 35(3), April 1983, pp. 465-487.

25. See Donald Rothchild and Robert L. Curry, *Scarcity, Choice and Public Policy in Middle Africa* (Berkeley: University of California Press, 1978), pp. 48-91 and pp. 301-335.

26. See Micah S. Tsomondo, "From Pan-Africanism to Socialism: The Modernization of an African Liberation Ideology," *Issue*, 5(4), Winter 1975, pp. 39-46; and Teti A. Kofi, "Principles of a Pan-Africa Economic Ideology," *Review of Black Political Economy*, 6(3), Spring 1976, pp. 306-330.

27. See Ravenhill (ed.), *Africa in Economic Crisis*.

28. James Mayall, "The OAU and the African Crisis," *Optima*, 27(2), 1977, p. 86.

29. See I. William Zartman and Yassin El-Ayouty (eds.), *The OAU After Twenty Years* (New York: Praeger, 1983).

30. See Elenga M'buyinga, *Pan-Africanism or Neo-Colonialism: The Bankruptcy of the OAU* (London: Zed, 1982).

31. Zdenek Cervenka, *The Unfinished Quest for Unity* (New York: Africana, 1977), pp. 176-190.

144

32. See Jerker Carlsson and Timothy M. Shaw (eds.), *Newly Industrializing Countries and the Political Economy of South-South Relations* (London: Macmillan, 1987).

33. See Timothy M. Shaw, "Debates About Africa's Future: The Brandt, World Bank and Lagos Plan Blueprints," *Third World Quarterly*, 5(2), April 1983, pp. 330-344.

34. See Julius Nyang'oro and Timothy M. Shaw (eds.), *Corporatism in Africa: Comparative Analysis and Practice* (Boulder: Westview Press, 1987).

35. See Robert Boardman, Panayotis Soldatos and Timothy M. Shaw (eds.), *The EEC, Africa and Lomé III* (Washington: University Press of America, 1984; Dalhousie African Studies Series Number 3).

36. See *ECA and the Development of Africa 1983-2008: Preliminary Prospective Study* (Addis Ababa, April 1983); and OAU, *Africa's Priority Programme for Economic Recovery 1986-1990* (Addis Ababa, July 1985).

37. *Biennial Report of the Executive Secretary of the United Nations Economic Commission for Africa 1977-1978* (Addis Ababa, February 1979, E/CN.14/695), p. 12.

38. See S.K.B. Asante, *The Political Economy of Regionalism in Africa: A Decade of ECOWAS* (New York: Praeger, 1986); "ECOWAS/CEAO: Conflict and Cooperation in West Africa" in Onwuka and Sesay (eds.), *The Future of Regionalism in Africa*, pp. 74-95; and "ECOWAS, the EEC and the Lomé Convention" in Domenico Mazzeo (ed.), *African Regional Organizations* (Cambridge: Cambridge University Press, 1984), pp. 171-195.

39. See Olatunde J.B. Ojo, "Nigeria and the Formation of ECOWAS," *International Organization*, 34(4), Autumn 1980, pp. 571-604.

40. John P. Renninger, "The Future of Economic Cooperation Schemes in Africa, with Special Reference to ECOWAS" in Shaw (ed.), *Alternative Futures for Africa*, p. 160.

41. *Ibid.*, p. 170. See also John P. Renninger, *Multinational Cooperation for Development in West Africa* (Elmsford, N.Y.: Pergamon, 1979).

42. James A. Sackey, "The Structure and Performance of CARICOM: Lessons for the Development of ECOWAS," *Canadian Journal of African Studies*, 12(2), 1978, p. 272.

43. *Ibid.*, p. 273.

44. *Ibid.*

45. See Peter Meyns, "SADCC and Regional Cooperation in Southern Africa" in Mazzeo (ed.), *African Regional Organizations*, pp. 196-224; Douglas G. Anglin, "Economic Liberation and Regional Cooperation in Southern Africa: SADCC

and PTA," *International Organization*, 37(4), Autumn 1983, pp. 681-711; and essays by L. Adele Jinadu, Thandika Mkandawire, Yash Tandon and Ibbo Mandaza in Timothy M. Shaw and Yash Tandon (eds.), *Regional Development at the International Level, Volume 2. African and Canadian Perspectives* (Washington: University Press of America, 1985), pp. 41-53 and pp. 93-144.

46. See Joseph Hanlon, *Beggar Your Neighbours: Apartheid Power in Southern Africa* (London: James Currey, 1986), especially pp. 17-90; Robert Davies, "Review Article: The Military and Foreign Policy in South Africa," *Journal of Southern African Studies*, 12(2), April 1986, pp. 308-315; and Phyllis Johnson and David Martin (eds.), *Destructive Engagement: Southern Africa at War* (Harare: Zimbabwe Publishing House, 1986), pp. 245-280.

47. See Adebayo Adedeji, "Inter-African Economic Cooperation"; and S.K.B. Asante, "Development and Regional Integration since 1980" in Adedeji and Shaw (eds.), *Economic Crisis in Africa*, pp. 59-99.

48. Langdon and Mytelka, "Africa in the Changing World Economy," p. 104.

49. See Boardman, Soldatos and Shaw (eds.), *The EEC, Africa and Lomé III*.

50. Ramphal, "Economic Cooperation and Collective Self-Reliance in Africa," pp. 11-12.

51. *Sub-Saharan Africa: From Crisis to Sustainable Growth. A Long-Term Perspective Study* (Washington D.C.: World Bank, 1989).

52. *African Alternative Framework to Structural Adjustment Programmes for Socio-Economic Recovery and Transformation* (Addis Ababa: Economic Commission for Africa, 1989).

53. *Africa's Adjustment and Growth in the 1980s* (Washington D.C.: World Bank, 1989).

54. This report was published by the ECA, Addis Ababa.

7

ECOWAS: Problems and Potential

Oliver S. Knowles

The Formation of ECOWAS

The economic logic behind the creation of ECOWAS is the conventional one that, within an integrated area, economies of scale can operate to make factors of production more efficient. But it could be argued that the real motivation for the establishment of ECOWAS was essentially noneconomic and stemmed from Nigeria's realization that, after Côte d'Ivoire's recognition of Biafra, Africa must be the focal point of Nigerian foreign policy.

Once Ghana was no longer a serious contender for West African leadership, Nigeria felt the need to counterbalance the influence of France, which had supported Côte d'Ivoire's recognition of Biafra. To this end, the Nigerian integrationists under General Yakubu Gowon, with some opportune assistance from "the spirit of Lomé" created by the negotiations to replace the EC Yaoundé convention, successfully lobbied for the establishment of a West African Economic Community in 1973. The economic benefits to Nigeria were far from clear. Nigeria was large enough to go it alone itself and some feared that a community might drain away Nigerian capital and resources which could be employed better in national development following its civil war. But in 1973 the Arab-Israeli "October War" had tripled the price of oil, Nigerian foreign exchange reserves had risen fivefold, and Nigerian diplomatic power and leverage were greatly enhanced. As a result the pressures to create a community prevailed. They were assisted by a realization in France that Nigeria had become France's primary export outlet in sub-Saharan Africa and that it was not obviously in French interest to support only a francophone grouping in West Africa.[1] This change in the political climate enabled negotiations for the establishment of a West African community to be concluded in 1975 with the signature of the Treaty of Lagos. The treaty was, however, largely based on theoretical assumptions about economic integration and integrative models for customs unions among developed countries and paid little attention to the geopolitical and administrative realities of West Africa. It also suffered grievously from the fallacious belief that by applying time pressures and pushing under the table difficult issues which required detailed negotiations, agreement and results on contentious issues could be more easily obtained. As a result many issues which should have been tackled at the negotiating stage only surfaced when the secretariat tried to implement them.

The main feature of ECOWAS is that it is a grouping of sixteen countries of uneven size with Nigeria providing over 65 percent of the population and the trade. Three other countries -- Côte d'Ivoire, Ghana and Senegal -- provide a further 20 percent, and the remaining twelve countries only provide some 15 percent between them. Secondly, it is a grouping of coastal and landlocked countries, with the landlocked countries very much dependent on their coastal partners for transport services and trade. Thirdly, there are linguistic barriers inherited from the colonial era: nine of the countries are francophone, five are anglophone, and two are lusophone. These barriers are reflected in a number of monolingual subregional institutions, notably the Communauté des Etats de l'Afrique de l'Ouest (CEAO) comprising six francophone countries, and the Banque Centrale des Etats de l'Afrique de l'Ouest (BCEAO). Another subgrouping, the Mano River Union (MRU), comprises one francophone and two anglophone countries.

The general objective of the Treaty of Lagos is to promote economic development by establishing a common market, and by harmonizing economic policies notably in agriculture, industrial development, and in money and banking. There is also provision for cooperation in the development of energy and mineral resources, and in infrastructure development. A Fund for Cooperation, Compensation and Development was established, to which is linked a scheme for fiscal compensation in relation to the common market. The common market is to be established by stages over a fifteen year period from the entry into force of the treaty, beginning with a two year standstill period for tariffs and trade restrictions, followed by an eight year period during which duties must be eliminated in intracommunity trade, and ending with a five year period over which a common external tariff is to be established.

Infrastructural and Technical Problems

To carry out and implement such a program within fifteen years would be a remarkable achievement even under the most favorable conditions. But conditions in West Africa are much less favorable than in Western Europe, whose Economic Community has now been in existence since the Treaty of Rome over thirty years ago. The fundamental problem in West Africa is that the partnership is a very unequal one, with a highly skewed distribution of benefits. The assumption of the treaty that fiscal compensation is an adequate instrument to ensure a fair distribution of benefits, even if it could be made to work which is by no means certain, is not an assumption which recommends itself to smaller countries. These see little possibility of participating in regional industrial development schemes and fear that a disproportionate share of the benefits will go to the larger countries, particularly to Nigeria. There has been a distinct lack of enthusiasm for implementing the provisions of the treaty. This is reflected in the lack of success which the secretariat has had in obtaining effective implementation of many of its proposals, and also of decisions taken by community institutions.

But even if country support were more enthusiastic, the logistical and infrastructural obstacles and problems in implementation are such that a much longer time scale would be required to make the program realistic. Running a common market is a sophisticated form of administration and requires a high standard of administrative skills and supporting services, as well as communications. Such services do not as yet exist in West Africa; they are still in the process of being created.

In Lagos, the ECOWAS secretariat has been working in conditions verging on the impossible. Office accommodation has been cramped. Power failures have frequently immobilized all electric office equipment, including typewriters, interpretation booths and air conditioning. Housing has been in short supply and the cost of living is high. Security is poor, and post and telephone communications to other ECOWAS countries have also been poor or nonexistent. The poor working conditions and lack of housing have in turn aggravated recruitment problems, particularly for francophone staff, in a situation where a system of national quotas already limits the scope for recruiting from the relatively limited number of qualified bilingual candidates available.

These conditions and the shortage of experienced staff have imposed great strains on the senior staff of the secretariat who have also had to cope with a system of rotating ECOWAS meetings between different ECOWAS capitals. This has made the administration of the secretariat very complex, even at time requiring the skill to organize a trans-African safari for office equipment and conference papers. Under such conditions it reflects considerable credit on senior ECOWAS staff that the organization has made the significant progress it has over the last fifteen years.

Poor communications have not been limited to postal and telephone links. Surface transport for goods is often nonexistent or unreliable, and air services are expensive or infrequent. Even linguistic communications can be difficult in a region where a United Nations study showed that there are fewer than forty professional translators and interpreters in sixteen countries.[2] Except between member countries of the BCEAO, the banking and monetary facilities fall far short of the minimum desirable standards. Complex exchange control systems exist, several currencies are overvalued, and clearing arrangements are slow and often inefficient.

Another series of problems has been the disparities in national customs procedures, and the poor quality of the work and lack of training in some of the customs administrations. A customs union cannot be sustained without a considerable degree of harmonization of procedures, which requires staff with both the training and ability to operate these procedures. Quite inadequate attention was given to these points by the architects of ECOWAS, as well as to the time needed to achieve them. An effective common market requires not only a common external tariff but also the prerequisites to the preparation of such a tariff, namely harmonized statistical procedures and systems, harmonized customs and statistical nomenclatures, harmonized valuation systems, and -- in this modern age -- harmonized systems of customs computerization. It also requires an extensive training program for customs staffs on these procedures. A study of customs training carried out by the ECOWAS secretariat showed considerable disparities in zonal customs training arrangements, in customs organization and entry and promotional arrangements. In some countries such arrangements are virtually nonexistent, and the quality and standards of customs administration fall far short of the minimum necessary to support an effective customs union and common market.

The ECOWAS secretariat has made considerable progress in the preparation and introduction of harmonized statistical procedures, customs and nomenclatures, as well as in the preparation and introduction of harmonized programs of customs computerizations. But the training of customs staffs to the requisite standards will be a lengthy and expensive business, and given the limited resources available it is certain that it cannot be achieved within the time scale imposed by the Treaty of Lagos. If an effective customs union and common market is to be established in ECOWAS there will have to be a major allocation of resources for a harmonized customs training program at all levels, as well as major technical and financial assistance by donor countries to this sector.

In addition to tackling infrastructural deficiencies, attention must be given to negotiating arrangements and tactics. In negotiations of this kind it is not possible for the smaller countries to give much away, and in the initial stages concessions have to be made by the more powerful partners; in practice this means mainly Nigeria. But the fall in oil prices has made such concessions difficult for Nigeria whose own economy is now beset with problems. Many of the negotiating problems have stemmed from two facts: i) the relationship of the CEAO to ECOWAS -- this relationship was not defined in the ECOWAS treaty; and ii) the tendency of ECOWAS to consider CEAO and MRU as institutions which will in due course disappear. Future negotiations can be greatly facilitated if a revised treaty spells out the relationship of these subgroups to ECOWAS. Experience has shown that this is not a problem which the heads of state can pass to the secretariats concerned with any hope of finding a workable solution.

Potential Growth and Cooperation

Greater flexibility is clearly needed in trade liberalization provisions before ECOWAS members can increase intraregional trade. While full liberalization might remain as the ultimate objective, a much more flexible time scale is needed with greater phasing of liberalization and the possibility of reviewing progress between phases, before a new phase is commenced. In this way the less developed countries would have the possibility of retaining some measure of protection until such time as they are clearly able to stand on their own feet. In considering possible approaches to greater flexibility the idea of a transfer tax or something analogous might be considered.

In the monetary sector there is room for improvement in the institutional arrangements for collaboration with the West African Clearing House (WACH), with the governors of central banks, and with the commercial banks.[3] Measures are also needed to improve the operational efficiency of the WACH, to strengthen commercial banking links, to promote collaboration in debt negotiations with developed countries, and to create a climate and conditions which will permit a reduction of exchange control restrictions on ECOWAS trade and investment, as well as movement towards more realistic exchange rates. However, it must not be forgotten that intraregional trade represents less than 5 percent of total trade and that the monetary system must primarily serve the needs of international trade. It is unrealistic to expect the countries to move other than gradually and step by step toward closer monetary cooperation. The monetary problems of an oil-based economy such as Nigeria are very different from those of non-oil producing countries.

The creation of the correct instruments and climate for industrial cooperation is perhaps the most difficult and politically sensitive task confronting ECOWAS. All experience so far in ECOWAS and elsewhere suggests that a scheme of mere industrial allocation will not be sustainable. It is also clear that there are definite limits to the amount of protection that countries are willing to concede to intraregional products. Any industrial production which is to achieve significant regional market penetration must enjoy a fair degree of comparative advantage and must maximize the use of local factors of production which offer such advantages.

The task of industrial cooperation is made doubly difficult by the ECOWAS rules of origin which are heavily loaded to ensure African ownership of the means of production. These rules pay little regard to the availability and distribution of indigenous capital, and operate very much to the disadvantage of the less developed countries which possess minimal quantities of industrial skills and capital. Much greater flexibility is needed in the approach to the problem of origin, and here also a phased approach would be desirable, with provision for a review at each stage before moving on to the next and with initial major concessions in favor of the less developed countries.

If industrial negotiations are to succeed, every effort must be made first to identify negotiating situations where industrialists from different countries might find a measure of common ground, and to create an appropriate negotiating forum. There is much useful experience of industrial complementarity schemes in other groupings of developing countries, such as in the Association of South East Asian Nations (ASEAN). A sector by sector approach to industrial complementarity should be started within the ECOWAS framework. The textile industry in ECOWAS would appear to offer considerable scope for developing complementarities and specializations, which could then be made effective by a sectoral approach to trade liberalization and by a common external tariff. Indeed, given the complexities of tariff negotiations involving sixteen countries, a sectoral approach to trade liberalization and a common external tariff in industrial products may be the only feasible approach.

The main obstacles to agricultural cooperation are the limitations of the ECOWAS transport system and the agricultural pricing and marketing policies pursued in some countries. The transport network is inadequate to support major movements of agricultural products across ECOWAS, and transport costs between countries may often be higher than to and from third countries for comparable products. Yet even in those situations where the transport system might permit trade, particularly border trade, there are often controlled marketing and price fixing systems which inhibit trade altogether. There is unanimous agreement that tariff barriers in agricultural products can be removed without difficulty, and the expansion of this trade therefore depends on a continuing program of transport improvements, and a progressive program of collaboration in the removal of inhibiting controls on prices and marketing. If such a program can succeed, producers would then have a greater incentive to develop the inherent comparative advantages in production in the region.

The possibilities for energy cooperation are considerable and some encouraging schemes have already been started in regard to the use of hydroelectricity. There is a need to tackle the problems of cooperation in production and marketing of petroleum products. In view of the strong position of transnational corporations in this industry, the next step might be a comprehensive survey of possibilities by a reputable firm of independent consultants.

Finally, attention must be given to the unsatisfactory secretariat arrangements, as well as the need to avoid duplication of effort with other organizations particularly in the monetary and the transport and communication sectors. There could be much merit in a more decentralized approach to secretariat organization, as in ASEAN. Such an approach might not only facilitate cooperation with other organizations, but also encourage a wide country interest in ECOWAS and strengthen support at a political level. An incidental benefit could also be to enable some countries to pay their subscriptions, or a part of their subscriptions, in local currency, and hence more easily than in hard currencies.

A number of decentralization arrangements might be envisaged. In view of the key role of Nigeria in the development of West African trade, industry and energy, as well as the presence in Lagos of the West African Chamber of Commerce, Industry, Mines and Agriculture, these subjects would appear best left in Lagos. However, there appears to be a good case for moving to other centers those divisions or sections of the secretariat responsible for transport and communications, for money and banking, for cultural affairs, for statistics and computer technology, as well as training schemes and research studies. The general criteria to be applied in redistribution should be to improve cooperation with other regional organizations, to increase operational efficiency, and to minimize operational costs.

No one should underestimate the very long and difficult path which lies ahead of any scheme for economic cooperation between developing countries lacking not only essential infrastructure but also a common language. At the same time ECOWAS has already achieved more in cooperation than would have been thought possible only two decades ago; the need for cooperation is now recognized, and given good will and the willingness to effect change, there is no reason why this rate of progress should not improve.

Notes

1. For a full account of the role of Nigeria in the formation of ECOWAS, see Olatunde J.B. Ojo, "Nigeria and the Formation of ECOWAS," *International Organization*, 34(4), 1980, pp. 571-604.

2. C. Dumbleton, "Language Services in ECOWAS" (Unpublished UNCTAD Report, 1982).

3. For an outline of the clearing house arrangements, see E. Osagie, "West African Clearing House, West African Unit of Account and Pressures for Monetary Integration," *Journal of Common Market Studies*, 17(3), March 1979, pp. 227-235.

PART TWO

Cooperation and Development

8

The Military Factor in West Africa: Leadership and Regional Development

Claude E. Welch, Jr.

West African states may be divided by what most have in common.

In no other part of Africa have the armed forces played such an extensive, long-standing direct role in politics. The sixteen member states of the Economic Community of West African States (ECOWAS) account for less than one-third of the members of the Organization of African Unity (OAU) -- yet they account for close to half of the successful coups d'etat that have affected the continent since 1958. As shown by the table at the end of this chapter, ECOWAS countries had experienced (by early 1990) half of the seventy-two successful forcible military overturns of governments.

Are these men interested in, and willing to support, significant steps toward regional links? More broadly, does the form of government and the background of political leaders have an impact on interstate cooperation? If so, is successful regional coordination the result of a particular style of rule, more likely to be enhanced by "democratic" governments presumably enjoying widespread legitimacy and popular support, or by "authoritarian" governments presumably profiting from an ability to make and implement potentially divisive decisions quickly? Is it appropriate to deem West African governments controlled by civilians as "democratic" and those dominated by military as "authoritarian"? Or is regional unity far more the consequence of leaders interested in promoting it, irrespective of their personal backgrounds and their styles of governing? Theoretical treatments of regional integration, to use a term common in the literature of the 1950s and 1960s, gave only limited attention to individual leaders: the "process" seemed to revolve more around foci of unity, complementary patterns of behavior, and economic gains than around particular persons and their

abilities.[1] Yet a basic characteristic of contemporary West
Africa (and, indeed, of the continent as a whole) is the
personalization of leadership.[2] We need, accordingly, to
examine the impact of personality on political links among
West African states.

This chapter, then, explores three areas. First, it
examines the causes, consequences and intraregional
distribution of coups d'etat in West Africa. The chapter
then considers the key issue of development, defined in terms
of the ECOWAS treaty, the Lagos Plan of Action, and the Addis
Ababa declaration of the OAU, to determine whether civilian-
or military-dominated governments in the region differ in
their approaches. Finally, it looks at obstacles to
interstate cooperation, as illustrated by the Defense
Protocol to the ECOWAS treaty and the Defense Commission of
the Organization of African Unity.

Causes and Consequences of Military "Intervention"

Brief review of the major approaches to military
"intervention" in politics should clarify basic issues.

Note, please, my use of quotation marks. "Intervention"
is the most marked, dramatic form of armed forces'
involvement in politics, but is far from the only type of
such involvement. As Colton has aptly shown,[3] the military's
role can be examined in terms of both "scope" and "means."
"Scope" refers to issues, in which four levels can be
distinguished: internal, affecting only the military and of
interest only to it; institutional, involving officers'
ideological self-image, status, and the like, but requiring
participation of civilian elites outside the military;
intermediate, primarily concerning other specialized segments
of society; and societal, dealing with the basic goals and
needs of the entire society. "Means" can be examined on four
levels as well: official prerogative; expert advice;
political bargaining; and force. A coup d'etat represents
the outermost form of both scope and means: it affects the
society as a whole; it involves the use, or threatened use,
of violence. Most other forms of military involvement in
politics fall short of overt seizure of power. Accordingly,
the full range of military "involvement" in politics -- and
civilian "involvement" in the armed forces -- is far larger,
and more complex, than the substitution of men in khaki for
those in mufti.

A second preliminary caution derives from the ubiquity of
many forms of military involvement in politics. Most West

African governments in general do not conform to
stereotypical views that contrast untrammeled military
"dictatorships" with civilian "democracies." Elements of
both are mingled in the region. For example, President J.S.
Momoh of Sierra Leone rose to the political heights in large
measure through his leadership of the armed forces: as the
military chief of staff under Siaka Stevens, Momoh not only
built a reputation of efficiency and personal honesty, but
also (perhaps more importantly) gained the respect of his
head of state for personal loyalty. Momoh was hand-picked as
Stevens's successor, and was duly elected president without
opposition. Exchange of his uniform for a suit did not
instantly convert him into a standard political party leader.
Yet is he all that different from Kountché of Niger or Traoré
of Mali, who seized power in bloodless coups d'etat, and who
remained in control with periodic elections? The contrasts
among leaders in West Africa may not derive directly from
their civilian or military backgrounds.

The final caution comes from the incidence of coups d'etat
in West Africa. They are assuredly not random phenomena,
distributed more or less evenly across the region. Two-
thirds of the successful interventions took place in five of
the sixteen ECOWAS member states: Benin and Burkina Faso
(six each), Ghana (five), and Mauritania and Nigeria (four
each). These countries seem trapped on a political merry-
go-round. Military seizure of power; a counter-coup against
the ruling officers; restoration of civilian government in
some instances; renewed intervention: such has been, in
brief, the cycle followed in Burkina, Ghana and Nigeria since
1966. By contrast, the Cape Verde Islands, Côte d'Ivoire and
Senegal have (to date of writing) maintained civilian control
of the armed forces; Guinea, Guinea-Bissau, Liberia, Mali,
Niger and Togo thus far have been marked by only one
successful coup d'etat.[4] We will need to ascertain whether
the scope, means and frequency of military involvement in
politics impact directly or indirectly on regional
cooperation.

In explaining the causes of forcible overturns of
governments, two leading schools of thought have been
identified.[5] One focuses on organizational characteristics.
According to this perspective, the armed forces in tropical
Africa, and indeed in developing countries as a whole, enjoy
significant opportunities for, and incentives to, direct
political involvement, due to their values and means of
organization. Their cohesion, communications, discipline,
esprit de corps and presumably national character give them
both the means and willingness to take direct political

action. Such an approach accordingly concentrates on factors internal to the military. By contrast, a second school of thought focuses on the social, economic and political environment in which the armed forces operate. Here, the weakness or absence of authoritative, effective national political institutions results in a fragmented political process. Members of the armed forces, often in conjunction with disaffected individuals or groups, come to exercise power. As can readily be seen, the first approach suggests that the *strength* of military institutions *pushes* them into seizures of control; the second approach presumes that the *weakness* of political institutions *pulls* segments of the armed forces into direct political roles. The latter seeks explanation through examining societal characteristics, such as ethnic fragmentation, rates of economic growth, or social mobilization; the former concentrates upon intramilitary values, patterns of socialization and means of control.

Two further schools of thought should also be noted, in a sense "macro" and "micro". The international environment, it has been argued, affects the scope and means of armed forces' political involvement. For example, external assistance that provides the wherewithal to take control, the transfer of norms between different national contexts, and covert or overt encouragement of coups d'etat by foreign powers have all appeared in major studies of African civil-military relations as causes of coups d'etat. Or, to flip the coin, the presence of an external garrison gives clear indication of a major power's interest in the health and survival of a particular government; the absence of successful seizures of power in Côte d'Ivoire and Senegal cannot by ascribed solely to chance![6] "Contagion" -- that is to say, the temporal clustering of seizures of power due to deliberate emulation -- fits in this approach as well. In stark contrast to this global and regional perspective is the final one to be reviewed, this focused on individuals. Personal rivalries, exacerbated by intraorganizational conflict, have been cited as the key factor in the sudden political prominence of military officers. In the words of Decalo, "An empirical examination of African military hierarchies, and a much more critical analysis of formal justifications for coups, thus reveals a bewildering array of very strong personal and corporate motivations for power grabs..."[7]

Wherein lies the truth among these four approaches? Major empirical studies by Jackman, with subsequent additions by Johnson, McGowan and Slater,[8] suggest that coups d'etat in Africa can be explained most satisfactorily by sociopolitical

variables -- in other words, by the second of the four
approaches sketched above. In Jackman's words, italicized in
the original, "instability of this kind is not random with
respect to political and social structure."[9] The chief
indicators of danger include rising levels of social
mobilization and presence of a numerically dominant ethnic
group, particularly as these may be intensified by
multipartyism. Johnson *et al.* found that factors internal to
the military entered into coup proneness as well: "When
other factors are equal, African states whose militaries are
large and ethnically homogeneous experience more military
involvement in politics, as predicted by Welch and Smith."[10]
Idiosyncratic or personal factors and international pressures
thus seem empirically to have limited relevance for a
systematic explanation of coups d'etat, although they may
illuminate the variety of reasons that enter into particular
military seizures of power.

Yet I remain puzzled by an imbalance, noted at the start
of this chapter. West Africa has experienced far more than
its share of coups d'etat than other parts of Africa.
Despite the heritage of violence and the ethnic fragmentation
of the larger states of southern Africa, successful coups
d'etat have been essentially absent from Zambia south; the
1986 change of regime in Lesotho apparently stemmed largely
from South African pressure on the enclave state. By
contrast, every state in the equally violent northeast corner
of the continent save Djibouti (where the French have
maintained a garrison) has experienced direct intervention.
The chronic instability of Uganda contrasts sharply with the
maintenance of governmental control over the military in
Kenya and Tanzania, despite mutinies in both the latter and
an abortive coup in Kenya in 1982.

In a similar fashion, among former French-ruled states,
a handful account for the lion's share of successful coups
d'etat: Benin, Burkina Faso, Congo/Brazzaville and
Mauritania, with twenty-one military seizures of power among
them, far outshadow the ten other former French-ruled
countries, which collectively have experienced only eleven
coups.[11] Within West Africa itself, a few countries account
for the majority of the successful interventions. Is there
empirical and theoretical significance in this apparent
clustering? The major reasons for multiple coups d'etat seem
to be national rather than regional or continental. A second
coup d'etat in a country appears to establish a continuing
process of instability that is difficult to arrest; the
"slippery slope" phenomenon seems clear, with repeat coups in
the second or third year after intervention -- likely a time

by which the promises of the coup-makers have proven hollow and intramilitary rivalries over governing have intensified. Conversely, the presence of external garrisons (Côte d'Ivoire, Senegal) serves as a clear deterrent to initial seizures of power.

Explanations of differing levels of incidence need to be linked to the element of leadership, despite the danger of circular argument. Some heads of government (for example, Houphouët-Boigny of Côte d'Ivoire and Banda of Malawi) remain unchallenged; peaceful transitions have occurred from one civilian to another (Senghor to Diouf in Senegal, Ahidjo to Biya in Cameroon, Neto to Dos Santos in Angola, or Kenyatta to arap Moi in Kenya). Their dominance is largely personal. I concur with Goldsworthy who, in his studies of civilian control of African armed forces, comments that such control does not rest on strongly institutionalized bases, because little evidence of a national consensus expressed in entrenched and legitimate institutions exists in tropical Africa. The loyalty of officers is to the person of the ruler, rather than to the abstraction of the state.[12]

Leadership qualities impact directly on the likelihood of regional unity, just as they affect the likelihood of military "intervention". To a great extent, however, the interests of analysts of interstate cooperation have lain elsewhere. More concerned with the "process" of integration or with background conditions to it, these scholars tend only to mention, rather than examine systematically, the contributions of individuals. In West Africa, and indeed in contemporary Africa as a whole, cooperation and conflict among states must be examined as a consequence, in large measure, of leadership styles.[13]

It is interesting to note that the initial steps toward ECOWAS were taken by military heads of state. Yakubu Gowon and Gnassigbe Eyadéma share credit for the community. Both had achieved the political heights through violence; each brought a distinctive style to governing; each came from an area heavily represented in the military rank and file. Gowon was the ranking surviving officer of northern Nigerian origin on 29 July 1966, when military personnel from that region overturned the southern-dominated government of General J.T.I. Aguiyi-Ironsi. He was thrust into greatness, in a sense: by all accounts a modest, somewhat retiring man, only thirty-two years old when he became head of state, Gowon strengthened his international position markedly through his success in the Nigerian civil war of 1967-70 and conciliatory policies after it. His internal position rested on seniority and geographic origin: born in the "Middle Belt", he enjoyed widespread good will among the soldiers. With the conflict over, and domestic reconstruction started, Gowon could turn his attention to Nigeria's international position and to potential military disengagement from politics.[14] The country's immense domestic market, and its swelling earnings from petroleum, heightened the challenges of rapid development; the country's population (well over half that of all West Africa) and its desire to achieve and exercise regional leadership led Nigeria toward a more active foreign policy, as Ojo has convincingly argued.[15]

But the necessary complement may well have been Eyadéma's leadership of Togo. This small republic had a distinctive history in West Africa, making it a potential bridge between anglophone and francophone states. Once Germany's "model colony", it had been divided during World War I: the western third was absorbed into the British-ruled Gold Coast, though it remained subject to international supervision; the eastern part was governed by the French (from 1919 to 1945 under the League of Nations Mandate system, then under the United Nations Trusteeship system) as an entity technically separate from the other colonies of French West Africa, although governed in essentially the same manner. Pulled economically and ethnically toward Ghana after independence, yet threatened by Ghanaian claims over its territory,[16] Togo clearly wished to gain allies against the threat to its west. On the other hand, Eyadéma, like his assassinated predecessor Sylvanus Olympio, shied away from close ties exclusively with French-speaking West African states. Togo was conspicuously absent from the Communauté Economique de l'Afrique de l'Ouest (CEAO), just as it had earlier forgone membership of the Union Douanière de l'Afrique de l'Ouest (UDEAO). A relative "outsider" among francophone countries after independence, Togo built upon the distinctiveness it had maintained in the colonial period.

Did the military backgrounds of Gowon and Eyadéma predispose them in any consistent way toward their support for regional cooperation, or directly influence their domestic political stances? The case, I believe, would be hard to make, given the contrasts in their careers and governing styles. Eyadéma rose from the ranks; an NCO in the French colonial army, he had combat experience in Vietnam and Algeria before being repatriated in 1962 as France broke up its overseas forces. Gowon profited from Sandhurst training and rose extremely rapidly without experiencing combat. (From his initial commissioning as a second lieutenant to his promotion to lieutenant colonel took less than eight years, due to the pell-mell pace of indigenizing the officer corps, scarcely 18 percent Nigerian at independence but totally Nigerian by the end of 1965.)[17] Gowon's father had been an educated Christian catechist, while Eyadéma's father was an uneducated farmer.

The two men varied in their approaches to leadership. Gowon frequently voiced his willingness to return the armed forces to the barracks, while Eyadéma consolidated his hold on power. Although the Nigerian civil war overshadowed all other concerns in his first three and half years as head of state, Gowon recognized that few of his fellow officers had been trained to govern. He had to wrestle with the problems of a grossly swollen military after the civil war, and of the ambitions of many colleagues. As is well known, Gowon was ousted barely two months after signature of the ECOWAS treaty, while he was attending the 1975 summit of the Organization of African Unity. The prime motivation for his removal seems to have been dislike among several senior officers for the slow pace of reform and recivilianization: the armed forces appeared to be losing its cohesion under the impact of governing, and a stepped-up program of change seemed necessary. Eyadéma never faced such a direct challenge from his fellow officers -- and, of course, never had to confront secession. His dominance was unquestioned among the Kabré, while potential rivals from other ethnic groups were eased out from the armed forces. The military, in other words, remained united. Although restiveness among the Ewe resulted in numerous plots and arrests, Eyadéma entrenched personal rule, using the cover of a single party, the Rassemblement du Peuple Togolais. The two leaders thus brought rather different styles of leadership to Nigeria and Togo; both confronted regional dissension, far more acute in Nigeria; Eyadéma profited from a stronger individual position, buttressed by the creation of a political movement, while Gowon professed remaining a soldier without active party affiliation or leadership. Indeed, in Decalo's judgment, "...direct military rule (since the 1967 takeover) under a remarkably cohesive army has brought Togo a measure of political stability, social tranquility, and economic development... Togo's experience with military rule is unique and instructive, because it is a rare exception to the generally negative record of military regimes."[18]

Their respective countries also differed in key respects. Nigeria potentially dominated West Africa, due to its large population and petroleum resources, and could readily take the lead role; Togo inherently would play a bit part, due to its size and limited resources. Both states, however, had significant disparities among regions, in common with most

West African countries: development was concentrated along
the coast and in areas of agricultural export. Neither Gowon
nor Eyadéma came from a "developed" area; indeed, the Angas
and Kabré followed traditional patterns of shifting
subsistence agriculture. Both leaders were fully aware of
the need for economic development. Nigeria benefited from
petroleum revenues, rising dramatically after the 1973 OPEC
price increases, but domestic manufacturing faced inherent
limits; Togo's tiny industrial base could grow if only far
wider markets could be found. But did the two countries have
similar approaches to economic growth? What, in fact, were
the major West African perspectives on development,
especially in the regional context? The question for them,
and for other leaders of the region, meant determining what
would be the most efficacious path to economic growth. The
Economic Community of West African States was their response.

Regional Views on Development --
and the Political Reality

The ECOWAS treaty sets forth far-reaching economic goals,
but rests these on a narrow political foundation. Based in
effect on a Polish parliament-type system, in which each
member has a veto, ECOWAS requires unanimity among the heads
of state, and stability in leadership, to progress toward its
objectives. The internal political dynamics of West African
countries make such unity and stability difficult to achieve.
Other chapters in this book examine in detail the aims of
the West African community, contrasting their sweeping nature
with the limited support provided them since the Lagos treaty
was signed in 1975. Economic progress on a regional basis
requires political will. In the absence of political will,
little accomplishment can be expected. As Asante comments,
"...neither economic integration nor economic progress can be
attained in West Africa without more dynamic policies and
better planned strategies of national and regional
development designed to tackle the most crucial and most
urgent economic and social problems. In the absence of such
reforms, the Treaty of Lagos and the procedures that it has
set in motion are bound to remain sterile and
unproductive."[19]
The general question I wish to pose in this section deals
with the role of governing officers in development and
regional cooperation: does widespread military involvement
in politics make government policies on economic development
pursued through regional means more likely than would

widespread civilian control? In other words, is there any basis for optimism about West African interstate cooperation, based on the prevailing distribution of power?

Let us start by recalling the approaches toward "intervention" mentioned in the preceding section. Four were identified: a "pull" approach, focused on military institutional norms and strengths; a "push" approach, based on social fragmentation and the weakness of central political institutions; an "international" approach, concentrated on the role of external powers or the "contagion" of violent political change in near-by states; and a "personalist" approach, aimed at the idiosyncrasies of individual coup leaders. Each appears to have significant limitations as a vehicle for economic growth and distribution. If "intervention" results from armed forces' desires to protect and enhance their corporate interests ("pull"), it stands to reason that government funds will be disproportionately directed toward the military. If a coup d'etat stems from rising tensions that divide the society along class, ethnic or regional lines ("push"), satisfying the perceived needs of the formerly disaffected but now dominant group or groups would seem paramount. If a government is toppled due to the machinations of another country ("international"), post-coup policies may be directed to benefit the patron, thereby deepening dependence and limiting the likelihood of self-reliant development or strong regional links; if deliberate emulation leads to intervention ("contagion"), serving corporate and personal interests may take first priority. Finally, if the change of leaders arises from personal ambitions and animosities ("personalist"), the new head of state may try for as rapid self-enrichment as possible, given the likelihood of other challenges to his position; long-term economic policies predicated on cooperation with other states would not likely be used.

The problem with this formulation is that the civilian-dominated states of West Africa suffer from identical problems. Major institutions supporting the head of state -- the single party; the bureaucracy; urban trade unions -- have corporate interests whose full satisfaction could transcend what a dispassionate economic adviser would recommend. Elected heads of government must satisfy their class, ethnic or regional bases of support; presidential home villages, like Yamassoukro, move to the head of the development queue. External trade or aid advantages -- the French or Libyan connection -- can also prop up a civilian regime, though at the cost of balanced or endogenous growth and of cooperation with neighboring states. Finally, men in mufti are certainly susceptible to corruption; fortunes have been (and are being) made by civilian as well as by military presidents.

These circumstances appear to hold generally throughout the Third World. Hence, it is not surprising to find the primacy of politics. "Political determinism" is paramount: "economic policies must get the blessing of the politicians before they can be implemented, and where political considerations clash with economic considerations the former usually prevail."[20] Equally, it is not surprising to learn that research in the mid-1970s found only marginal differences between (using McKinlay and Cohan's terms) "military regime systems" and "non-military regime systems" in their achievement of economic development.[21] Although these studies have been faulted for their simple dichotomization of types of government,[22] given the multiple forms of military involvement in politics, they highlight an important point. There may in fact be little difference, empirical or theoretical, between the economic policies pursued by "civilian" and by "military" governments in West Africa.

What have been the major policies they have pursued? The severe economic problems of many African states in the past decade have led to new, critical examination of strategies of development.[23] In the face of drought and famine, escalating debt burdens, erratic and falling international prices for commodities and major minerals, and fiscal mismanagement of state enterprises, African presidents and external commentators have been looking for new solutions. The Organization of African Unity, the World Bank, and the UN General Assembly have all offered suggestions. The 1975 creation of the Economic Community of West African States was an early effort to cut across the different currency zones that mark Africa and build a regional foundation for growth.

The ECOWAS treaty loosely exemplifies collective self-reliance. Its stress on promoting "cooperation and development in all fields of economic activity" is intended as an alternative approach to what most West African states had been following prior to 1975 (and, even today, what most favor): economic growth on national bases, including modest import substitution; heavy reliance on comparative advantage through a major export (or exports); and essentially bilateral ties with a developed capitalist country or the European Community (EC) as a whole. Some successes did result up to the late 1970s -- that is, until overly ambitious schemes, widespread corruption, further OPEC cost escalation, and falling world prices for major products intervened.

Nothing in the institutional structure of ECOWAS can preclude inept planning, peculation, or international price trends outside the direct control of West African states. Collective self-reliance starts with domestic conditions, but progresses through favorable international conditions. The political will of member states, able and willing to work closely with each other, is the necessary starting point, though not a necessary guarantee of success.

The Lagos treaty was followed, five years later, by the OAU Lagos "Plan of Action"; this, in turn, was followed by the 1981 World Bank report, "Toward Accelerated Development in Sub-Saharan Africa", by the 1984 OAU Addis Ababa Declaration, and by the 1986 special session of the United Nations General Assembly devoted to African economic problems. The Lagos declaration stressed self-reliance; it focused on cooperation among African states and with other parts of the Third World. The World Bank report (often called the Berg report, after its chief author) took a different approach, emphasizing more extensive links to developed countries and specialization. "Toward Accelerated Development" has been widely criticized by African leaders and many scholars for its repetition of what they consider an inappropriate strategy of potentially exacerbating dependence on export of primary products to the West; they prefer a strategy marked by greater self-reliance, preferences for African processed products in access to major markets, and significantly expanded aid and investment from developed countries without the proverbial strings attached. The Addis Ababa declaration, while taking note of the disappointing results of the early 1980s, renewed African stress on links among developing countries, while the UN resolution sought major financial commitments from affluent UN members. Regional cooperation among African states continues to be seen as a way of diminishing the weaknesses inherent in the "neocolonial" prescriptions of the Berg report. But such cooperation depends on political will. Do West African leaders possess it? In particular, have men who gained control through coups d'etat demonstrated interest and efforts toward regional cooperation?

In the eyes of at least one West African military head of state, ECOWAS has been suspect. When Master Sergeant Sammy Doe seized power, he meted out summary executions to a dozen major politicians -- including the chair of the OAU, President William Tolbert. Doe's violent actions against former politicians were not unprecedented: less than a year earlier, Flight-Lieutenant Jerry Rawlings had sent three former Ghanaian presidents before the firing squad.

Nonetheless, the killings stirred a hornets' nest of opposition within ECOWAS. When Doe flew to Lomé for the May 1980 ECOWAS meeting (in Sékou Touré's jet, one should note), he was informed privately he would not be permitted to attend. Nor was the ECOWAS action unprecedented: less than a decade earlier, the OAU had refused to recognize the Amin coup, an action that temporarily isolated Uganda but in no way affected its internal situation nor solved the OAU's dilemma of what to do in cases of forcible change of regime.[24] As might have been expected, the twenty-eight year old Liberian head of state reacted angrily to the snub, threatening to suspend his country's participation.[25] For understandable reasons, Liberian participation in ECOWAS has been less than enthusiastic since these events, despite the speed with which the boycott was ended.

More broadly, the commitment of West African states to regional unity has continued to wax and wane with the personal commitment of individual presidents. While Eyadéma has remained at the helm in Togo, his own support and leadership within the organization have diminished somewhat. Several changes of government in Lagos have installed heads of state far cooler to ECOWAS than Gowon. His immediate successors, Murtala Mohammed and Olusegun Obasanjo, concentrated on recivilianization; the elected Shagari governments seemed bent on using petroleum revenues for national growth (plus, of course, the enrichment of the politicians), and directly attacked a major principle of the community by expelling over two million citizens of other West African states; the subsequent Buhari and Babangida governments wrestled with severe economic problems, also expelled illegal aliens of ECOWAS countries, and (despite hosting the 1986 and 1987 summits) showed little enthusiasm for ECOWAS. Indeed, none of the shifts in presidential leadership in West Africa after 1975 seemed to produce leaders enthusiastic about regional economic cooperation. The most likely candidate, Diouf of Senegal, spent a great deal of time travelling as OAU chair in 1985-86. One of his major triumphs was presenting the African case for significantly expanded development aid at the special session of the UN General Assembly in May 1986. His continent-wide commitment did not translate into major direct support for ECOWAS, however; by the late 1980s, his government was mired in disputes over elections and relations with neighboring states.

Enthusiasm and commitment of the heads of state are essential, since decisions binding ECOWAS member states can be made only by the presidents -- formally, by "The Authority of Heads of State and Government." An unstated rule of unanimity prevails at the annual summits. Coupled with the need for ratification by the sixteen states, paralysis results.[26] I believe the fault is not only institutional, but is inherent in the structure chosen. The ways in which military officers become presidents militate against emergence of strong support for regional economic cooperation. The overwhelming majority of coup makers respond to domestic problems and interests. They must build a nation -- or satisfy powerful groups -- and find the long-term potential benefits but short-term actual costs of regional collaboration disincentives. To put the matter bluntly, it is doubtful whether the processes of internal political change in West African countries advance the processes of regional economic development. Even when the heads of state turn to collective security, their paramount interest remains national sovereignty.

The Defense Commission and Obstacles to Cooperation

Among regions of Africa, West Africa is distinctive in having a mutual defense pact that cuts across the distinctions among states of different colonial backgrounds. On the one hand, its existence seems to manifest a high degree of intraregional willingness to cooperate. On the other hand, the agreement may introduce additional complications in an already troubled situation. Which is closer to the truth?

ECOWAS leaders, Ravenhill observed, "have unnecessarily complicated their task by adopting the politically sensitive protocol on Defence. Why this should be part of the baggage of an economic organization which has no commitment towards political integration is unclear, except as a means of appeasing the long-standing ambitions of certain heads of state."[27] To understand this skeptical comment, several questions should be answered. Why did the ECOWAS heads of state adopt the protocol in 1981? Has the distribution of power and influence among civilian and military heads of state in West Africa impacted upon the protocol? What institutions have been established as a result? How do these relate to periodic OAU discussions of the need for African collective security? Do the "main conditions" for regional security -- which Imobighe summarizes as a community of interest and perception of a common threat[28] -- currently exist in the area?

The interest in regional security in Africa as a whole

grew from three mutually reinforcing sources. One was the general recognition of the threat posed by division and weakness: a continent balkanized into fifty plus states, most small and impoverished, would be prey to external manipulation. A second was aggression, particularly by former colonial powers or their agents and by South Africa, against independent African states. The third was the escalation of internal conflict into international confrontation.

Well before the OAU was formed, crisis within an African state resulted in calls for collective security for the continent. President Kwame Nkrumah of Ghana, the strongest proponent of integration among African states, suggested creation of an African high command in November 1960, owing to dissatisfaction with the actions of the UN in reintegrating the Congolese secessionist province of Katanga.[29] Nkrumah carried his crusade to the Addis Ababa conference at which the OAU was created. His suggestion of an African high command attracted little support at that time; it smacked of derogating the sovereignty just gained; it collided with the bilateral military arrangements many countries maintained, particularly with their former colonial powers. An agreement to "co-ordinate and harmonize" general policy was adopted without debate -- but also without commitment.[30] As a sop, the OAU Charter was drafted to include five specialized commissions, one dealing with defense. Nkrumah continued to press his ideas at the first meeting of the defense commission, held in Accra five months after the establishment of the OAU. Manifest distaste for a unified high command led Ghana, with Nigeria as a co-sponsor, to propose the alternative of establishing a small, permanent military headquarters located in the same venue as the OAU secretariat, which would carry out planning and liaison. This idea, too, was buried.[31] A 1965 OAU resolution to create a Pan-African force that might deter colonial armies from attacking OAU member states had no teeth: members were supposed voluntarily to designate units of their armed forces that could be placed at the disposal of the OAU, but no machinery was set up to organize and deploy such units.[32]

The notion of organizing collective security on regional rather than continental lines emerged at the fourth (1971) session of the defense commission, its first session in six years. Portuguese aggression against Guinea in November 1970 revived interest. Participants at the meeting, who represented thirty of the then forty-one OAU members, concurred in the potential creation of regional defense units (composed of units provided by states in the area), an executive secretariat for each region, an Office of National Defense Advisers within the OAU secretariat to coordinate security questions for all OAU states and gather military intelligence, and a permanent defense committee which would meet every six months.[33] The proposals were placed before the heads of state at the 1972 OAU summit; no action was taken. A 1977 proposal by the OAU secretary general to form a collective intervention force, which could deter attacks on Frontline states, also evoked no response.[34] The 1978 OAU summit resolved to take further steps, but these were vaguely defined and primarily focused on southern Africa. Specifically:

(a) The summit asserts that the responsibility for defending Africa and ensuring its security should be shouldered by the African peoples alone;

(b) Announces officially that the formation of an African military force should be within the context of the objectives and the priorities which were defined by the OAU for overthrowing the racist minority regimes;

(c) Urges all the member countries to settle their disputes in a peaceful way and also by making approaches to the mediation and reconciliation committee of the OAU;

(d) Calls for the reactivation of the OAU's Defence Commission in preparation for considering the need to establish an African military force under the supervision of the OAU.[35]

Occupation of the Kagera salient by Ugandan forces in November 1978, and the subsequent advance of Tanzanian troops into Uganda, lent even further urgency to the matter.

The defense council met in April 1979. After six days of often tense debate, it proposed linking creation of a Pan-African interventionary force with military support to Frontline states feeling pressure from South Africa.[36] At best the compromise was an uneasy one, fraught with difficulties. The logistical and political problems became evident at the 1979 OAU meeting of the OAU council: although participants expressed their "political determination" to establish a Pan-African defense force, they sent the proposal back for further study. Details about the structure of the force and financial implications remained unclear, the benefits uncertain. Overall, minimal progress had been made on either cooperative protection against civil strife or effective moves against apartheid. A formula for defense outside the organization's framework thus appeared appropriate.

The ECOWAS initiative arose, accordingly, in a context of disappointment about what the OAU had accomplished, intensified by concern over the mounting violence in Chad and its potential spillover into West Africa, and uncertainty unleashed by the Tanzanian assault on Uganda. Space precludes a detailed recounting of either set of events; however, owing to the direct impact of the conflict in Chad on Nigeria, the major power in ECOWAS, brief note of Chad's kaleidoscopic ethnic, political and regional tensions must be made.[37] Lemarchand aptly described Chad as a state "only by legal fiction or diplomatic courtesy,"[38] owing to its acute internal disparities. The French troops that helped maintain internal stability were withdrawn in 1975, on the request of General Malloum, who had himself seized control in 1970. Internecine conflict escalated. Political groups fragmented into personalist cliques; truces were short-lived. OAU efforts to mediate in 1979, with the Nigerian government of General Obasanjo providing extensive backing, proved fruitless. Frustration with OAU lack of progress on either forming an effective force in southern Africa or containing internal conflict in Chad encouraged ECOWAS members to take their own steps.

A foundation for regional military cooperation existed within West Africa. In 1977, seven francophone states (Burkina Faso, Côte d'Ivoire, Mali, Mauritania, Niger, Senegal and Togo) signed a nonaggression pact. Meeting in Nouakchott in October 1979, they noted their agreement "could be extended" to other states in the region.[39] This invitation was soon taken up; nonaggression was extended into mutual protection. In February 1980, the five-state ECOWAS defense committee (Nigeria, Togo, Liberia, Senegal and Côte d'Ivoire) drafted an agreement on nonaggression and assistance in defense matters among the sixteen members. It was discussed at the Lomé ECOWAS summit, with objections being raised by Benin, Cape Verde, Guinea-Bissau and Mali; President Eyadéma described the act as a "logical follow-up to the signing of the non-aggression protocol."[40] These objections were overcome, or at least muted, by the 1981 ECOWAS summit in Freetown, at which the defense protocol was signed. Participating states agreed to establish two bodies -- a defense commission composed of defense ministers and chiefs of staff, and a defense council composed of heads of state and governments -- and two positions -- a chief of staff and a deputy executive for defense within the ECOWAS secretariat; the defense council would meet within forty-

eight hours, either on the request of a member state being
attacked by a nonmember state, or when conflict existed
between two member states; external aggression would be
countered by joint military action, while conflict within
ECOWAS would be mitigated by having the allied forces act as
a peacekeeping force.[41] Thereby the organization's defense
arm came into formal existence. How significant a commitment
it represents for regional cooperation remains to be
determined.

Conclusion

The states of West Africa have accomplished what the
states of the entire continent have not: acceptance of a
mutual security agreement.   The regional rather than
continental approach to joint peacekeeping appears -- at
least in paper terms -- somewhat more successful in gaining
approval by heads of state. Yet whether the ECOWAS defense
protocol has major long-term significance for regional
cooperation remains open to question.

ECOWAS is not purely an economic organization, despite
Ravenhill's assertion. Indeed, no interstate organization
in Africa can avoid politicization. The domestic interests
and basic attitudes of heads of state provide the basic
agenda for any African international organization. ECOWAS
started its life with difficult issues, such as the free
movement of persons among member states and the defense
protocol. These necessarily involve political decisions.
ECOWAS, like the OAU, rests on the concurrence of presidents.
Leadership provides the key to cooperation in West Africa--
its nature, extent and objectives.

An agreement on mutual defense does not require prior
full-scale agreement on amalgamation. Recall the distinction
Deutsch and his associates drew between "amalgamated" and
"pluralistic" security communities. Successful creation of
the former rested on a dozen factors; successful
establishment of the latter, by contrast, appeared to rest on
three -- on compatibility of major values relevant to
political decision-making, on capacity to respond to needs
and messages quickly, adequately, and without violence, and
on mutual predictability of behavior. Here the personalist
style of national leadership serves as boon and bane. An
idiosyncratic leader out of step with his colleagues -- as
was President Nkrumah of Ghana when he pressed in the early
1960s for an African high command -- cannot easily persuade
others of the need for change when such change appears to

threaten basic state interests. Nkrumah challenged the bases of sovereignty among countries that had just achieved independence; African leaders were not ready then, nor are they ready now, to derogate substantial amounts of sovereignty to interstate bodies. On the other hand, the experiences of thirty years of independence have modified the attitudes on which the OAU was created. In 1963, there was little dissatisfaction with the bilateral military links many OAU members maintained with the former colonial powers, limited experience with coups d'etat, and (with the obvious exception of the former Belgian Congo) slight impact of great power rivalry and secessionist threats. The conditions under which the ECOWAS protocol was drafted and accepted differed dramatically from the conditions under which the OAU African high command was proposed and rejected. Establishment of a "pluralistic" security community in West Africa is indeed possible.

The mutual security initiative within ECOWAS came, as was noted above, from a core of francophone countries. These states cooperated far more extensively and readily than did former British-administered countries. The alphabet soup of organizations they created after independence -- UAM, CEAO, OCAM -- reflected their willingness to work together; the common currency most shared, like the joint airline they created, testified as much to the ease with which the heads of state could work with each other as to the heritage of a common colonial ruler. The nonaggression pact signed in 1977 signaled their mutual recognition of potential threats to security. Interestingly, three of the signatory leaders (Houphouët-Boigny in Côte d'Ivoire, Ould Daddah in Mauritania and Senghor in Senegal) were the men under whom these states had gained independence; the other four signers were the leaders of the initial coup d'etat in each (Traoré in Mali, Kountché in Niger, Eyadéma in Togo, and Lamizana in Burkina Faso). All these leaders were experienced and reasonably confident of their ability to rule, but also were aware of the fragility of their position.

Ironically, the least predictable behavior came in Nigeria, whose initiative had been central to the creation of ECOWAS. The removal of Gowon shortly after signing of the Lagos treaty was a sign of serious internal problems. Nigeria experienced five changes of head of state between 1975 and 1985; this turbulence and lack of predictability in by far the most important member state seriously compromised progress in the community. The massive expulsion of ECOWAS immigrants, under Shagari and later under Buhari, gave the lie to Nigeria's support for free movement of nationals among member states. To be certain, there may be no more sensitive political issue than granting political rights and job opportunities to nonnationals, as Houphouët-Boigny learned in the 1960s when riots greeted his effort to provide Ivorian citizenship to Council of the Entente nationals.[42] In the absence of clear, consistent support from Nigeria, ECOWAS will find significant progress difficult.

Ultimately, accordingly, national policies and international cooperation reflect predilections of major leaders. That West African heads of state will continue to be drawn heavily from the armed forces in the 1990s seems unquestionable. I am not aware of any compelling empirical evidence, nor any convincing theoretical argument, that presidents drawn from the military are necessarily any more oriented toward, or conversely more opposed to, interstate cooperation than are their civilian counterparts, however. Both seem readily to deal with regional security when they are reasonably secure in their grasps on power but well aware of the challengeable nature of their positions. Cooperation within West Africa thus rests fundamentally on the perceptions of heads of state regarding their domestic bases of support, and does not appear as directly affected by the civilian or military nature of leaders, or by the development strategy pursued.

Table 8.1
Successful Coups d'Etat in Africa, 1958-1989

Date	Country
Nov. 17, 1958	Sudan
Sept. 14, 1960	Zaire
Jan. 13, 1963	Togo*
Oct. 28, 1963	Benin*
Jan. 12, 1963	Zanzibar*
Oct. 26, 1964	Sudan
June 19, 1965	Algeria
Nov. 25, 1965	Zaire
Nov. 29, 1965	Benin
Dec. 22, 1965	Benin
Jan. 1, 1966	Central African Republic
Jan. 3, 1966	Burkina Faso

(continued)

Jan. 15, 1966	Nigeria
Feb. 24, 1966	Ghana
July 8, 1966	Burundi*
July 29, 1966	Nigeria
Nov. 28, 1966	Burundi
Jan. 13, 1967	Togo
March 21-3, 1967	Sierra Leone
Dec. 17, 1967	Benin
April 18, 1968	Sierra Leone*
Aug. 28, 1968	Congo/Brazzaville
Nov. 19, 1968	Mali
May 25, 1969	Sudan
Sept. 1, 1969	Libya
Oct. 21, 1969	Somalia
Dec. 10, 1969	Benin
Jan. 30, 1970	Lesotho*
Jan. 25, 1971	Uganda
Jan. 13, 1972	Ghana
May 18, 1972	Madagascar
Oct. 26, 1972	Benin
July 5, 1973	Rwanda
Feb. 8, 1974	Burkina Faso
April 15, 1974	Niger
Sept. 12, 1974	Ethiopia
Jan. 25, 1975	Madagascar
April 13, 1975	Chad
July 29, 1975	Nigeria
Aug. 3, 1975	Seychelles
Nov. 1, 1976	Burundi
March 18, 1977	Congo/Brazzaville
June 4-5, 1977	Seychelles
July 5, 1978	Ghana
May 5, 1978	Comoros
July 10, 1978	Mauritania
Feb. 5, 1979	Congo/Brazzaville
Apr. 6, 1979	Mauritania
June 4, 1979	Ghana
Aug. 4, 1979	Equatorial Guinea

(continued)

Sept. 20, 1979	Central African Republic
Jan. 4, 1980	Mauritania
April 12, 1980	Liberia
May 11, 1980	Uganda
Nov. 15, 1980	Guinea-Bissau
Nov. 24, 1980	Burkina Faso
Sept. 1, 1981	Central African Republic
Dec. 31, 1981	Ghana
Nov. 7, 1982	Burkina Faso
May 18, 1983	Burkina Faso
Aug. 4, 1983	Burkina Faso
Dec. 31, 1983	Nigeria
April 23, 1984	Guinea
Dec. 12, 1984	Mauritania
Apr. 6, 1985	Sudan
July 27, 1985	Uganda
Aug. 17, 1985	Nigeria
Jan. 20, 1986	Lesotho
Jan. 26, 1986	Uganda**
Oct. 15, 1987	Burkina Faso
Nov. 7, 1987	Tunisia
June 30, 1989	Sudan

*ouster of previous government followed by installation of new government not headed by military officers.

**date of capture of Kampala by National Resistance Army

Notes

1. For example, consider the twelve conditions Deutsch and his associates found historically "essential" for the creation of what they deemed amalgamated security-

communities: mutual compatibility of main values; a distinctive way of life; expectations of stronger economic ties or gains; a marked increase in the political and administrative capabilities of at least some participating units; superior economic growth on the part of at least some participating units; unbroken lines of social communication, both geographically between territories and sociologically between different social strata; a broadening of the political elite; mobility of persons, at least among the politically relevant strata; a multiplicity of ranges of communication and transaction; a compensation of flows of communications and transactions; not too infrequent interchange of group roles; and considerable mutual predictability of behavior.

In the case of pluralistic security-communities, however, their list was far shorter: compatibility of major values relevant to political decision-making; capacity of participating governments to respond to each other's needs, messages and actions quickly, adequately, and without resort to violence; and mutual predictability of behavior. Karl W. Deutsch *et al.*, *Political Community and the North Atlantic Area*, reprinted in *International Political Communities: An Anthology* (Garden City: Anchor, 1966), pp. 37-38, 45.

2. Robert Jackson and Carl G. Rosberg, Jr., *Personal Rule in Black Africa: Prince, Autocrat, Prophet, Tyrant* (Berkeley and Los Angeles: University of California Press, 1982).

3. Timothy S. Colton, *Commissars, Commanders, and Civilian Authority: The Structure of Soviet Military Politics* (Cambridge: Harvard University Press, 1979), pp. 221-249.

4. The placement of Togo among single-coup countries may surprise some readers, given the military acts of 13 January 1963 and 13 January 1967. Both are customarily counted as coups d'etat, and indeed appear as such in the table. The first, however, was in essence an assassination, carried out by unemployed Togolese veterans of the French army, who had unsuccessfully demanded that President Olympio hire them. With the head of state dead, the soldiers turned to two former political leaders, Nicholas Grunitzky and Antoine Meatchi, who ruled uneasily as president and vice-president until Eyadéma's full assumption of power in 1967. During this period, the armed forces expanded from approximately 250 to 1,200 men, 80 percent of them from the north. Figures from Samuel Decalo, *Coups and Army Rule in Africa: Studies in Military Style* (New Haven: Yale University Press, 1976), p. 99.

5. The two schools of thought are summarized and contrasted in Samuel Decalo, "Military Rule in Africa: Etiology and Morphology" in Simon Baynham (ed.), *Military*

Power and Politics in Black Africa (London: Croom Helm, 1986), pp. 40-42; Decalo, *Coups and Army Rule*, pp. 7-13; and Donald L. Horowitz, *Coup Theories and Officers' Motives: Sri Lanka in Comparative Perspective* (Princeton: Princeton University Press, 1980), pp. 4-6.

6. In the words of Professor Martin, "Ultimately one expects that the main objective [of French policy] is to help pro-French regimes stay in power, as the remarkable political stability and exceptional elite longevity of several francophone states seems to indicate." Guy Martin, "Bases of France's African Policy," *Journal of Modern African Studies*, 23, 1985, p. 206. Also see Pierre Lellouche and Dominique Moisi, "French Policy in Africa: A Lonely Battle against Destabilization," *International Security*, 3, 1978, pp. 108-133; George Moose, "French Military Policy in Africa" in William J. Foltz and Henry S. Bienen (eds.), *Arms and the African: Military Influences on Africa's International Relations* (New Haven: Yale University Press, 1985), pp. 59-97.

7. Decalo, "Military Rule in Africa," pp.44-45.

8. Robert H. Jackman, "The Predictability of Coups d'Etat: A Model with African Data," *American Political Science Review*, 72, 1978, pp. 1262-1275; Thomas H. Johnson, Robert O. Slater and Pat McGowan, "Explaining African Military Coups d'Etat: An Historical Explanation," *Journal of Modern African Studies*, 22, 1984, pp. 633-666; and rejoinders in *American Political Science Review*, 80, 1986, pp. 225-249.

9. Jackman, "Predictability," p. 1273.

10. Johnson *et al.*, "Explaining African Military Coups d'Etat," p. 634, citing Claude E. Welch, Jr. and Arthur K. Smith, *Military Role and Rule* (North Scituate MA: Duxbury Press, 1974), pp. 14-15.

11. See Table 8.1 at the conclusion of this chapter.

12. David Goldsworthy, "Armies and Politics in Civilian Regimes" in Baynham, *Military Power*, pp. 97-128 (paraphrase from p. 106); also see David Goldsworthy, "Civilian Control of the Military in Black Africa," *African Affairs*, 80(318), 1981, pp. 49-74.

13. I do not wish, to be certain, to reduce my argument, à la Decalo, to a simple question of personality. Leadership and personal characteristics do not exist in a vacuum. Analysts must give particular attention to the relationships between environmental factors (incentives and obstacles to leadership; resources; levels of institutionalization; etc.) and individual factors (self-confidence; levels of affluence and education; activity; positive or negative characteristics; etc.). The relatively brief period of

independence, political turmoil, and the small size of the political elite in many West African states interact to allow a significant impact for leadership -- but presentation of events in a "great man" sort of way misreports the dynamics.

14. The Nigerian disengagement is explored at length in chapter 6 of my book, *No Farewell to Arms? Military Disengagement from Politics in Africa and Latin America* (Boulder: Westview Press, 1987). Also see Valerie P. Bennett and A.H.M. Kirk-Greene, "Back to the Barracks: A Decade of Marking Time" in Keith Panter-Brick (ed.), *Soldiers and Oil: The Political Transformation of Nigeria* (London: Frank Cass, 1978), pp. 13-26; and Toyin Falola and Julius Ihonvbere, *The Rise and Fall of Nigeria's Second Republic, 1979-84* (London: Zed, 1985), pp. 18-45.

15. Olatunde J.B. Ojo, "Nigeria and the Formation of ECOWAS," *International Organization*, 34, 1980, pp. 571-604.

16. Dennis Austin, "The Uncertain Frontier: Ghana-Togo," *Journal of Modern African Studies*, 1, 1963, pp. 139-146; David Brown, "Borderline Politics in Ghana: The National Liberation Movement of Western Togoland," *Journal of Modern African Studies*, 18(4), 1980, pp. 575-610; David Brown, "Who are the Tribalists? Social Pluralism and Political Ideology in Ghana," *African Affairs*, 81(322), 1982, pp. 37-69; Claude E. Welch, Jr., *Dream of Unity: Pan-Africanism and Political Unification in West Africa* (Ithaca: Cornell University Press, 1966), pp. 37-147.

17. Robin Luckham, *The Nigerian Military: A Sociological Analysis of Authority and Revolt 1960-67* (Cambridge: Cambridge University Press, 1971), pp. 163, 175.

18. Decalo, *Coups and Army Rule*, p. 87.

19. S.K.B. Asante, *The Political Economy of Regionalism in Africa: A Decade of the Economic Community of West African States* (New York: Praeger, 1985), pp. 196-197. Also see Edem Kodjo, "Need for Political Will," *West Africa*, 30 June 1986, pp. 1364-1366.

20. S.K.B. Asante, "ECOWAS, the EEC and the Lomé Convention" in Domenico Mazzeo (ed.), *African Regional Organizations* (Cambridge: Cambridge University Press, 1984), p. 179.

21. R.D. McKinlay and A.S. Cohan, "Performance and Instability in Military and Nonmilitary Regime Systems," *American Political Science Review*, 70, 1976, pp. 850-864; also by the same authors, "A Comparative Analysis of the Political and Economic Performance of Military and Civilian Regimes: A Cross-National Aggregate Study," *Comparative Politics*, 8, 1975, pp. 1-30; Kim Quaide Hill, "Military Role vs. Military Rule: Allocations to Military Authorities," *Comparative Politics*, 11, 1979, pp. 371-377; Robert W.

182

Jackman, "Politicians in Uniform: Military Government and Social Change in the Third World," *American Political Science Review*, 70, 1976, pp. 1078-1097.

22. John Ravenhill, "Comparing Regime Performance in Africa: The Limitations of Cross-National Aggregate Analysis," *Journal of Modern African Studies*, 18(1), 1980, pp. 124-125.

23. As recent examples, see Robert J. Berg and Jennifer Seymour Whitaker (eds.), *Strategies for African Development* (Berkeley and Los Angeles: University of California Press, 1986); and Richard Sandbrook (with Judith Barker), *The Politics of Africa's Economic Stagnation* (Cambridge: Cambridge University Press, 1985).

24. Claude E. Welch, Jr., "The OAU and International Recognition: Lessons from Uganda" in Yassin El-Ayouty (ed.), *The OAU After Ten Years* (New York: Praeger, 1975), pp. 103-117.

25. *Africa Research Bulletin*, 17(5), May 1980, p. 5664A.

26. See the pointed discussion in Asante, *Political Economy*, pp. 69-73 regarding the "slow and inadequate" means of ECOWAS decision-making.

27. John Ravenhill, "The Future of Regionalism in Africa" in Ralph I. Onwuka and Amadu Sesay (eds.), *The Future of Regionalism in Africa* (New York: St. Martin's, 1985), pp. 215-216.

28. Tom Imobighe, "ECOWAS Defence Pact and Regionalism in Africa" in *Ibid.*, p. 118.

29. Catherine Hoskyns, *The Congo since Independence, January 1960-December 1961* (London: Oxford University Press, 1965); T.A. Imobighe, "An African High Command: The Search for a Feasible Strategy of Continental Defence," *African Affairs*, 79(315), 1980, p. 241; W. Scott Thompson, *Ghana's Foreign Policy 1957-66: Diplomacy, Ideology, and the New State* (Princeton: Princeton University Press, 1969), pp. 119-161.

30. Michael Wolfers, *Politics in the Organization of African Unity* (London: Methuen, 1976), pp. 92-93.

31. Imobighe, "African High Command," pp. 244-245; Wolfers, *Politics in the OAU*, p. 93.

32. Imobighe, "African High Command," p. 246.

33. *Africa Research Bulletin*, 8(12), 1971, pp. 2303-2304.

34. Imobighe, "African High Command," pp. 248-249.

35. *Africa Research Bulletin*, 14(7), 1978, p. 4914C.

36. *Ibid.*, 16(4), 1979, p. 5218C. Later progress on creation of the Pan-African force was negligible. The defense ministers met for a week in late March-early April 1979, without agreement on the text of a protocol, although

participants did recommend basic organs for the force, including a defense council of ten OAU heads of state, a committee of chiefs of staff, and the office of a military adviser. Problems remained with finance, since initial contributions of a billion dollars would be needed to establish the force (*Ibid.*, 18(4), 1981, p. 6011B). In January 1984, a military protocol was adopted, calling for a "defense organ" (*Ibid.*, 21(1), 1984, p. 7089A). However, when Sierra Leone proposed that the OAU establish "a principal and permanent forum capable of responding with the required promptness and efficiency to crises which occur in the political and security sectors of the African continent" at the 1985 meeting of the OAU council (the foreign ministers), no vote was taken, and the proposal died (*Ibid.*, 22(3), 1985, p.7561C). In May 1986, the defense commission met in Zimbabwe, with South African pressure lending a sense of urgency but not overcoming members' hesitation to reach agreement. Despite the complaint of Ghana's defense minister -- that the OAU had after twenty-three years yet to establish "a viable system for our collective security in the event of external aggression and mounting peace-keeping expenditures in times of intra-African conflicts" -- the participants failed to agree on proposals for submission to the OAU council (*Ibid.*, 23(5), 1986, p. 8107AB). No progress has been recorded over the years since then.

37. Rene Lemarchand, "The Crisis in Chad" in Gerald J. Bender, James S. Coleman, and Richard L. Sklar (eds.), *African Crisis Areas and U.S. Foreign Policy* (Berkeley and Los Angeles: University of California Press, 1985), pp. 239-256; Virginia Thompson and Richard Adloff, *Conflict in Chad* (Berkeley: Institute of International Studies, 1981); Samuel Decalo, "Chad: The Roots of Center-Periphery Strife," *African Affairs*, 79(317), 1980, pp. 491-509.

38. Lemarchand, "Crisis in Chad," p. 241.

39. *Africa Research Bulletin*, 16(6), 1979, p. 5431B.

40. *Ibid.*, 17(2), 1980, p. 5664A

41. *Ibid.*, 18(6), 1981, p. 6072A.

42. Virginia Thompson, *West Africa's Council of the Entente* (Ithaca: Cornell University Press, 1972), pp. 143-163.

9

Intraregional Trade in West Africa

Mary E. Burfisher and
Margaret B. Missiaen

Trade among developing countries has generated
considerable interest for economic and political reasons.
Growth in exports has an important role in growth of
developing economies, but trade among less developed
countries (LDCs) could hold greater potential for supporting
broad economic growth than does world trade in general.[1]
Trade among LDCs can be beneficial in the following ways: a
wider array of export markets can support the evolution of a
developing country's comparative advantage, product demand
may be similar among developing countries, exports can be
diversified, and LDCs can provide alternative markets as
economic growth and import demand of developed countries
slow. Increased trade among LDCs is also politically
desirable, as evidenced by its prominence among the
objectives of many regional groupings of LDCs, including the
Economic Community of West African States (ECOWAS).

This chapter focuses upon intraregional trade in West
Africa and its prospects for supporting economic growth and
development in that region. The paper documents
intraregional trade during 1970-82 in the eighteen developing
countries of the wider West African region: Benin, Burkina
Faso, Cameroon, Cape Verde, Chad, Côte d'Ivoire, Gambia,
Ghana, Guinea, Guinea-Bissau, Liberia, Mali, Mauritania,
Niger, Nigeria, Senegal, Sierra Leone and Togo. We
emphasize trade in agricultural commodities, especially in
livestock, grains, vegetable oils, cola nuts and cotton. We
also discuss intraregional trade in petroleum.

Intraregional Trade

The eighteen West African countries had a population of

Table 9.1
Recorded and unrecorded trade of major West African countries[1] (1,000 U.S. dollars)

	Unrecorded Trade					Recorded trade	Total trade	% share of trade unrecorded
	Mali	Cameroon	Ghana	BCEAO[2]	Nigeria	Total			
1970:	1,802	54	3,603	86,355	10,369	102,183	111,930	214,113	48
1971:	1,780	153	2,559	128,820	12,678	145,990	142,228	288,218	51
1972:	78	2,497	2,735	135,405	20,373	161,088	174,801	335,889	48
1973:	5,369	624	3,712	140,118	18,240	168,063	229,070	397,133	42
1974:	4,218	1,738	3,363	202,709	21,489	233,517	418,347	651,864	36
1975:	1,449	846	2,174	268,200	21,447	294,116	555,828	849,944	35
1976:	80	6,204	4,973	304,009	2,973	318,239	489,375	807,614	39
1977:	17	3,121	7,365	506,329	11,924	528,756	682,800	1,211,556	44
1978:	2,069	2,663	10,679	434,960	39,105	489,476	667,943	1,157,419	42
1979:	NA	10,006	6,906	472,800	53,481	543,193	755,205	1,298,398	42
1980:	2,996	17,945	10,365	252,423	49,057	332,786	1,268,660	1,601,446	21
1981:	NA	NA	8,652	446,160	72,973	527,785	1,113,739	1,641,524	32
1982:	NA	NA	2,815	410,246	13,785	426,846	788,526	1,215,372	35

NA = Not available

[1]Includes Benin, Burkina, Cameroon, Ghana, Mali, Niger, Nigeria, Senegal, and Togo, accounting for 95 percent of regional trade during 1970-80.
[2]BCEAO members are Benin, Burkina, Côte d'Ivoire, Niger, Senegal, and Togo. Mali became a full member in 1984.

Source: Banque Centrale des Etats de l'Afrique de l'Ouest, *Statistiques Economiques et Monétaires* (Dakar: various years); and United Nations, *Commodity Trade Statistics,* ST/EAS/STAT/Series D (New York: United Nations, annual 1970-82).

172 million in 1982. Nigeria's size caused it to dominate a region of otherwise small economies. Nigeria accounted for 53 percent of West Africa's population and 68 percent of the region's combined gross national product (GNP). Per capita incomes in West Africa were low, ranging from $77 in Chad to $914 in Côte d'Ivoire in 1982. All of these economies remained heavily dependent on international trade. World exports were relatively undiversified, with one or two commodities accounting for the bulk of foreign exchange earnings in most West African countries.

Data Sources for Recorded and Unrecorded Intraregional Trade

An analysis of West African intraregional trade immediately confronts the problem of how to document it accurately because a sizeable proportion is unrecorded by customs or official trade statistics. Unrecorded trade is partly composed of smuggled or underinvoiced goods. But it also results from the traditional nature of production and marketing systems for some of the region's most important traded commodities, notably live cattle. The limited administrative and statistical capabilities of some countries also result in poor or unavailable trade data.

The primary data source was the commodity trade statistics of the United Nations (UN). These data were supplemented with country trade statistics and Food and Agriculture Organization (FAO) trade yearbooks. We also estimated unrecorded intraregional trade using two methods. One source of information was the Banque Centrale des Etats de l'Afrique de l'Ouest (BCEAO), which estimates unrecorded trade within the BCEAO community (Benin, Burkina Faso, Côte d'Ivoire, Mali, Niger, Senegal and Togo. Mali joined in 1984). BCEAO estimates are based on assessments and, if necessary, a reevaluation of officially reported export unit prices. The BCEAO also reconciles customs trade data with the distribution of Communauté Financière Africaine (CFA) currency[2] within member countries. All CFA notes are tagged with member country designations. For example, foreign CFA notes in circulation in excess of the amount reasonably warranted by official export statistics would cause the BCEAO to revise upward its estimate of total exports.

A second basis for estimating unrecorded trade is to examine country trade data discrepancies between exporters and importers. The difference between the value of trade as reported by exporters and importers can occur for many reasons, but such a discrepancy is generally viewed as

Table 9.2
All commodities: West African trade market shares

	Burkina Faso	Ghana	Côte d'Ivoire	Mali	Niger	Nigeria	Senegal	Other	Total
					Percent				
Exports:									
1970-72	6.3	1.1	21.1	11.1	9.1	11.8	21.9	17.1	100.0
1975-77	3.1	1.8	26.1	3.4	4.9	33.2	17.4	10.1	100.0
1979-81	3.4	0.7	26.6	3.7	5.9	40.8	10.6	8.3	100.0
Imports:									
1970-72	5.4	8.4	24.6	8.0	3.6	10.9	11.7	27.4	100.0
1975-77	6.9	15.4	20.4	12.0	4.6	9.5	9.9	21.3	100.0
1979-81	8.3	21.9	15.4	11.0	4.4	10.0	6.5	22.5	100.0
Share of Exports to Regional market:									
1970-72	49.4	0.5	6.6	49.6	34.6	1.0	20.8	NA	NA
1975-77	38.3	1.4	9.8	29.9	23.4	2.0	17.5	NA	NA
1979-81	42.3	0.8	10.4	8.2	13.0	2.2	24.9	NA	NA
1986-87	22.1	NA	11.2	11.0	10.4	2.6	17.1	NA	NA

NA = Not available
Source: BCEAO and UN, as cited in Table 9.1. The 1986-87 data from International Monetary Fund, *Direction of Trade Statistics* (Washington D.C.: IMF, 1987 and 1988).

indicating illegal trade.[3]   Trade data discrepancies were
used to estimate unrecorded trade for Ghana, Cameroon, Mali
and Nigeria. Estimates of unrecorded trade, therefore, cover
only ten of eighteen countries. These countries, however,
accounted for 95 percent of the recorded trade within the
region during 1970-80.

Intraregional trade among these West African countries was
worth $1.6 billion in 1981, a more than sevenfold increase in
nominal value since 1970. Unrecorded trade accounted for an
average of 40 percent of their intraregional trade during
1970-82 and was worth about $500 million annually in recent
years. Some countries have an especially high proportion of
trade that is unrecorded.   Benin's unrecorded exports
accounted for nearly 80 percent of its total exports in the
late 1970s. Burkina's unrecorded exports accounted for over
60 percent of the total in 1978. Nigeria's estimated
unrecorded trade varies greatly, ranging from 222 percent of
official trade in 1970 to only 1 percent in 1977.   This
disparity reflects poor data quality rather than real trade
flows.   Nigeria's unrecorded trade estimates should be
treated as particularly speculative, given the weakness of
its official trade data.

Unrecorded trade flows among the BCEAO members appeared to
drop sharply in 1980 (Table 9.1). Almost all of the change
was due to a shift by Côte d'Ivoire from underreporting
exports (by $200 million in 1979) to overreporting exports
(by $130 million in 1980). This is due to Côte d'Ivoire's
balance of payments deficit from 1979-82. The deficits in
1980 and 1981 were met by overdrafts from the French
treasury. In balancing accounts, BCEAO counted part of the
injection of Ivorian francs as an overreporting of exports.
Consequently, some of the apparent drop in unrecorded trade
in 1980 does not reflect real changes in trade flows within
the BCEAO community.

Major Intraregional Trade

Based on recorded trade data, intraregional trade is
concentrated among less than half of the countries and became
more concentrated over the study period (Table 9.2).
Nigeria, Côte d'Ivoire and Senegal are by far the region's
top exporters. These three countries accounted for about 50
percent of recorded intraregional exports in the early 1970s
and 75 percent by the late 1970s. The livestock-exporting
countries of Mali, Niger and Burkina Faso also accounted for
a large proportion of recorded intraregional trade.   Togo

Table 9.3
Agricultural commodities: West African trade market shares

	Burkina Faso	Cameroon	Ghana	Côte d'Ivoire	Mali	Niger	Nigeria	Senegal	Other	Total
Exports:										
1970-72	15.3	1.4	0.7	15.3	24.0	22.4	1.0	12.4	7.6	100.0
1975-77	11.8	3.3	1.7	27.5	12.9	19.6	0.9	15.9	6.5	100.0
1979-81	14.8	2.1	0.5	33.1	9.2	31.5	0.4	6.6	1.7	100.0
Imports:										
1970-72	2.2	0.6	9.2	31.8	3.2	2.2	22.4	14.3	14.1	100.0
1975-77	5.0	2.4	4.7	24.3	3.8	5.2	29.9	13.0	11.7	100.0
1979-81	8.2	1.2	2.1	19.8	5.8	6.3	37.2	7.9	11.5	100.0
Share of Exports to Regional market:										
1970-72	51.8	0.5	0.2	2.7	45.8	38.1	0.1	7.8	NA	NA
1975-77	33.7	1.0	0.4	3.3	25.2	61.9	0.2	7.3	NA	NA
1979-81	37.7	0.6	0.2	3.3	8.7	88.1	0.2	12.7	NA	NA

NA = Not available

Source: BCEAO and UN, as cited in Table 9.1.

became a major exporter to other West African countries in the late 1970s when projects in its industrial development program began production; by the early 1980s, many of Togo's projects proved inefficient and began to fail.

Intraregional trade is an important export market for several West African countries, particularly the cattle-exporters. Burkina Faso, Mali, Niger and Senegal rely on regional markets for 20-50 percent of their total export sales, although totals vary considerably from one year to the next. Recorded trade data probably understate their real dependence on the regional market, because much of their cattle exports are unrecorded. The leading regional exporters are also the region's major importers, for the most part. Just three countries -- Côte d'Ivoire, Nigeria and Senegal -- imported nearly half of intraregionally traded goods during 1970-72. Ghana and Mali became more important importers during the study period. The leading importers by 1979-81 were Ghana, Côte d'Ivoire and Mali, and together they accounted for about half of intraregional imports.

The region's five major agricultural exporters (Mali, Niger, Côte d'Ivoire, Burkina Faso and Senegal) accounted for about 90 percent of recorded intraregional agricultural trade during the 1970s (Table 9.3). The pattern appears to have changed somewhat in the 1980s when Cameroon became an important agricultural exporter. The recent data, however, are less reliable because fewer countries reported. The major import markets for West African agricultural products were Côte d'Ivoire, Nigeria and Senegal during 1970-72. Ghana ranked fourth during the early 1970s, but was replaced by Burkina Faso and Mauritania in the second half of the decade. Niger emerged as an important agricultural market in the 1980s but reexports from Nigeria are a major factor in this development.

Three of the major agricultural exporters -- Burkina Faso, Mali and Niger -- are heavily dependent on live animal trade which accounted for about two-thirds of their recorded agricultural exports to the region in the 1970s. The two other major regional exporters, Côte d'Ivoire and Senegal, supplied a variety of agricultural products to a number of countries in the region. Côte d'Ivoire was the region's leading agricultural exporter during most of the study period, doubling its market share from 15 percent to 30 percent during the 1970s. In the early 1970s, cola nuts and coffee accounted for 75 percent of the country's exports of agricultural products to the region. A decade later, this trade had expanded to include a wider range of commodities following the development of its agricultural processing

Table 9.4
Agriculture's role in West Africa's regional exports

	1970	1972	1974	1976	1978	1980	1982
				Million dollars			
Agriculture's share of intraregional exports:	56	62	95	123	152	211	109
Total	125	190	435	511	698	1308	841

Source: United Nations, as cited in Table 9.1.

industries. These industries enabled Côte d'Ivoire to meet regional demand for some products that had previously been imported from outside the region. Some of these items are cigarettes, bread and pastas, beer, instant coffee, sugar, dried soups and broths and other miscellaneous food preparations (Standard International Trade Classification [SITC] Code 09). Côte d'Ivoire's market expansion also rested on increased regional demand for its palm oil, as neighboring countries shifted from being vegetable oil exporters to importers. Coffee accounted for more than 30 percent of Ivorian regional agricultural exports by 1978-80, palm oil was second with 15 percent. Senegal also provides a variety of agricultural products to its neighbors, but its share of intraregional agricultural trade declined from 12.4 percent in 1970-72 to 8.6 percent during 1978-80. Senegal has traditionally exported processed products, from both domestic and imported raw materials, to other West African countries. Like Côte d'Ivoire, Senegal's exports showed some diversification during the study period. In the early 1970s, Senegal's most valuable agricultural export to neighboring countries was cigarettes, followed by peanut oil and wheat flour. In the 1980s, Senegal's regional agricultural exports also included animal feed stuff (SITC code 08), mostly peanut cake, peanut oil, fruits and vegetables, and cereal preparations (mostly pasta and bakery items). Cigarette exports had declined in importance, and wheat flour exports became insignificant as most West African countries built their own flour mills. Some items, such as peanut meal, were clearly of domestic origin; other categories, such as fruit and vegetables, appear to include reexports.

Commodity Composition of Intraregional Trade

Trends in the commodity composition of intraregional trade in West Africa during 1970-81 were strongly affected by developments in the world petroleum market. The increase in quantity and unit price of intraregional trade in petroleum caused the relative importance of all other intraregionally traded commodities to decline.[4] The role of agricultural commodities in intraregional trade fell sharply in the early 1970s, from 45 percent in 1970 to 22 percent in 1974. It remained at about 20 percent through 1979 before declining slightly again in 1980-82 (Table 9.4).

In absolute terms, intraregional agricultural trade performed well in West Africa during 1970-81. Because of

Table 9.5
Annual export growth in West African countries: Regional, rest of world, and
total exports (in percent)

	1970-75			1976-81		
	Regional	Rest of World	Total	Regional	Rest of World	Total
Benin[1]	10.3	-4.1	-0.5	5.5	10.9	10.1
Burkina Faso	17.4	7.5	12.4	15.1	2.0	5.8
Cape-Verde	NA	6.1	6.1	NA	19.4	19.4
Côte d'Ivoire	28.3	14.1	15.4	12.0	6.8	7.4
Gambia[1]	43.5	18.6	19.0	-16.9	6.5	5.7
Ghana	45.2	8.7	8.9	3.7	2.7	2.7
Guinea[1]	-8.8	18.0	15.9	11.7	27.7	26.7
Guinea-Bissau[1]	NA	14.2	14.6	-99.3	17.1	14.3
Liberia	11.1	8.7	8.7	13.6	2.3	2.4
Mali[1]	0.1	0.9	0.5	5.5	20.3	19.1
Mauritania[1]	-24.8	11.8	11.4	22.7	1.7	1.7
Niger	15.1	18.8	17.7	14.1	22.1	20.4
Nigeria	57.8	31.0	31.2	16.7	10.2	10.3
Senegal	24.6	23.2	23.5	15.0	-5.6	-1.2
Sierra Leone[1]	16.3	3.0	3.2	2.3	11.9	11.7
Togo	27.9	13.2	13.8	26.1	9.5	11.2
Total region	25.6	22.2	22.4	13.5	9.3	9.5

[1]Growth rates are for 1970-75 and 1976-80;
Source: United Nations, as cited in Table 9.1.

agricultural trade's sharp expansion in 1980, its share of intraregional trade declined only slightly despite the increase in petroleum prices in 1979-80. The increase in agricultural trade within West Africa during 1980 was mostly accounted for by developments in Niger and, to some extent, in Côte d'Ivoire, Senegal and Mali. The large increase in Niger's exports to Nigeria in 1980 was accounted for by more than a $20 million jump in cowpea shipments. This increase reflects exports through official channels; a change from earlier years when exports were in the hands of private traders and not recorded in official statistics. Diversification of agricultural trade to include processed food products, by Côte d'Ivoire in particular, also helped buoy the role of agriculture in intraregional trade.

Export Market Growth, 1970-81

West Africa's intraregional trade grew faster than its trade with the rest of the world throughout 1970-81 (Table 9.5). Annual growth in intraregional exports during 1970-75 was only slightly higher than growth in West Africa's other markets. Much of the export growth in both markets was accounted for by Nigeria's booming oil export revenues following the sharp increase in world oil prices in 1973. When Nigeria is excluded, the intraregional market vastly outperformed other markets during the early 1970s. The annual growth rate of West Africa's intraregional trade was 21 percent, nearly double the growth rate of West Africa's other trade.

The region's three major exporters, Nigeria, Côte d'Ivoire and Senegal, accounted for about three-fourths of intraregional exports, and experienced faster growth in their regional market than in the world market. The countries most dependent on intraregional trade for export markets -- Burkina Faso, Niger and Mali -- had mixed experiences. Burkina's regional exports grew faster than its other trade, while the reverse occurred for Niger and Mali. Niger's uranium exports accounted for its more favorable market performance outside the region. Rapid growth in Mali's world cotton exports outpaced growth in recorded livestock exports, its most important regional export.

West Africa's export growth began to slow during 1976-81, but its world market exports slowed even more than its intraregional trade. Growth in regional exports fell from 26 percent annually during 1970-75 to 14 percent during 1976-81. Growth in its other world markets fell more sharply, from 22 percent to 9 percent during the same periods. Developments in the Nigerian oil market dominated trade during 1976-81. Proportionally smaller oil price hikes caused annual growth in Nigeria's exports to drop from 30 percent to only 10 percent.

Other major regional traders whose exports boomed in the early 1970s experienced less favorable world market conditions during 1976-81. Côte d'Ivoire's exports outside the region slowed as world prices for cocoa and coffee weakened; its regional trade also slowed. Senegal's earnings from trade outside the regions declined during the late 1970s as peanut export revenues fell, but its continued strong growth in regional exports helped offset these losses. Growth in world exports from Cameroon and Niger was buoyed during 1976-81 by nontraditional commodities. Cameroon started to export oil in 1978-79, which offset falling prices for its cocoa and coffee exports. Cameroon's regional exports (mainly wood, textiles, and chemical and iron products) slowed considerably during this period. Niger's strong world export growth reflected its uranium sales.

Intraregional Livestock Trade

Livestock is the highest valued agricultural commodity in intraregional trade. West Africa's livestock trade is characterized by a complementarity[5] in production and consumption between the Sahel countries and the coastal states, by a responsiveness of trade patterns to drought and to changing economic and political conditions, by its importance to national economies, and by its large informal or unrecorded component. Most of the trade is composed of live animals including cattle, sheep, goats, donkeys, camels and horses. Intraregional trade of prepared meats is very small and development efforts in this industry have not met with much success.

The quality of data for cattle is poor. This situation mainly reflects the nature of the traditional livestock production and marketing system. Herds are dispersed over large, often remote and inaccessible areas and are frequently moved across borders. Monitoring or estimating herd sizes and exports is, therefore, difficult. The Sahelian countries also have limited administrative capability in operating customs stations and in patrolling the large, remote areas between stations. Finally, there is smuggling activity to avoid taxes, inspection fees, or trade prohibitions. Perhaps the most that can be expected of trade data on cattle is that they reflect in a general, but accurate, way the reasonably expected quantities and cyclical trends in this sector. Caution should be used in trying to interpret the data more rigorously.

The major sources of data for this study of aggregate intraregional trade are the UN trade system, supplemented with FAO trade data and national accounts. Comparison of UN and FAO data on cattle exports indicates that the UN system provides only limited coverage of cattle trade, so that total trade as reported by the UN is undoubtedly too low. For example, FAO estimated the value of intraregional cattle exports at $214 million in 1980; however, UN data for all agricultural commodities within the region was only $211 million. The value of cattle trade, according to FAO, is far greater than indicated by UN trade data (recorded intraregional flows). Most of the difference represents the efforts of FAO to estimate unrecorded cattle exports by some countries, which is a large component of our estimated unrecorded trade.

To evaluate the comprehensiveness of FAO cattle export data, we compared those data with the UN series and with national accounts for Burkina Faso, Mali and Mauritania. FAO data for Burkina Faso are generally four to six times greater than that of the UN. FAO data on cattle exports approximate Burkina's official, recorded export series. No data on unrecorded trade are available. Reported increases in Burkina exports to Nigeria since the mid-1970s are mostly unrecorded.[6] This shift would account for some of the apparent decline in Burkina's cattle exports since that time.

The government of Mali estimates unrecorded trade at about four times the volume of controlled exports. FAO began to incorporate uncontrolled trade into its trade series in the late 1960s. The two series are not always consistent; the FAO data still were much greater than Mali's statistics in 1970-73, but even greater since 1977. The limited comparative data for Mauritania during 1962-70 appear to confirm that FAO series began to estimate total, not just recorded, exports beginning in 1970.

Nonstatistical factors may spuriously account for trends in estimated cattle trade. Better administrative capability can improve customs control and give the appearance that traded volume increased. Mali, for example, instituted tighter border controls with Mauritania in the late 1960s, in an effort to control animal disease. Consequently, legal entry was believed to approximate total entry and to account for some of the increase in Mauritanian cattle exports to Mali. In recent years, however, the quality of statistical

Table 9.6
Cattle exports by country (1,000 head)

	1970	1972	1974	1976	1978	1980	1982	1984
Burkina	58.8	72.9	79.9	35.1	49.1	66.1	31.0	18.0
Cameroon	5.5	7.2	2.0	3.0	8.0	3.7	3.0	3.0
Cape Verde	0.8	0.4	0.0	0.0	0.0	0.0	0.0	0.0
Chad	200.0	220.0	136.0	200.0	220.0	255.0	200.0	130.0
Guinea	32.0	35.0	25.0	25.0	30.0	35.0	37.0	37.0
Mali	190.0	220.0	122.0	111.0	193.0	396.0	479.0	490.0
Mauritania	100.0	124.0	99.0	80.0	92.0	90.0	90.0	80.0
Niger	202.0	184.1	130.4	150.0	215.0	175.0	160.0	200.0
Nigeria	0.2	0.0	0.2	0.0	0.0	0.0	0.0	0.0
Senegal	5.0	2.3	0.1	0.0	0.2	0.1	0.1	2.0
Togo	0.0	0.0	0.7	0.1	0.0	0.0	0.0	0.0
TOTAL	794.4	865.9	595.3	604.2	807.3	1020.9	1000.1	960.0

Source: Food and Agriculture Organization, *Trade Yearbook* (Rome: FAO, annual 1970-84).

reporting has deteriorated in many countries.

The major producers and exporters of live cattle are Burkina Faso, Chad, Mali, Mauritania and Niger (Table 9.6). The dry climate and vast land area of these Sahelian countries make them well suited for production of livestock. The primary advantage of the Sahel is the absence of the tsetse fly, which transmits trypanosomiasis (sleeping sickness), a disease that is fatal to cattle. Tsetse infest the wetter regions south of latitude 14 degrees north (including all of coastal West Africa), inhibiting livestock production in those areas. The southward movement of cattle from the Sahel states is also accounted for by the generally higher incomes in coastal countries. In 1982, the average per capita GNP in the eight Sahel countries combined was $270, compared with an average of $750 in the remaining ten countries of the West African region. As a result of their higher effective demand, these countries absorb a disproportionate amount of West African meat production. The five surplus meat producers hold about 45 percent of the West African herd, yet consume only about 25 percent of meat production. The meat-deficit countries account for the remaining 75 percent.[7]

Cattle production is an important economic activity in the major producing states of the Sahel. It makes a significant contribution to their export earnings and export tax revenues. Cattle exports accounted for an average of 64 percent of Chad's export earnings, 58 percent of Mali's, 11 percent of Niger's, 8.3 percent of Mauritania's and 2.8 percent of Burkina's during 1980-84. The role of cattle in Burkina's exports is underestimated, because FAO trade data for this period are lower than the officially recorded value of cattle exports. The contribution of cattle exports to tax revenues is an important feature of the livestock sector in the resource-poor countries of the Sahel, because their national budgets depend heavily on income from import and export taxes. For example, livestock export taxes in Burkina Faso accounted for an average of 75 percent of export tax revenues in 1977-79.

Changing Trade Patterns, 1970-82

The pattern of intraregional cattle trade in West Africa shifted during 1970-82. Two factors have been particularly important in accounting for changed regional trade patterns. Drought has caused both cyclical variations in trade and a gradual, long-term change in the location of cattle production. Changing economic conditions have altered the distribution of import demand among the coastal consumption points. In addition, national policies (such as changes in export and import taxes) may have caused some apparent shifts in trade patterns as unrecorded exports rise.

The effect of drought on regional patterns is not fully captured by the available trade data. One reason is the general weakness of cattle data. Another reason is that animals in the more remote and marginal areas, which are most vulnerable to drought, are the most likely to be unaccounted for in official statistics. Drought also induces greater unrecorded movements of herds across borders. Some are exports, while others eventually return to their country of origin. Prolonged drought in Mauritania has forced producers to move their herds farther south across the Senegal River to pastures in Mali and Senegal. Some herds from Niger in the dry season cross the borders and move south into Benin, Nigeria, Chad and Cameroon. This border movement has intensified in recent years. An estimated 50 percent of Niger's herd left the country in search of pastures during the 1984 drought.[8]

Prolonged drought is also creating longer-term changes in the areas suitable for traditional livestock raising. Rainfall in Mauritania has remained below average since the 1973 drought. The 150 millimeters (mm) precipitation isohyet has moved over 100 kilometers to the south during the past decade. Traditional livestock raising practices continue, but the most permanent southward movement of herds and their compression into smaller areas are causing competition for, and deterioration of, feed and land resources. Cattle deaths and herd movement into Senegal and Mali account for some of the decline in Mauritania's herd size and export availability. The climate has gradually deteriorated in Niger with a decrease in average rainfall and an increasingly erratic distribution of rains. The pastures of the pastoral and intermediate zones, where cattle production is concentrated, are becoming degraded.

Long-term climate change in some of the Sahelian countries is upsetting the ecological equilibrium of crop and livestock production both in wetter and drier zones. Southward and more permanent movements of herds into areas suitable for crop cultivation intensifies competition for land and water and contributes to erosion and degradation of resources. This competition limits the possibilities for expanding livestock production. Any potential for increased livestock production is increasingly viewed by Sahelian states as being dependent on efforts to improve the quality, rather than the quantity, of existing herds.

Another aspect of regional drought has been its impact on opening up Sahelian export markets to non-African suppliers. Drought has disrupted meat supplies in the region and has generated significant price variability. Sahelian meat supplies decreased to the coastal states following the 1973 drought prompting them to find new sources of supply from outside the region, and inducing the development of infrastructure to handle chilled and frozen meat imports from Latin America and Europe. Côte d'Ivoire, a major Sahelian market, began to substitute imported meats from other countries in an effort to assure meat supplies and keep prices low. The introduction of new meat suppliers to the West African region still provides a relatively small component of the region's meat supply. But it means that the Sahelian exporters' market position has begun to be affected more by their price competitiveness with non-African suppliers.

The most notable change in intraregional trade patterns is the shift away from Ghana and toward Côte d'Ivoire and Nigeria as the major cattle importing countries of the region (Table 9.7). The shift in import markets is accompanied by changes in the traditional transit routes within the region. Transit trade through Burkina from Mali and Niger has declined. Trade has been redirected through Niger to the Nigerian market. Ghana was the main export market for cattle from Mali and Burkina Faso until the late 1960s and early 1970s. Several factors, including falling incomes, the overvalued Ghanaian currency and policy barriers to trade, caused Ghana's meat import demand to decline sharply. Cattle imports during 1970-75 plummeted by 70 percent. Ghana's cattle imports by 1984 were only 2 percent of the 1970 level. This shift away from exports to Ghana is reflected in Burkina's export statistics. Ghana received 60-80 percent of Burkina's recorded cattle exports in the early 1960s with Côte d'Ivoire receiving most of the remainder. It was the reverse by 1977, with Côte d'Ivoire receiving 77 percent and Ghana receiving 9 percent.

Large cattle imports by Côte d'Ivoire reflect its relative prosperity within the region. Growth in real per capita income, which averaged 2 percent annually during 1970-80, increased consumer demand for meat. Because livestock production in the country is limited by tsetse, growth in meat demand has been met primarily by an increased dependence on imports. Live cattle imports in 1970 provided 73 percent of the Ivorian total meat supply and 84 percent of its beef supply.[9] Until 1974, live cattle imports from neighboring

Table 9.7
Cattle imports by country (1,000 head)

	1970	1972	1974	1976	1978	1980	1982	1984
Benin	4.6	4.0	3.0	5.0	8.0	9.5	10.0	10.0
Burkina	20.0	29.5	38.6	0.9	0.6	2.4	6.2	5.0
Cameroon	46.9	20.0	37.0	40.0	43.0	55.5	14.8	20.0
Cape Verde	0.0	0.0	0.0	0.0	0.0	0.0	0.0	0.0
Côte d' Ivoire	230.7	280.0	160.0	145.0	170.0	225.0	165.0	200.0
Gambia	0.2	0.1	0.1	0.0	0.0	0.0	0.0	0.0
Ghana	61.9	37.0	47.3	1.3	1.1	4.0	1.1	1.2
Guinea-Bissau	0.4	0.0	0.0	0.0	0.0	0.0	0.0	0.0
Liberia	18.0	22.0	15.0	13.0	23.0	22.0	25.0	25.0
Mali	10.0	10.0	10.0	0.0	0.0	0.0	0.0	0.0
Niger	10.0	8.0	3.0	20.0	5.0	13.0	38.0	80.0
Nigeria	264.0	293.0	229.0	175.0	315.0	356.0	300.0	300.0
Senegal	60.0	19.8	6.8	8.2	20.0	5.0	20.0	35.0
Sierra Leone	24.0	25.0	25.0	25.0	25.0	25.0	25.0	25.0
Togo	11.6	5.8	9.9	4.7	0.1	2.0	5.0	5.0
TOTAL	762.3	754.3	584.7	438.1	610.8	719.4	610.1	706.2

Source: Food and Agriculture Organization, *Trade Yearbook* (Rome: FAO, annual 1970-84).

West African suppliers constituted most of both total meat imports and total meat supply.

This pattern of supply shifted considerably during the 1970s with the introduction of non-western suppliers of chilled and frozen meats. Disrupted cattle imports following the 1973 drought and higher Sahelian cattle prices prompted the Ivorian government to import chilled and frozen beef from Latin America and Europe beginning in 1975. These imports supplied about 3 percent of Ivorian meat consumption during 1970-74, but they jumped to 16 percent in 1975 and 38 percent in 1976.[10]

Cattle imports by Nigeria increased significantly between 1970 and 1980 when Nigerian cattle imports peaked. Growth in consumer demand for meat was spurred in the 1970s by boom conditions in this oil-exporting country. Constraints to expanded domestic production resulted in growth in cattle imports from the region. Domestic meat production met only an estimated 60-70 percent of consumption during the early 1970s.[11] Imports rose to meet expanded consumer demand. Unlike Côte d'Ivoire, however, Nigerian meat import requirements were met mainly by Sahelian suppliers. The strong demand for slaughter animals in Nigeria raised Nigerian prices to 50 percent above comparable prices in Abidjan in 1976. This price differential was another factor in the shift in transit trade from Burkina Faso to Niger and the Nigerian market. Nigeria drew animals out of the Ivorian market, primarily from northern Burkina Faso, eastern Mali, and western Niger.[12]

National policies and regulations may account for some shifts in intraregional trade patterns for live cattle, but the causality is difficult to distinguish. Because a large proportion of this trade is unrecorded, it is not discernible whether a policy affects trade volume or simply the distribution of trade between recorded and unrecorded components. Burkina Faso provides an example of the effect that tariff policies can have on shifting trade patterns. During 1976-80, Burkina's policy objectives changed from protectionism toward domestic cattle production by discouraging imports to active encouragement of imports to augment herd sizes. Cattle import duties were slashed from 38 percent to only 4 percent by 1980. Cattle export duties were being increased during 1975-80, rising 261 percent. Import taxes, which had formerly been higher than export taxes, were in 1980 only one-eighth of comparable export duties. FAO trade data for this period show that Burkina's official cattle exports declined sharply following the export tax hikes, except for drought years. Cattle imports rose sharply with the 1980 import tax cut. These trends probably reflect some shifts from legal to illegal cattle trade as a result of these policy changes.

Regional Grain Trade

Recorded intraregional grain trade increased more than four fold during the study period (1970-82), but nevertheless it remained less than 1 percent of total imports. Trade in corn, rice and sorghum among the West African countries increased from an average of 4,000 tons in 1970-72 to 18,000 tons in 1980-82. Total imports of these commodities more than tripled from 738,000 tons to 2.6 million tons during the same period. Although several West African countries exported small quantities of grain during the 1970s, all countries are net importers. Complementarity is difficult to achieve in these countries, since most are affected by drought in the same year. In recent years, corn surpluses have tended to be in coastal countries, while shortages of millet and sorghum occur in Sahelian countries.

Inefficient transportation systems also increase West African grain prices. Transportation networks are poorly developed and are not set up to move grain from surplus to deficit regions. Burkina Faso, for example, has trouble moving grain from one region to another within the country, let alone moving it into another country. Moving surplus Ghanaian corn into Burkina Faso and Mali is difficult because most corn is produced in the south and has to be moved a long distance before reaching Burkina Faso and even further to reach Mali. Also most of the roads connect with the ports, restricting grain movement in other directions.[13]

Most West African countries attempt to restrict food exports to keep available supplies within the country. Information on production, stocks and trade is so poor that most governments have no way of knowing whether domestic supplies are adequate. Differing tariff structures, quantitative import restrictions, and exchange controls discourage official transactions but may encourage unrecorded trade. Imports from suppliers outside the region are easier to arrange because of traditional ties and reliability of supplies. West African countries are not considered reliable suppliers of grain because their production varies too much.

Importance of Unrecorded Trade

There are no estimates, reliable or otherwise, of unrecorded grain trade. It is expected that grain will move to high priced and to hard currency countries from lower priced and soft currency countries. The situation, however, can also be complicated by other factors such as trade policies. For example, locally produced corn and imported rice from neighbor countries move into Nigeria where food prices are higher. The Nigerian naira earned in this exchange are then used to purchase imported consumer goods and petroleum products that are subsidized by the overvalued naira (although this trend has altered in the late-1980s with the devaluation of the naira). Despite a weak Ghanaian currency, little grain was sold in neighboring countries because of high food prices in Ghana. Adequate grain supplies in neighboring Côte d'Ivoire and Togo also kept their prices relatively low. Southern Nigeria imports rice and corn from Benin and Cameroon, while northern Nigeria exports sorghum to Niger.

An analysis of producer grain prices converted to dollars at both the official and unofficial exchange rates also gives an indication of the direction of grain flows. Even though sorghum prices are high in Nigeria, converting sorghum prices to dollars at the unofficial rates brings the prices below those in Niger in most years. Mali's prices for rice, sorghum and millet are consistently below those of its neighbors. Poor harvests for several years in Mali have probably encouraged grain transactions within the country at prices far above the official level. It is unlikely that large quantities of grain have moved from Mali to neighboring countries. Recent policy changes in Mali have brought grain prices in line with those of its neighbors. In the early 1980s, the high-producer price for rice in Liberia and the strength of its currency (pegged to the U.S. dollar) generated an inflow of rice from neighboring Sierra Leone and Guinea, creating severe financial problems for Liberia's swamped cereal purchasing agency.

Corn Trade

Small quantities of corn have been traded among the West African countries every year during the study period. Trade increased from 1,200 tons in 1970-72 to 3,200 tons in 1980-82. Imports from outside the region, however, increased much more dramatically, from 66,000 tons in the early 1970s to over 500,000 tons in 1982.

Imports are a relatively small component of West Africa's total corn availability, which included production of about 3 million tons per year in the early 1970s. Intraregional trade accounted for 8 percent of the total trade during this period. Corn movements within the region picked up as the intensity of the Sahel drought increased in the mid 1970s. Ghana was the major exporter, while Burkina Faso and Cape Verde were the major importers. This trade tapered off in the late 1970s, falling to less than 1 percent of the total. Nigeria dominated the total trade during 1976-82, accounting for half of total imports; much of this was for Nigeria's rapidly expanding modern livestock sector.

Rice Trade

The share of intraregional trade in total rice imports remained constant at about 0.5 percent during the 1970-82 period. Rice trade among the West African countries grew from 2,300 tons in 1970-72 to 8,000 tons a decade later. The volume of trade ranged from 2,000-8,000 tons a year. Côte d'Ivoire exported 90 percent of the region's rice trade in 1976 and 70 percent in 1977. Cameroon supplied the other 30 percent in 1977.

Except for a few countries, there is no clear pattern to the recorded trade. The major exporters are Côte d'Ivoire, Ghana (in the early years) and Cameroon (in recent years). Burkina has been an importer throughout the period, while Nigeria has imported from the region only recently. Intraregional trade patterns since 1980 suggest reexport of imported rice. Niger, Cameroon and Senegal were the major exporters during the early 1980s. Niger produces very little rice, but it shows exports in 1981, a year of unusually high imports. Cameroon exported rice to Nigeria and Chad, traditional markets for transshipped rice. Senegal's exports are dwarfed by its imports. The data also show Senegal exporting to and importing from Gambia. Trade data from rice exporting countries show Cameroon to be one of the largest rice importers in West Africa -- 300,000-400,000 tons in 1982-84, while Cameroon reports purchases of 20,000-50,000 tons. It is likely that most of this rice is consumed in Nigeria. Exports to Cameroon quadrupled in 1979, the year Nigeria banned rice imports.

Sorghum and Millet Trade

Nigeria is by far the most important regional exporter of sorghum and millet, showing significant shipments in most years during 1970-82. Niger, Mali and Burkina Faso are also exporters. Mali was the most important importer with significant purchases in seven years. Other importers were Chad, Niger, Nigeria and Cameroon. Many countries appear in both importer and exporter columns.

Sorghum follows the same pattern as other cereals in that record shipments were reported in the mid-1970s. Intraregional trade has been an insignificant share of the total since 1970. The West African share of imports averaged less than 1 percent during 1970-72 and peaked at 15 percent in 1976. The unusually large import volume in 1976 included 30,000 tons exported by Mali. Sorghum and millet are much more important than corn and rice in the overall availability picture. Production of these grains in 1970-72 was 10.5 million tons, compared with 2.8 million tons of corn and 1.4 million tons of rice. Of all the other cereals, only rice imports contributed significantly to total availability.

Intraregional trade in sorghum remained small during the worst years of the Sahel drought, because shortfalls in production caused deficits in all countries. Imports from the world rose from 122,000 tons in 1970 to a peak of 500,000 tons in 1974. Some recovery in West African production reduced imports to 200,000 tons in 1975, but the region never approached self-sufficiency.

Intraregional trade reached a record 35,000 tons in 1976 when Mali exported sorghum and millet to Niger, Senegal and Gambia. Good harvests in 1974 and 1975 enabled the Office des Produits Agricoles du Mali (OPAM), the Mali grain marketing agency, to purchase over 40,000 tons of millet and sorghum in 1976 and again in 1977. Because of limited financial resources and low market prices, OPAM was forced to export rather than store this grain. Official statistics show the 1976 exports, but the 1977 shipments were not recorded. Producer prices in Mali were lower than in neighboring countries -- encouraging both recorded and unrecorded exports.

Palm and Peanut Oil Trade

Palm oil is a commodity that has seen an increase in intraregional trade during the study period. Palm oil trade averaged 5,000 tons during 1970-72 and rose to 13,800 tons

ten years later. In 1971, Côte d'Ivoire replaced Nigeria as
the leading palm oil exporter to the region. Most countries
in the region import palm oil. The major importers are
Senegal, Niger and Ghana. Other importers are Côte d'Ivoire
(early years), Cameroon, Mali, Nigeria (after 1975),
Mauritania and Burkina Faso.

Most of the palm oil trade came from within the region
through 1976. West African countries were important
suppliers in world trade. Nigeria exported as much as
150,000 tons of palm oil in the 1960s. When Nigeria's
vegetable oil imports began to grow rapidly in the late
1970s, suppliers outside the region became more important.
Singapore and Malaysia supplied most of Nigeria's palm oil in
the 1980s, reaching 168,000 tons by 1982, before imports were
restricted. The regional share has fallen to less than 20
percent of Nigeria's total palm oil imports.

West African producers should be able to compete
with other palm oil suppliers to the region because of lower
transportation costs. Because African oil palm stands are
wild and scattered, production costs are higher than in
Malaysia. In the past, the quantity of palm oil processed in
modern plants has been small, also leading to higher costs.
Côte d'Ivoire is now modernizing its palm oil industry and is
becoming more competitive. For palm oil shipped to Nigeria,
Ivorian export prices (f.o.b.) for 1983 were below those of
Singapore. Lower transportation cost would make Ivorian
prices (c.i.f.) significantly cheaper; however, soybean oil
from Germany and Brazil is still lower priced than palm oil.
With Nigeria importing smaller quantities of vegetable oil,
Côte d'Ivoire should be able to meet a larger share of the
demand.

Several West African countries are important peanut
producers and exporters of peanut oil. Senegal, Nigeria,
Gambia, Niger and Mali have all exported significant
quantities of peanut oil during the last twenty years. Most
of this oil moved outside the region. Senegal and Nigeria
were by far the major exporters within West Africa. The
importers were led by Mauritania followed by Sierra Leone,
Côte d'Ivoire, Benin, Chad and Nigeria (since 1976).

While demand for vegetable oil imports has increased in
most West African countries in recent years, the higher price
of peanut oil has tended to make it less competitive with
other oils such as palm and soybean. All of the other
importers have shown declining purchases in recent years.
During the early 1970s, Sierra Leone purchased small
quantities from Nigeria. When Nigeria stopped exporting,
Sierra Leone switched to other oils from suppliers outside

the region. Chad has also stopped importing peanut oil. Côte
d'Ivoire's imports of peanut oil from the region tapered off
as Mali stopped exporting. Nigeria started importing peanut
oil in 1976 and bought it from Senegal and Niger for a few
years before shifting to other cheaper oils in the 1980s.
Nigeria will not resume importing peanut oil as long as the
prices are significantly higher than other oils' prices.
Senegal will continue to export peanut oil and import cheaper
oils, but it is unlikely that a market for peanut oil will
develop in other West African countries. Prospects for
increased intraregional trade are much better for palm oil.

Unrecorded trade in vegetable oil is probably less than it
was for livestock and grains because the oilseeds must be
processed in a modern plant before oil can be easily
transported. Some unrecorded trade of peanuts takes place
depending on the relative prices among countries. This trade
is most important between Senegal and Gambia.

Cola Nut Trade

The coastal countries of West Africa have traded cola nuts
with the savanna countries of the region for centuries.
Traditionally, cola nuts were consumed by travelers and
presented to visitors. Today, the nuts are popular both as
a snack and for ceremonial occasions. The nuts for export
are wrapped in leaves to preserve them and packed in 50 kg
bags.

Côte d'Ivoire is by far the largest exporter of cola nuts
to the West African countries. Ivorian exports averaged
26,000 tons, worth $3.5 million during 1970-72, and Senegal
took more than half these nuts. Ivorian cola nut trade
expanded during the 1970s, and exports reached an annual
average of 43,000 tons valued at $8.2 million in the early
1980s. The markets however, shifted away from Senegal to
Mali, Burkina Faso and Niger during the 1980s. Ghana is the
second largest exporter, but its shipments have declined
sharply since 1975. There are no recent data available for
Ghana. Its sales appear to have leveled off at about 2,000
tons, the same as in the early 1970s.

Cotton and Textile Trade

Raw cotton is an important traded commodity for a number
of West African countries, including Nigeria, Ghana, Chad,
Mali, Burkina Faso and Benin. Despite a growing potential

for complementarity within the region among the exporters and importers of raw cotton, intraregional trade has been relatively unimportant. In the past, all West African producers were either exporters or self-sufficient in raw cotton. Because few countries have spinning and weaving capabilities, most countries exported raw cotton, mainly to Europe, and imported cloth for finishing. This situation has changed dramatically since the early 1980s when both Nigeria and Ghana began importing raw cotton for their developing textile industries. Nigeria's and Ghana's textile mills are operating at a fraction of their capacity because foreign exchange shortages have limited their ability to import raw materials. At the same time, West African cotton exporters have begun to experience burdensome surpluses because world cotton prices have fallen below their production costs. This has made their exports noncompetitive in the world market.

If transportation problems and policy obstacles could be overcome, there is potential to expand intraregional raw cotton trade. Given Nigeria's and Ghana's shortage of foreign exchange, barter arrangements might be beneficial to both importers and exporters within the region. Nigeria could trade petroleum for cotton, while Ghana has corn and palm oil available for export.

Intraregional trade in textile yarn and fabric among some West African countries grew during 1970-82. Textile yarns and fabrics account for a significant proportion of the nonagricultural intraregional trade of Burkina Faso, Côte d'Ivoire, Senegal, Nigeria and Cameroon. Côte d'Ivoire has the leading textile industry in West Africa. Textile production includes yarns, fabrics and miscellaneous products such as jute bags and strings. Producers use both domestic and imported inputs. Imported inputs are primarily from West African countries. Burkina Faso, Nigeria and Senegal export cotton yarns to Côte d'Ivoire and, in turn, Côte d'Ivoire exports fabrics and other textile goods to Mali, Benin, Niger, Senegal and Togo. Cameroon has a fully integrated textile industry that uses mainly local inputs in the production of cloth and finished goods. Cameroon exports a small amount of its textiles to Nigeria and Chad. Exports from Nigeria's textile industry go to Ghana and Côte d'Ivoire.

Further development of the textile industry within the region is inhibited by the high-producer prices for cotton, which increase the costs of local inputs for textile mills. High costs of local textile production make it difficult for African fabrics to compete with imports. Protective import tariffs in many countries have not been completely effective,

because smuggled imports, mainly from East Asia, keep
domestic prices low.

Petroleum Trade

Petroleum and petroleum products became the dominant
commodity in the foreign trade of many West African countries
during the study period (1970-82). Petroleum was also the
highest valued component of intraregional trade in West
Africa. Petroleum's share of export earnings rose sharply
with the oil price increases of the 1970s. In 1970, oil
contributed no more than 58 percent to any West African
country's export income. By 1980, oil accounted for 95
percent of the export revenues of Nigeria and 11 percent of
Côte d'Ivoire's.

There is a complementarity within West Africa between the
producers and consumers of crude and refined petroleum, and
it has benefited most West African countries. Nigeria and
Cameroon are the region's only net exporters of crude oil.
Côte d'Ivoire and Senegal are important suppliers of refined
petroleum products to the region. By the end of the 1970s
most of the coastal countries were importing crude oil and
refining it for domestic use or for export to Mali, Burkina
Faso, Niger and Chad. Importing countries save on
transportation costs by purchasing petroleum products from
neighboring countries.

By the early 1980s, 50 percent of Ivorian petroleum
exports valued at more than $200 million went to neighboring
countries. West African countries are also important markets
for Senegal, taking more than 35 percent of its petroleum
product exports in the early 1980s. These sales accounted
for more than 20 percent of Senegal's export earnings.
Nigeria also found markets for its oil in West African
countries. Nigeria's annual sales of crude to other West
African countries, mainly Ghana, Côte d'Ivoire, Senegal and
Sierra Leone, averaged $350 million during 1978-80. Because
of the huge volume of Nigeria's petroleum exports, this
amounted to only 2 percent of its total oil export earnings.
Petroleum trade between Nigeria and Côte d'Ivoire is highly
complementary. Nigeria had a chronic shortage of refining
capacity as demand for petroleum products grew very rapidly
in the 1970s. Nigeria was a major supplier of crude to Côte
d'Ivoire, which then refined the oil and returned some of it
to Nigeria.

There is some recorded trade in refined petroleum products
among most of the West African countries. Senegal, Togo,

Benin and Côte d'Ivoire are both importers and exporters of petroleum products. No estimates of unrecorded petroleum trade are available. Heavily subsidized products in Nigeria are reported to have moved into neighboring countries, especially Niger. Even though Nigeria did not report any shipments of petroleum products to Niger, Niger reported imports from Nigeria that averaged $20 million in 1980-81.

Recent trends in petroleum prices have reduced the value of this trade. Nigeria's exports to West African countries peaked at more than $500 million in 1980, dropped to an average of only $300 million during 1982-84, and has fallen markedly since then. The West African share increased slightly to 3 percent because Nigeria's world exports also fell. Côte d'Ivoire managed to increase the value of its West African petroleum exports during 1982-84 by shipping larger volumes. The unit value of these exports held constant despite declining world prices, indicating a shift in composition of Ivorian petroleum exports from crude to refined products.

Conclusion

Growth in exports became an important element in the economic stabilization and development strategies of many West African countries during the 1980s. Prospects for growth in intraregional trade have taken on an added importance in this context.

Reliable trade data are available for only a few countries in the region after 1982. Data for 1980-87 that are available for selected countries (Burkina Faso, Côte d'Ivoire, Mali, Niger, Nigeria and Senegal) show that trends in the share of exports going to the regional market are mixed (see Table 9.2). The share of regional trade in the exports of Côte d'Ivoire, Mali and Nigeria rose, while the share fell for the other three countries. Slower regional export growth is consistent with unfavorable economic conditions in the region during the 1980s, which weakened regional import demand. Policy reforms adopted by many countries in the region may have contributed to reduced output from protected industries, which had provided the basis for much of the growth in intraregional trade in processed products during 1970-82. On the other hand, policy developments in the region have probably fostered intraregional trade based on comparative advantage, as limited financial resources reduce the ability of West African countries to protect domestic industries, and create incentives for them to import from lower cost sources, including their West African neighbors. There continue to be some advantages held by the regional market, in terms of similarity in product demand, lower transportation costs, and the successful development of marketing channels within the region during the 1970s and early 1980s.

While intraregional trade is likely to remain a small component of West Africa's world trade in the 1990s, the region will continue to be a significant export market for some countries and commodities. It is particularly important for the Sahelian countries because of their heavy dependence on regional export earnings, and for Côte d'Ivoire and Senegal, for whom regional exports have supported industrial development.

The role of exports in West Africa's growth has become more important as its alternative engines of growth, such as foreign borrowings, falter. The role of West Africa's intraregional trade in the future will depend on its dynamic role in the process of growth and modernization of its industries. Policies to support regional trade need to address carefully product choice. Researchers should attempt to identify the sectors or industries in which intraregional trade could be most effectively exploited, looking, for example, at differences in the costs of production within West Africa, the magnitude of scale economies, the nature of product demand in regional markets versus world markets, and comparative transportation costs. Some existing sectors that are important in intraregional trade, cattle in particular, cannot easily expand output. Other industries will require regional coordination to avoid many countries developing identical industries, such as textiles. New industries and products that satisfy regional tastes, such as Ivorian processed foods, have the potential to achieve economies of scale in the regional market. In general, any efforts to capitalize on the identifiable benefits of intraregional trade need to address the existing barriers to this trade, due to tariff barriers within West Africa, weak regional institutions, and divergent monetary policies that make currency convertibility difficult.

Notes

1. See Bela Balassa, "The Changing Pattern of Comparative Advantage in Manufactured Goods," *Review of Economics and Statistics*, 61, 1979, pp. 259-266; W.A. Lewis, "The Slowing Down of the Engine of Growth," *American Economic Review*,

70(4), September 1980, pp. 555-564; S.B. Linder, *An Essay on Trade and Transformation* (Stockholm: Almquist and Wikesell, 1961).

2. The CFA franc is the common currency used by BCEAO countries and pegged to the French franc at a rate of 50 CFA francs equal 1 French franc. In 1989, there was intense speculation over the possible devaluation of the CFA franc.

3. J.N. Bhagwati (ed.), *Illegal Transactions in International Trade* (Amsterdam: North Holland, 1974).

4. Petroleum is the leading nonagricultural commodity in intraregional trade. Nigeria and Cameroon are producers and regional exporters of crude petroleum. Several West African countries refine imported crude for reexport to neighboring West African countries.

5. Generally the Sahel countries are livestock exporters, while the coastal countries are importers.

6. Larry Herman, "The Livestock and Meat Marketing System in Upper Volta: An Evaluation of Economic Efficiency" in Kenneth H. Shapiro (ed.), *Livestock Production and Marketing in the Entente States of West Africa* (Center for Research on Economic Development, University of Michigan, Ann Arbor, 1979), pp. 232-327.

7. Kenneth H. Shapiro, "The Livestock Economies of West Africa: An Overview" in Shapiro (ed.), *Livestock Production and Marketing*, pp. 4-69.

8. Food and Agriculture Organization, *Republic of Niger: Report of the FAO Multidonor Mission Assessment of the Food, Agriculture and Livestock Situation*, OSRO Report No. 14/84/E (Rome: FAO, 1984).

9. Société d'Etudes pour le Développement Economique et Social (SEDES), *Approvisionnement en Viandes de l'Afrique de l'Ouest*, Volumes 1 and 2, Paris, 1975.

10. John Staatz, "The Economics of Cattle and Meat Marketing in Ivory Coast" in Shapiro (ed.), *Livestock Production and Marketing*, pp. 144-231.

11. Harold D. Nelson, *Nigeria: A Country Study*, 4th Edition (Washington D.C.: The American University, Foreign Area Studies, 1982).

12. Staatz, "The Economics of Cattle and Meat Marketing in Ivory Coast."

13. Mahmoud Allaya, "Etude des Marchés et des Perspectives d'Echanges Céréaliers des Pays de l'Afrique de l'Ouest: Senegal, Mali, Haute Volta, Côte d'Ivoire, Ghana, Nigeria, Cameroun," *Africa Development*, 1984, pp. 93-143.

10

Islam and Development in West Africa

William Miles

If trade, to paraphrase a famous economist, is the engine of economic growth, then Islam, at least in the context of West Africa, has been its motor. From the outset, the extension of the creed of Mohammed to the deserts, savannas and forests of the Western Sudan has been attendant with profound changes in the economic (as well as political) structures of the societies within this same region. The territorial regrouping of these societies into colonies, and then independent states, has not eradicated the influence and significance that Islam has historically wielded in the sahelian (and even coastal) areas of West Africa. Neither has the creation of postindependence interstate regional organizations and associations, such as the Economic Community of West African States (ECOWAS). The purpose of this chapter is to examine the role of Islam in those countries which are also members of ECOWAS, and proffer some tentative conclusions concerning the role of Islam in the developmental process of these states and this organization.

The Religion of Commerce

The spread of Islam, both in the Crescent-bearing nations of yesteryear as well as the "fundamentalist" revolutions of today, is popularly associated with a militant brand of the Islamic faith. *Jihad* -- "holy war" -- is for many indissolubly linked with the penetration of Islam wherever that religion has so taken root. It is not surprising that the Islamicization of West Africa is also remembered in terms of violent conquest and wars of spiritual (i.e. Muslim) purification. The tales of Usman dan Fodio in Hausaland and

Alhaji Umar of the Senegambia are easily (and justifiably) invoked in this context. Yet exclusive attention to these more spectacular examples of West African *jihad* masks a more longstanding (and, perhaps, ultimately more important) reality: that these nineteenth-century movements of radical Islamicization were preceded by eleven centuries of gradual and, for the most part, peaceful conversion to Islam by the political and commercial elite of the West African empires.

Rather than *jihad*, perhaps the terms *Wangara*, *Dyula*, and *Yarse* should be recalled as the major forces spreading Islam throughout West Africa. For each of these terms refers to Muslim traders, for whom the teaching of the faith was at least as important as the sale of merchandise. Muslim traders may have been white (Berber) from the Maghreb, or black (especially Mande) from the Upper Niger; their aims and means, nevertheless, were identical. Trade and commerce were the major vehicles by which the Muslim faith originally penetrated into, and took root in, the ancient empires of West Africa; trade and commerce remain major factors in strengthening the regional ties of member states of the West African community.

Islamic and economic development in the Western Sudan were thus inextricably linked in their origin. Gold, slaves and cola nuts may no longer be major sources of trans-sahelian exchange; but even as other, more modern clusters of goods have replaced these ancient goods, the principle of economic exchange and interdependence giving rise to broader foundations of political and social unity has been maintained. For ECOWAS no less than the caliphates and empires of the precolonial era, material prosperity and social unity are believed to thrive when a) physical, political and economic *barriers* to trade are lessened, and b) a social or moral *consensus* emerges according to which norms and rules of material interchange may be conducted.[1]

Postjihadic, postcolonial, and indeed postindependence changes have far from sundered this relationship between Islam and economic development. As we shall see below, particularly in terms of economic links between West African states (and believers) and oil-rich Arab governments, some of the ties between religious and economic development have become increasingly important. Whether the correlation between Islam and development in West Africa proves ultimately positive, however, must await consideration of various other economic and political factors.

The "Islamicity" of ECOWAS

The Economic Community of West African States is, of course, a secular association, eschewing any official links to religious faiths or organizations. Yet of the sixteen member nations of ECOWAS, Islam is the single most important religion in twelve of them, claims more than half of the population in six of them (seven, if Nigeria is included), and is the official creed of one of them (the Islamic Republic of Mauritania). All but one of the ECOWAS countries, Cape Verde, have significant numbers of Muslim citizens. (Cape Verde joined ECOWAS in 1977, two years after the original fifteen members established the organization.) In fact, given the overall diversity of the countries in the subregion -- extreme diversity in terms of size, topography, colonial affiliation, population density, gross national product, distribution of wealth, purchasing power[2] -- Islam is one of the few factors (besides geographical proximity) which does offer some unifying link for these otherwise disparate states.

The actual percentage of Muslims living in ECOWAS states is less than 50 but greater than 40 percent; 47 percent seems to be a reasonably accurate figure (see Table 10.1).[3] (The difficulty of obtaining accurate demographic data for Africa is well-known; when population statistics are broken down by ethnic or religious affiliation, numerical reliability is all the more precarious.) Collectively, the Muslims of the ECOWAS states represent at least 17 percent of the world's total Muslim population (approximately 124 million out of 720 million).

Sheer numbers and percentages alone do not reflect the significance -- both economic and political -- of Islam in the ECOWAS community of nations; for not only do Muslims represent the single largest religious community throughout West Africa, but Islam is by far the strongest *organized* religion in the entire subregion. We shall see below how the institution of Islam functions as an important transnational actor throughout West Africa -- and perhaps rivals ECOWAS itself in that same transnational capacity.

Islam not only unites, however loosely, the sundry states and millions of residents of West Africa; more importantly, it manages to transcend the manifold ethnic divisions which characterize the region. At least thirty-six ethnic groups living within the ECOWAS borders share in the Muslim *umma*, or

Table 10.1
Muslims in ECOWAS Countries

Country	Number of Muslims	% of Population
Benin	49,968	15
Burkina Faso	3,088,759	39
Cape Verde	--	--
Côte d'Ivoire	2,240,867	23
Gambia	591,498	85
Ghana	490,228	12
Guinea	5,035,950	95
Guinea-Bissau	283,500	35
Liberia	485,070	23
Mali	5,333,900	65
Mauritania	1,306,343	98
Niger	5,543,850	98
Nigeria	43,257,390	47
Senegal	5,757,300	90
Sierra Leone	879,382	25
Togo	206,025	8
ECOWAS TOTAL	74,550,300	47

Source: Compiled from data in *Africa South of the Sahara 1987* (London: Europa Publications, 1986); and George Kurian (ed.), *Encyclopedia of the Third World* (New York: Facts on File, 1986, 1984, 1982).

Table 10.2
Ethnic Groups With Muslim Populations -- ECOWAS Countries

	Number of Muslims in Thousands	% of Group Who Are Muslim	Number of Countries in Which Found	% of ECOWAS Muslims
Hausa	16,053	80	3	31
Fulani	10,459	93	13	20
Yoruba	6,990	50	3	13
Kanuri	3,432	100	2	7
Manding	3,349	40	10	6
Wolof	1,916	93	3	4
Mossi/ Mole- Dagbani	1,540	25	3	3
Songhai	1,373	100	5	3
Moor	1,319	98	3	3
Tuareg	859	100	3	2
Susu	830	100	2	2
Nupe	799	100	1	2
Serer	695	82	1	1
Soninke	675	67	6	1
Tukulor	589	100	2	1
Senufo	509	23	3	1
TOTAL	51,387			100

Note: Table excludes twenty other ethnic groups with Muslim populations less than 500,000.

Source: Compiled from data in R. Weekes (ed.), *Muslim Peoples. A World Ethnographic Survey* (Westport: Greenwood Press, 1978).

community: this represents over 12 percent of ethnic Muslim groups worldwide (see Table 10.2). There are many subethnic groups as well which have not been included in this calculation.

Certainly disputes and controversies between and among different Islamic "sects" have arisen over the course of time, but never have they taken on the explosive proportions that they have in the Middle East or Near East. As Amadou Hampate Ba, a noted Malian religious leader put it, Islam "takes on a much less combative and aggressive tone" in West Africa than elsewhere in the Muslim world.[4] There is little danger of pan-Islamic or radical Muslim movements challenging the legitimacy of inherited state boundaries in West Africa, and "no effort to erase existing sovereignties in favor of a revived caliphate."[5] (Neither do regional economic associations in Africa -- such as ECOWAS -- seriously entertain the dismantling of borders, and the creation of a single, unified political unit.) Yet the transpolitical grip of Islam in West Africa is such that it may have as important an influence in terms of social and economic development as do state policies, governmental ideologies and regional formations. Thus, we must examine the relationship between Islam as a religion and a way of life, and development as a holistic process of societal change.

Islam and Development: A Theoretical Critique

Western scholarship has come a long way since the days of Max Weber, when Islam was rather uncritically perceived as a creed which, by its very essence, hindered social and economic progress. Contrasted with the individualistic, diligent and thrifty work ethic of the Christian (and particularly Protestant) West, Weber felt that Islam, with its:

> thoroughly traditionalistic ethic...directed the conduct of life into paths whose effect was plainly opposite to the methodical control of life found among Puritans.[6]

Weberian assumptions about the incompatibility of Islam with development can be found in the more contemporary scholarly literature. McClelland's aside that "Arabs as Moslems are probably generally low in achievement"[7] may be cited as an embarrassing example. *Any* religious intrusion into modern societal evolution gets short shrift from Almond and Powell, who refer to such a phenomenon as "negative development."[8] Nevertheless, scholars in the 1970s and 1980s are more prone to examine the compatibility of Islam and development than presuppose their incompatibility. Such investigations have been as fruitful to the study and analysis of development as they are to a more refined understanding of contemporary Islam. That this heightened awareness of the developmental implications of Islam has occurred since the post-OPEC trauma of the early 1970s can only, at this stage, be inferred. Basically, these newer reinterpretations challenge the assumption that Islam -- and Muslims -- need take a passive, submissive, and fatalistic approach to life. In contrast, they find evidence of a more creative, innovative, and indeed entrepreneurial dimension to modern-day Islam. Far from being *dépassé* in this age of international finance and high-tech postindustrialization, these scholars find remarkable adaptability on the part of both adherents to the Faith, and the Faith itself.

Cummings, Askiar and Mustafa find that Islam is not only compatible with "modern economic change," but has flourished in countries whose economic system is capitalistic in orientation. Their examination of those aspects of economy governed by the Koran (taxation, income distribution, interest, banking, private ownership and rent) leads them to the conclusion that:

> Islam not only does not rule out economic progress...it clearly endorses several of the basic factors cited frequently by Western commentators as essential in historic economic transformation -- private property, recognition of the profit incentive, a tradition of hard work, a link between economic success and eternal reward. Thus Islam seems unlikely to rule out rapid economic growth or even the construction of a strong system more or less capitalist in essence.[9]

Yet Islamic economics is not to be equated with capitalism *in toto*. For capitalism is seen to ignore or dismiss some of the basic principles of Islamic justice: justice as conceived in material, as well as transcendent, terms.

Long before western developmental revisionists rejected the "development as economic growth" thesis, Islamic moral economists have recognized that while societal or aggregate prosperity is desirable, redistribution of wealth is also fundamental to the notion of development. (It is to be noted in passing that while the discipline of "political economy" has waxed and waned [and waxed!] in western scholarship, "moral economy" has never had any comparable career. The very term "moral economist" would strike most academics as a veritable oxymoron.) Any introduction to the basic tenets of Islam stresses the principle of *zakkat*. One of the five pillars of Islam, *zakkat* -- the duty to transfer a portion on one's wealth (not just income) to disadvantaged Muslims -- may be thought of as a religiously-inspired social security and insurance institution. Individual wealth is acceptable, and should even be admired, as long as ultimate admiration and appreciation is rendered to Allah; nevertheless, unmitigated or excessive luxury in the face of poverty, which we shall later refer to as "skewed development," is unIslamic. Thus, while those preconditions of (capitalistic) economic growth and development noted above are congruent with Islamic norms of material behavior, laissez-faire capitalism, untempered by a redistributive system of *zakkat*, is not.

An uncritical reading of the above might lead one to believe that Islamic development -- especially its concern with distribution -- is but a form of divinely sanctioned socialism. Yet while the term "Islamic socialism" might be attractive to some, there are irreducible differences which render the formula "Islam equals socialism" untenable.

For one, the *source* of the distributive imperative cannot be reconciled between the two systems. Depending on the variety of socialism one is entertaining, economic justice *qua* redistribution of wealth is the result of either a) human (i.e. moral) conscience or b) dialectical materialism. In Islam, however, economic justice *must* be a matter of divine injunction. To question the relevance of the source of the distributive imperative is itself a reflection of secular, if not atheistic, thought -- and hence intolerable to Islam. The issue transcends mere theological or philosophical quibbling over the sources of morality: when dealing with a choice between a human-reasoned basis of economic decision-making, and one inspired by a vast, divine-oriented body of law and commentary replete with binding precedent, the allowable range of means, no less than goals, is at stake.

A second incompatibility between Islam and socialism relates to the question of private, and the ownership of productive, property. To the extent that socialism forbids, excludes or denies this, Islam must depart from socialism. The Koran (and its interpretations) may set conditions on the use of private property, but does not countenance collectivization in the sense that socialism conceives it.

Although there are several other Islamic concepts which may be invoked in reformulating classical notions of development, space only allows mention of one more: *tawhid*.

Private property is condoned (and encouraged) in Islam; *absolute* ownership, on the other hand, belongs to God alone. Mortal owners of goods, property and resources are actually trustees for what belongs, ultimately, to Allah. They thus have certain duties concerning, and responsibilities for, that to which they may otherwise claim legal possession. Especially in the case of natural resources, Muslims (especially, one may suggest, oil-rich Muslims) may certainly exploit their minerals *for* profit, but only if they do so consistently with the teachings *of* the prophet.

Even this summary sketch of the theoretical interstices of Islam and development should help clarify the important decoupling which advocates of Islamic-oriented economic change make: "development" is not the same as "westernization." The paths to development that European nations have taken -- be they capitalistic or socialistic-- need not be the models for Muslim nations in their particular quest to achieve modern social and economic progress and change. Nor can they be. For neither the preconditions of capitalistic oriented development, nor the ideological imperatives of socialistic development, can be blanketly incorporated into societies whose commitment to Islamic principles of justice and faith are genuine. Islam does not resist or obstruct development; it does, however, establish a more rigorous standard for it.

Islam as a Transnational Actor

Students of international relations acknowledge that the state is no longer the sole, or indeed always the most important, global actor. "Transnational actors," such as international organizations (e.g. the United Nations) or transnational corporations (TNCs) may also exert influence or pressure on governments; at times, they may even challenge the latters' presumed sovereignty. Religious organizations, no less than the more usually acknowledged secular transnational actors, may also exercise this role. In West Africa, two types of denominational transnational actors are a) those organizations set up to promote Islam and to assist materially those states with significant Muslim communities, and b) traditional Islamic brotherhoods and associations, which advance a particular cause or version of Islam (sometimes referred to as sects). We shall examine first the traditional brotherhoods in their capacity as transnational actors, and then the multilateral and bilateral Islamic organizations functioning in West Africa.

Turuq

Turuq (s. *tariqa*) is the term given to the Sufi brotherhoods which, from the fifteenth century to the present, have so successfully spread Islam throughout West Africa. (*Turuq* have existed elsewhere, and for even longer periods of time, throughout the Muslim world.) The world brotherhoods' facility for organizing their adherents into tightly knit communities has been a factor in both resisting and adapting to change in the West African Muslim world. Although their primary *raison d'être* is of course religious, the economic influence and power of the Islamic brotherhoods has been considerable. In particular, *tariqa* success at forming and promoting commercial networks of and for brotherhood members has been a major factor in the region's trade.

The two most powerful brotherhoods in West Africa are the Qadariyya and the Tijaniyya. Qadariyya came to West Africa in the fifteenth century, as the original impetus for Islamic conversion. Qadari leaders were thought to possess a kind of divine power or grace (*baraka*) which they could pass on to their followers. They also were responsible for imparting Islamic mysticism, law and science to their disciples.

It is the Tijaniyya, however, which, in terms of Islamic transnational and developmental potential, is the more interesting *tariqa*. Brought to West Africa in the nineteenth century, the Tijaniyya gained adherents modestly in Mauritania, more significantly in the Senegambia, and most recently in Hausaland. Indeed, Tijaniyya influence spans the region from Senegal to northern Nigeria. Offshoot branches continue to propagate ever more particularistic brands of the brotherhood. Much of the international impact of Tijaniyya is due to Ibrahim Niass (1900-1975), who founded what is known as "Reformed" Tijaniyya. Niass believed in spreading Islam peacefully, regardless of national boundaries, and by using scientific and technological innovation to do so. The use of radio, tapes and cassette recordings to disseminate Koranic readings, commentaries and preaching was thereby condoned; the supposed incompatibility between "anachronistic Islam" and "modern technology" was disproven.

In his attempts to bridge the gap between the West African and non-black African Islamic worlds, Niass undertook many trips abroad to spread pan-Islamic links. His meeting in Mecca with Abdullahi Bayero, Emir of Kano, resulted in the expansion of Tijaniyya throughout Nigeria,[10] if not without ensuing friction with the Sokoto Qadariyya establishment. Niass became vice-president of the World Muslim Congress

(WMC), whose sixty-seven branches and affiliates throughout the world today include ten in ECOWAS countries alone. Students of Tijaniyya history will recognize the significance of the postal address of the WMC's West African Regional Office: H.E. Ibrahim Niass, P.O. Box 1, Madina, Kaolack, Senegal.

Although regarded as a populist movement, Niass-style Tijaniyya has also attracted "wealthy merchants, businessmen and professionals.... It is... often very difficult to make a clear distinction between spiritual and material interests."[11] Far from being an ascetic doctrine, Niass's teachings have linked material success and financial fortune to divine blessing. The Tijaniyya brotherhood has accordingly organized and acted to increase such blessings (at least among Tijaniyya followers). One powerful example of how this Islamic brotherhood blossomed into a prosperous commercial network is the migrant Muslim community in Ibadan. In this southern Nigerian (and non-Islamic city), the *tariqa* has grown proportionately with the need to consolidate the migrant northerners' position as merchant intermediaries in the livestock/cola trade.[12]

Another example of *tariqa* influence in West African economic networks is the case of the Muridiyya of Senegal, a subgroup of the Qadariyya. In Senegal, the Mourides transformed a religio-agricultural institution -- the *dara* -- into a modern export-oriented commercial network. The *dara* initially was the collective farm upon which Mouride followers worked, passing on (for hopes of *baraka*) the bounty of their labor to their marabout leaders. When the French colonized Senegal, both the *dara* institution and the Mouride hierarchy were utilized to organize and systemize the export groundnut cash crop trade. After independence, Mouride marabout influence on the rural economy (especially the groundnut industry) remained strong, even if Senegalese industrialization and urbanization have necessitated a further adaptation in the *dara*: their conversion into *da'ira*, or urban associations of Mouride brothers.[13]

Although recent works have indicated a weakening of Mouride influence in the modern Senegalese economy,[14] their acquiescence to government-led programs of rural development is still seen as critical.[15] Furthermore, the implications of the Muridiyya for development are ambivalent: whereas the Mouride brotherhood has been instrumental in promoting the international groundnut trade, an important foreign exchange provider and early foundation for the Senegalese economy, marabout resistance to modern medicine and western education is also seen as having antidevelopmental consequences.[16] Most important, however, the Muriddiya in Senegal, no less than the Qadariyya and Tijaniyya brotherhoods elsewhere throughout West Africa, remain Islamic associations, operating at the grassroots level, whose economic and developmental influence, both positive and negative, should not be underestimated.

International Islamic Organizations

Unlike the Islamic brotherhoods, whose relationship to national governments is often ambivalent (occasionally opposing, sometimes competing with state and secular authorities), international Islamic organizations which are development-oriented generally function in tandem with national governments. Although younger than, and operating at a very different level from, the traditional *turuq*, these multilateral and bilateral developmental institutions similarly rely on pan-Islamic principle and networks to promote religious *and* economic goals.

The Organization of the Islamic Conference (OIC) was set up in 1971, with the aim to "strengthen the struggle of all Muslim people with a view to safeguarding their dignity, independence and national rights" and to "promote Islamic solidarity among member States [and] consolidate cooperation among member states in economic, social, cultural, scientific and other vital fields of activity."[17] Within the OIC system, a host of "Muslim Associations" have been set up to promote development in both member and nonmember (but Muslim-populated) countries. Specialized committees of the OIC thus include the Islamic Commission for Economic, Cultural and Social Affairs (est. 1976), the Standing Committee for Social and Technical Cooperation (est. 1981), and the Standing Committee for Economic and Trade Cooperation (est. 1981). Subsidiary organs of the OIC include the Islamic Center for the Development of Trade, the Islamic Center for Technical and Vocational Training and Research, the Islamic Foundation for Science, Technology and Development, and the Statistical, Economic and Social Research and Training Center for Islamic Countries. The Islamic Chamber of Commerce, Industry and Commodity Exchange, the Islamic Reinsurance Corporation, and the Islamic Development Bank (see below) belong to the OIC system. The Third Islamic Conference of 1981 also set up a Committee of Islamic Solidarity with the People of the Sahel, which provided assistance to ten African nations -- only one of which (Chad) is not an ECOWAS member, and one of which (Cape Verde) is not an OIC member.

Over a fifth of the forty-five members of the OIC are ECOWAS countries (Burkina Faso, Gambia, Guinea, Guinea-Bissau, Mali, Mauritania, Niger, Nigeria, Senegal and Sierra Leone). For at least one of these nations, membership in OIC has been, to put it mildly, rather controversial. When President Babangida announced in March 1986 that Nigeria had become a full OIC member (elevating it from observer status), vociferous debate erupted throughout the country, much of it (especially from southern and Christian sources) condemning this "Islamicization" of Nigeria. One source even attributed the violent demonstrations at the Ahmadu Bello University campus in May 1986 (which resulted in at least fifteen deaths) to, in part, "alarm about Islamic pressures" and "fear" that Babangida wanted to turn Nigeria into an Islamic state.[18]

The uproar to which disclosure of Nigerian OIC membership gave way impelled Babangida to set up a twenty-two member presidential committee to investigate the ramifications and implications of the move, although the committee itself split on religious grounds. Four years after the decision, there are no indications that the government is contemplating withdrawal. The heated reactions against an official relationship with the OIC may be surprising, in light of Nigeria's longer standing memberships in the International Islamic Organization and the International Islamic Federation of Student Organizations.

In 1975, the Islamic Development Bank (IDB) was set up "to encourage economic development and social progress of member countries and Muslim communities, in accordance with the principles of the Islamic Shari'ah."[19] Beginning its operations with $2.4 billion in startup capital,[20] the IDB has become one of the world's largest multilateral development organizations. Nine ECOWAS countries are members of the IDB: Burkina Faso, Gambia, Guinea, Guinea-Bissau, Mali, Mauritania, Niger, Senegal and Sierra Leone. Nigeria, too, has availed itself of IDB loans.[21] Although criticism has been made that much of the IDB holdings have been earmarked according to political criteria rather than developmental need (i.e. to Arab "frontline" states rather than poor African nations),[22] IDB activity in West Africa has not been inconsequential.

Afro-Arab Ties

On religious no less than geopolitical grounds, Islam and the Arab world are inseparable. Although West African Islam has striven (and rather successfully so) to maintain its culturally specific autonomy, it cannot ignore that its supra-Saharan and Middle Eastern brethren possess two vital holdings: holy cities and petroleum reserves. The first of these connections will be discussed in the next section; here, we will examine the second.

The Islamic Development Bank was in fact originally set up by oil-rich Arab nations to cushion for developing nations the price rise shock that followed OPEC production cutbacks

Table 10.3
Arab Bank For Economic Development In Africa (BADEA) Loans To ECOWAS Countries -- 1975-1987 (in millions of U.S. dollars)

Benin	38.7
Burkina Faso	33.3
Cape Verde	28.2
Côte d'Ivoire	3.3
Gambia	9.1
Ghana	46.8
Guinea	35.5
Guinea-Bissau	22.2
Liberia	10.6
Mali	39.7
Mauritania	0
Niger	35.9
Nigeria	0
Senegal	41.0
Sierra Leone	25.1
Togo	8.6
TOTAL	378.0
% of total to Africa (sub-Saharan Africa only)	36%

Source: Compiled from data in *Africa South of the Sahara 1989* (London: Europa Publications, 1988) p. 192.

in 1973. It was not the only organization functioning with that aim, and it is not the only Arab constituted institution providing assistance to West African nations on the basis of Muslim ties.

The Arab Bank for Economic Development in Africa (BADEA) was chartered in 1973 "to reinforce economic, financial and technical cooperation between the African and Arab countries."[23] In the first five years of its operations, the BADEA lent out a total of over $130 million to thirteen ECOWAS nations for heavy infrastructure projects (cement factories, port and airport extensions, electric power facilities, road and dam construction (see Table 10.3). In 1985, the BADEA extended four of its ten loans to ECOWAS countries: $10 million to Guinea (for artisinal fisheries), $4.7 million to Guinea-Bissau (for a power station), $4 million to Niger (for livestock development), and $4 million to Senegal (for urban electrification). Two other Arab multilateral agencies which have benefited ECOWAS countries are the Fund for Arab-African Technical Assistance, which provides investment loans to promote technical cooperation, and the Special Arab Fund for Africa, begun in 1974 to disburse low interest or "service expense" loans to compensate low income African countries for losses due to higher oil prices.

In addition to these Muslim/developmental multilateral organizations, individual Arab nations have also established bilateral development agencies that have assisted, *inter alia*, West African states with Muslim majorities and minorities. The Saudi Development Fund (SDF) was set up in 1974 to provide soft loans to Arab and non-Arab developing nations for the purposes of economic development and financial assistance. Between 1975 and 1982, thirteen ECOWAS countries (all except Benin, Côte d'Ivoire and Nigeria) received a total of sixty-one financial loans, amounting to $809 million (see Table 10.4). The Kuwait Fund for Arab Economic Development (KFAED), although in existence for much longer than the SDF (est. 1961), has had a more limited impact in West Africa: only Senegal among ECOWAS countries has benefited from KFAED loans. KFAED is worth noting, however, inasmuch as it is the most explicitly religious of the bilateral (and perhaps even multilateral) Islamic development organizations. Its stated purpose is to "spend in the way of Allah," and acknowledges a Koranic duty upon Kuwait to share her oil wealth among less fortunately-endowed nations.

Hajj and West African Development

"[During the pilgrimage to Mecca, there] is no fault in you, that you should seek bounty from your Lord." -- Sura II, v. 194.

No one who has witnessed the return of the *alhazai* (s. *alhaji*) to their West African homes from the pilgrimage to Mecca can fail to have noted the extensive and bountiful loads of goods which the faithful do bring back from the holy city. As the above passage from the Koran has been interpreted, there is no contradiction in Islam between engaging in large-scale commerce, and actualizing the fifth pillar of the Muslim faith.[24] Applied to the context of West Africa, the *hajj* has become a veritable business.

The extent to which the economic ramifications of the *hajj* are conducive or disfunctional to development has been discussed in the literature.[25] On the one hand, the work and savings necessitated to purchase a plane ticket to Jeddah can be seen as an incentive to "rational accumulation of capital."[26] On the other hand, "it can be argued... that financing a pilgrimage to Mecca represents a nonproductive use of capital."[27] Neither of these views, however, takes into account the economic ramifications of the pilgrimage *after* the pilgrim has arrived in Saudi Arabia, or indeed after he (or she, for Muslim women in West Africa most certainly do undertake the *hajj*) returns home.

Fieldwork in rural Nigeria and Niger has revealed the powerful economic potential the *hajj* presents, even for members of modest farming communities.[28] *Hajj* is not only a most powerful incentive to purchase, enlarge, fatten and resell livestock for their cash value, but also to engage in cash crop cultivation for monetary income. Equally important from an economic point of view, however, are the occupations that these *tukruni* (the Saudi word for West Africans) take on once they arrive in Saudi Arabia. For many, it is small scale, short-term trading, to tide them over until their pilgrimage is over. Yet for others, it has become a major livelihood, as they trade in anything from prayer mats and embroidered carpets (potential dowry gifts) to foreign currency. For some, the *hajj* has become something akin to a business trip, undertaken several times a year, and assuming major commercial proportions. However, it must be stressed that such multiple pilgrimage performance, even when linked to business activities, is not in the least inconsistent with perceived religious norms of duty and obligation, and entails little or no local opprobrium. Indeed, at least in Nigeria, the very term *alhaji* is now used to designate a rich merchant; it is a term of material admiration *and* religious respect.

Not all pilgrims from West Africa, of course, become major entrepreneurs. But even the modest *tukruni* who become mere laborers manage to accumulate savings from their wages which,

Table 10.4
Saudi Development Fund (SDF) Loans to ECOWAS Countries --
1975-1982

	Number of Loans	Amount (in millions of $ U.S.)
Benin	0	0
Burkina Faso	2	32
Cape Verde	2	10
Côte d'Ivoire	0	0
Gambia	3	15
Ghana	2	39
Guinea	7	90
Guinea-Bissau	5	10
Liberia	2	21
Mali	12	140
Mauritania	5	174
Niger	6	49
Nigeria	0	0
Senegal	12	204
Sierra Leone	1	15
Togo	2	10
TOTAL	61	809
% of total to Africa (includes Egypt and North Africa)	40	32

Source: Compiled from data in A. Gresh, "L'Arabie Saoduite en Afrique non Arabe," *Politique Africaine*, 10, 1983, p. 73.

when transferred back to their villages, become extremely important assets. It is impossible to determine the number of illegal West African aliens occupying menial jobs in Saudi Arabia, but indications are that this is a significant phenomenon.[29]

The days are long gone since occasional, intrepid West Africans would set out overland, on foot or donkey, joining caravans in transcontinental treks towards Mecca. Air travel from West Africa to Jeddah is today brisk -- sometimes crushing -- as official statistics from the Saudi government

attest. Nigeria may be unique in having a major governmental
Pilgrims Board to facilitate the *hajj*; even so, it has
difficulty completely monitoring or controlling the flow.

The trend towards air lift pilgrimages from West Africa to
Saudi Arabia is clearly on the upswing, skyrocketing from as
recently as the early 1970s (see Table 10.5). In 1980, for
instance, well over 95,000 pilgrims from ECOWAS countries
accomplished the *hajj* -- nearly triple the number from 1970.
In 1981, with over 100,000 pilgrims arriving from Nigeria
alone, a record-breaking 120,000 pilgrimages were undertaken
by ECOWAS country Muslims. Thus, averaging the years in the
1980s for which data are available, between one and two out
of every ten Muslims worldwide performing the pilgrimage
hails from an ECOWAS nation; ECOWAS Muslims thereby comprise
almost 90 percent of all Muslims arriving in Saudi Arabia
from sub-Saharan Africa.

This immense contemporary wave of West African visitors
has been examined for its political ramifications. Certainly
the *hajj* was controlled and regulated by the British and
French during the colonial era, so as to eliminate any pan-
Islamic resistance to colonial rule. It has been claimed,
for instance, that "the pilgrimage tends to radicalize those
who make it, so that when they return they begin to seek for
ways and means of reviving 'pure' Islam in their own
country."[30] It would be hazardous, however, to link causally
whatever Muslim fundamentalism in West Africa is there (and
it is relatively contained) to the burgeoning *hajj*, or even
to claim that Afro-Arab international relations and diplomacy
are significantly affected by the enormous numbers of *tukruni*
arriving and residing in Saudi Arabia. In terms of
developmental impact, however, one other possible result of
the *hajj* may at least be briefly explored.

One of the tangential notions accompanying developmental
theory is that of the "demonstration effect." Exposure to
"modern" or "developed" ways is thought to lead to imitation
of, or behavior modeled after, these more efficient or
attractive ways. Implicitly, the demonstration effect is
linked to western agents and modes of activity and behavior.
After all, it is the West that has presumably been
responsible, in modern times, for exposing less developed
societies and their peoples to technologically advanced
instruments, and to behavior (including consumer patterns)
thought of as "modern."

In the context of West African Muslims, and particularly
rural ones, it can be argued that the *hajj* now provides the
demonstration effect that western societies do not, and that
Saudi Arabia is replacing the West as the demonstrative

Table 10.5
Pilgrims From ECOWAS Countries Arriving in Saudi Arabia --
Selected Years

	1965	1970	1975	1980	1981	1983
Benin	--	356	419	--	--	--
Burkina Faso	--	630	1,540	1,853	3,669	1,545
Cape Verde	--	--	--	--	--	--
Côte d' Ivoire	--	683	1,771	1,796	1,543	915
Gambia	--	--	--	458	410	662
Ghana	--	518	2,708	1,329	1,454	1,058
Guinea	1,257	1,786	986	--	--	4,710
Guinea-Bissau	--	--	--	--	--	--
Liberia	--	126	61	128	124	5
Mali	654	998	2,719	3,192	3,068	2,861
Mauri-tania	--	416	--	960	1,445	1,241
Niger	--	2,810	685	3,285	3,623	1,335
Nigeria	3,438	24,185	92,593	78,043	100,300	76,153
Senegal	1,801	2,097	3,832	4,437	4,237	4,213
Sierra Leone	--	284	377	--	512	276
Togo	--	94	--	218	251	331
TOTAL	7,150	35,983	107,686	95,699	120,646	95,305
% of Sub-Saharan Africa	40	73	n.a.	88	90	90
% of World Total	3	9	12	11	14	9

Source: Compiled from data in *Statistical Yearbook*, 1983, 1981, 1980, 1975, 1970, 1965, Kingdom of Saudi Arabia, Ministry of Finance and National Economy, Central Department of Statistics.

agent. For many rural West Africans, Mecca and Saudi Arabia
is the outside world, and they derive much of their first-
hand experience of modern, foreign ways and means from this
(unwestern) source. Luxury and consumer products and goods
brought back from the *hajj* which provide a more chronometric
and outward outlook (watches, radios, cassette players, slide
viewers, etc.) are only one side of this; more important,
from a developmental point of view, is the experience gained
in construction, factory work and wage-labor employment, and
general exposure to a relatively complex urban lifestyle and
environment. The village carpenter who returns home with
more sophisticated tools of his trade (tools which are
perhaps in fact available in his own country, but to which he
had never been exposed) is one illustration of how Islam, via
the demonstration effect resulting from the *hajj*, can play a
positive role in rural West African development.

Islamic Responses to Skewed Development

In West Africa as elsewhere, the relationship between
Islam and development is not always so fortuitous. To the
extent that development *is* linked to westernization, and is
associated with the familiar set of social ills (hyper-
urbanization, overcrowding, rural depopulation, food-chain
irregularities, unemployment, rising distributive inequities,
super-stratification, communal breakdown, crime), Islamic (or
quasi-Islamic) responses have been forthcoming. Some of
these responses have been positive; others, negative and
destructive. An example of each kind of response will be
briefly presented below. The overriding point, however, is
that even where Islam is incapable of controlling the form
and direction of development, it is not therefore powerless
to respond to it.
Ahmadiyya is an Islamic sect, founded in the Indian
subcontinent in the late nineteenth century. Although
periodically suspected and rejected by Islamic orthodoxy
because of their veneration of Ahmadiyya's founder, Ghulam
Ahmad, whom they consider a prophetic figure, Ahmadis do
consider themselves as Muslims. Ahmadiyya has taken root
and grown in West Africa, particularly because of its
developmental infrastructure. Ahmadiyya appeals principally
to uprooted, dispossessed, and disadvantaged urban men, and
Muslim women unhappy with the more orthodox strictures and
practices of Muslim culture (seclusion, polygamy and
segregated prayer).[31]
"An integral and essential part of Ahmadi belief is the

establishment and maintenance of schools, colleges and hospitals. This has been especially important in establishing Ahmadiyya in West Africa."[32] Ahmadiyya has modernized the notion of *jihad* into a holy war against illiteracy, and thus promotes education -- for women as well as men. *Lejna* is an organization of Ahmadiyya women, which involves them in issues relating to urban life and improvement. They are bound to inform themselves on, and disseminate information about, health, nutrition, education, and even prison conditions.[33] Yacoob, based on her research in Côte d'Ivoire, sees Ahmadiyya principally as a "strategy... to deal with a new urban environment and a new world view."[34] It remains, nevertheless, an Islamic (however liberalized) strategy, reconciling the exigencies of a developing society *within* the framework of religious faith. These urbanites have not rejected Islam as others, particularly francophone elites, have as an impediment to individual success and improvement; they have reoriented Islam to become a means for achieving the same.

In Nigeria, the urban dispossessed have also reacted, however symptomatically, to skewed development in their own society. Again, the response has been cast in a quasi-Islamic mode; tragically, the Maitatsine revolts, as they have come to be known, have taken on millenarian, negativistic and violent dimensions.

Originating in northern Cameroon, Alhaji Mohammed Marwa Maitatsine attracted a following of Koranic students, youths and unemployed migrants throughout Niger Republic and northern Nigeria. His locus of strength, however, was the metropolis of Kano. Here, Maitatsine gathered a veritable cult about him, "preach[ing] and... condemn[ing] the widespread corruption of existing secular and religious elites and especially the orgy of western consumption enjoyed by Kano's privileged classes during the brief but socially disruptive petroleum boom (1974-81)."[35] Physical objects of Maitatsine wrath (beyond the religious and governmental authorities whom he "damned") included cars, televisions, radios, watches and even buttons -- all symbols of western consumerism and luxury. Money too was seen as evil (if a necessary one), with Maitatsine followers enjoined from accumulating all but a subsistence level amount. Maitatsine considered himself a prophet. So did his thousands of followers, who waged a veritable war against the Nigerian army and police in 1980. Maitatsine himself perished -- along with thousands of others -- in the ensuing bombardment and riddling of his stronghold in old Kano. Nevertheless, Maitatsine sentiment has erupted into violence in northern

Nigeria periodically since then. Nigeria is the one West African country where skewed development, manifested by spectacular oil wealth amidst widespread poverty, is perhaps most glaring. It is also one country where there is a distinct developmental gap along religious and regional lines, with the Christian south historically being more developed than the Muslim north. Yet it is the only West African country, populated by significant numbers of Muslims, where economic dissatisfaction is deep, and arguably growing. Accepting that West African Islam is less "combative and aggressive" than Islam in the Near and Middle East, Islamic responses to skewed development in West Africa are likely to be more a function of developmental success (or failure) than Islamic militancy. As such, they will probably continue to manifest themselves more in localized, nation-specific forms rather than general, region-wide movements.

Conclusion

The present chapter has but skimmed the surface of the manifold and intertwining relationships between Islam and development in West Africa. A host of other important issues have only been mentioned in passing, or not at all. These include: Islamic organizations and associations at the *national* level[36]; Islamic responses to western and secular education[37]; rural-urban ties and changes fostered by Islamicization[38]; other Islamic brotherhoods operating in the region[39]; patron-client relations within *turuq*, and their impact on socioeconomic change; and brotherhood networks functioning within the informal economy (especially in terms of black market, smuggling and contraband operations).[40]

To conclude, the expansion of the Muslim faith throughout West Africa, coincident with the growing interdependence of the world at large, will tend to strengthen the relationship between Islam and development in this region. Economy of scale is critical to commercial expansion and development; so is the consciousness of a wider world, which regional and international Islam has been expanding. Economic trade and commercial links helped bring Islam to West Africa: in its turn, Islamic networks -- and principles -- will be tapped to promote the material and spiritual development of the Faithful. For, as even the Koran teaches, "Never will God change the condition of a people until they change it themselves" (Sura II, v. 143).

Notes

1.   This second point has been argued in the context of Adam Smith's analysis of capitalistic development. According to Smith, even laissez-faire competitive self-interest requires a "moral base" which society accepts as a guide to behavior.

2.   Uka Ezenwe, *ECOWAS and the Economic Integration of West Africa* (New York: St. Martin's Press, 1983), pp. 14-15; and Ralph Onwuka, *Development and Integration in West Africa: The Case of the Economic Community of West African States (ECOWAS)* (Ibadan: W. Girardet, undated), p. 1.

3.   Weekes presents figures which, averaged together, amount to 42 percent; from Table 6 on p. 31 in Peter Clarke, *West Africa and Islam. A Study of Religious Development from the 8th to the 20th Century* (London: Edward Arnold, 1982), a figure of 46 percent may be extrapolated.

4.   Quoted in Jon Kraus, "Islamic Affinities and International Politics in Sub-Saharan Africa," *Current History*, 456, 1978, p. 155.

5.   Michael Hudson, "Islam and Political Development" in John Esposito (ed.), *Islam and Development. Religion and Sociopolitical Change* (Syracuse: Syracuse University Press, 1980), p. 15.

6.   Weber quoted in Claude Sutcliffe, "Is Islam an Obstacle to Development? Ideal Patterns of Belief Versus Actual Patterns of Behavior," *The Journal of Developing Areas*, 10, 1975, p. 77.

7.   *Ibid.*

8.   Cited in Hudson, " Islam and Political Development," p. 3.

9.   John Cummings, Hossein Askari, and Ahmad Mustafa, "Islam and Modern Economic Change" in Esposito (ed.), *Islam and Development*, p. 46.

10.   Clarke, *West Africa and Islam*, p. 207.

11.   *Ibid.*, p. 208.

12.   See Abner Cohen, *Custom and Politics in Urban Africa. A Study of Hausa Migrants in Yoruba Towns* (Berkeley and Los Angeles: University of California Press, 1969).

13.   Nehemiah Levtzion, "Rural and Urban Islam in West Africa: An Introductory Essay," *Asian and African Studies*, 20, 1986, p. 20.

14.   See M.C. Diop, "Les affaires mourides à Dakar," *Politique Africaine*, 1, 1981.

15.   Lucy Creevey Behrman, "Muslim Politics and Development in Senegal," *Journal of Modern African Studies*, 15, 1977, pp. 261-277.

238

16. *Ibid.*
17. *Yearbook of International Organizations 1986-87* (Munich: K.G. Saur, 1986).
18. *Africa Research Bulletin*, 23(6), July 1986, p. 8121.
19. *Africa South of the Sahara 1987* (London: Europa Publications, 1986), p. 199.
20. Victor Le Vine and Timothy Luke, *The Arab-African Connection: Political and Economic Realities (Boulder: Westview Press, 1979), p. 49.*
21. *Ibid.* Nigeria contemplated membership in 1987, but opposition from many quarters forced the government to shelve its proposal.
22. *Ibid.*
23. *Arab Economist*, 1977, p. 38, quoted in Le Vine and Luke, *The Arab-African Connection, ibid.* The Special Arab Assistance Fund for Africa (SAAFA) merged with BADEA in 1977. It had by then disbursed $214.2 million.
24. Cummings, Askari and Mustafa, "Islam and Modern Economic Change," p. 39; and Richard Bell, trans. *Qur'an* (Edinburgh: T.& T. Clark, 1937), p. 193.
25. See Edward Stockwell and Karen Laidlaw, *Third World Development: Problems and Prospects* (Chicago: Nelson-Hall, 1981), especially pp. 145-146.
26. *Ibid.*, p. 145.
27. *Ibid.*, p. 146.
28. See William Miles, "Islam and Development in the Western Sahel: Engine or Brake?" *Institute of Muslim Minority Affairs Journal*, 7, 1986.
29. See Ziauddin Sardar and M.A. Zaki Badawi (eds.), *Hajj Studies, Volume 1* (London: Croom Helm, undated), pp. 126-127.
30. Clarke, *West Africa and Islam*, p. 274.
31. See May Yacoob, "The Ahmadiyya: Urban Adaptation in the Ivory Coast" (Boston University Ph.D. thesis, 1980).
32. *Ibid.*, p. 90.
33. *Ibid.*, p. 102.
34. *Ibid.*, p. 159.
35. Paul Lubeck, "Islamic Protest under Semi-Industrial Capitalism: Yan Tatsine Explained," *Africa*, 55, 1985, p. 370.
36. Such as the *Jama'atu Nasril Islam* and Muslim Students Organization in Nigeria, or the *Union Culturelle Musulmane* in Senegal.
37. See Clarke, "The Religious Factor in the Developmental Process in Nigeria;" also Akbar Muhammed, "Islam and National Integration through Education in Nigeria" in Esposito (ed.), *Islam and Development*, for case studies dealing with Nigeria. See Behrman, "Muslim Politics and Development in Senegal" for Senegal.

38. See *Asian and African Studies*, 20(1), 1986, for a special issue devoted to this theme.

39. Such as the Hamaliyya, the Sanussiya, Wahabiyya and Yan Izalla.

40. See Diop, "Les affaires mourides à Dakar" concerning the Mourides and the Occas market in Touba.

11

Gender and the Development Agenda

Barbara J. Callaway

The analysis of the structure of gender subordination across cultures in general and in Africa in particular during the late 1960s and early 1970s brought a sharply different focus to an understanding of the interrelationship between African social structure, sex roles, gender relations and public policies designed to foster economic development.[1]

The revival of western feminism in the 1960s sparked a broad attack on existing male privilege and a concomitant scholarly examination of the bases of universal gender inequality. It highlighted belief systems and practices which limited women's access to socially valued resources and public statuses and concluded that the legal and cultural practices of marriage in particular limited women primarily to reproduction and long years of childcare and consequent economic dependency, and thus to limited public roles.[2]

While the women's suffrage movement early in this century stressed political participation as the key to gender parity, feminists in the 1970s stressed the importance of self-determination gained primarily through economic self-sufficiency. They emphasized that economic self-sufficiency permits women the choice of marrying or not and creates the prerequisite stake necessary to demand access to public resources. Emphasis on domesticity and the home extolled in Africa by Victorian colonialists (whether of the government or of the church) were deemphasized in favor of the rewards to be gained and the status and power to be obtained by women in the public sphere. And, beyond that, the importance of the sense of self, status and autonomy accruing from personal economic independence was stressed. Some feminist scholarship focusing on Africa asserted that in fact these values did exist to some measure in precolonial (i.e. precapitalist) African societies.

During the 1980s the deepening economic crisis in Africa led to a broad critique of dominant development strategies and, partly in consequence, to a focus on Africa's failing agriculture, particularly domestic food production.[3] Much of the continent struggles with a fragile resource base, exploding population and declining per capita food production. Inadequate production is a result of declining fertility of the land, production priorities that emphasize cash crops at the expense of food crops, inappropriate and low levels of technology, and a system of cultivation based historically on extensive agricultural modes carried out by women.

This focus on domestic food production has, however, highlighted the role of women in African agriculture. In this context, feminist revisionism and the basic human needs approach to development share a commitment to promote greater growth with equity. Both attempt to combine theory and policy in the effort to promote effective interventions benefiting women (as well as men). Nonetheless, an understanding of how best to accomplish these goals remains elusive. This chapter attempts to outline the considerations which structure this challenge both to theory and to policy. If considerations of gender equity in the 1990s are highly unlikely to alter the priorities of international development donors and host governments, ways to improve women's agricultural productivity nonetheless are recognized as essential in addressing Africa's domestic food production problems.

The Focus on Women and Agriculture

The theoretical critique by feminists of previous scholarship on Africa seeks in part to end the invisibility of women, particularly in the labor force as farmers, food processors and retailers of both crops and cooked food.[4] The policy critique makes a fundamental point: accumulated data on African women's activities reveal that with no public assistance whatsoever women play the dominant role in domestic food production.

Most observers now acknowledge that many African women work more hours than their spouses, even excluding cooking and childcare. They play a more important role in the rural labor force than women on any other continent, and dominate in food crop production.[5] Yet, despite African women's unquestionable centrality to family survival, observers agree that social organization and agricultural, educational and administrative policy marginalize women in a number of ways.

The colonial economy forced or drew men into cash cropping for export and wage labor in mining, urban and agricultural enterprises. Due in part to this demand for men's labor, women in many regions came to dominate food production for domestic consumption. Because many men do not earn enough to support their wives and children, women's food farms often make family survival possible. Nonetheless, women have faced increasingly difficult conditions in their efforts to feed their families. As more of their children attend school, for example, women lose an important labor resource. As population increases and the expansion of cash cropping causes increasing land scarcity, the land allocated to women is often of poor quality or far from their homes. Declining yields in some areas reflect overcropping. Where men cash crop, their wives are often obliged to assist them. They are sometimes given cash by their husbands when the produce is sold, but the money involved neither equals the labor market value of a hired substitute or compensates the women for the labor withdrawn from their own crops. Where men migrate for work, women are *de facto* heads of household and must provide for their families without husbands' help even in clearing or plowing land.

The international attention to declining agriculture and concomitant famine in Africa in the 1980s has brought African food production and national policies affecting food production under scrutiny. This convergence of an international focus on women's agricultural work and international concern with Africa's growing food deficits provides policy-makers with a significant opportunity to design assistance programs targeting women. But policies designed to affect women's agricultural contribution may increase women's productivity without enhancing their earning power or empowering them in their households and communities. In order for policy to be effective in either domain (public economy or private household), an accurate understanding of women's role and status in culture and society is essential. Such understanding is difficult to attain, however.

The standard interpretation of the role women play in agriculture in West Africa takes as its starting point the work of Ester Boserup.[6] According to this interpretation, African women in the precolonial period enjoyed considerable independence which was disrupted by the arrival of the colonialists and their introduction of cash crops. In the precolonial traditional system, it is assumed, most West African women were responsible for the bulk of agricultural work. They labored in the male-run family fields and in most societies had their own plots as well. Women then as now provided almost all of the family food except for meat and grain. They sold their own surplus and generally decided what household necessities they would buy with it (such as clothing or condiments).

As colonialism progressed, men received new tools and advice on how to grow cash crops. Men thus profited from the new crops while women did not. Increasingly, too, men migrated to the cities. Simultaneously, birth rates rose and death rates decreased. As a result, women had to feed more people and had more work to do (to replace migrating men) while the work they did -- in the subsistence food production and processing sector -- lost value relative to the higher prestige and higher productivity of the modernized commercial crop sector controlled by men. When postindependence government interest turned back to food crop production, furthermore, it was again men who received tools and technical advice. Women, therefore, may have been somewhat relieved from their labors by the introduction of small innovative appropriate technologies such as plows, hoes and more efficient cook stoves, but they lost most of the economic independence they had had.[7] While accurate on many counts, there are problems with this perspective which should be acknowledged if effective policies to aid women, as well as promote food production, are to be formulated.

Reassessing Women and Agriculture

The first problem with this interpretation comes from the assumption that there was a fixed and immutable position for all African women in a traditional precolonial system when clearly precolonial societies were infinitely varied and the role of women in them changed continuously over time. In Nigeria, for example, Yoruba women lived in large urbanlike communities where they controlled large markets and sold food grown by men on surrounding farms; the Igbo lived in small villages and women had a monopoly in the production of certain crops, some of which became cash as well as food crops;[8] the Hausa resided in both large cities and small villages, while the Fulani were both pastoralists and nomads, and women had very different roles to play in each type of society. Traditional society was neither fixed nor unresponsive to outside factors or varying internal conditions unrelated to colonialism per se.

Long before European colonialists appeared in northern Nigeria, different ethnic groups had migrated into the area and changed their ways of life. Some became sedentary where they had been nomadic (the Fulani). Some settled where the land was relatively fertile and water less scarce (the Hausa). Some stayed for a time in drier zones which became even drier as desertification progressed [a process which did not begin in 1980] (the Kanuri). Trade routes across the Sahara from North Africa and the Sudan introduced new tools and ideas. As the focus of trade shifted to the coast after the Europeans arrived there, other influences filtered into the inland cultures. Muslim reform movements arose. Christian missionaries proselytized.

For instance, in Kano, a large homogeneous Hausa/Fulani emirate in northern Nigeria, wars were fought between the fourteenth and twentieth centuries to establish emirate or territorial boundaries, to reform Islam, and to establish colonial rule. Throughout the period various economic hardships such as droughts and trade blockades were overcome. The institution of slavery was greatly expanded. Internal organization of family and economic structures changed to adapt first to the intrusion of neighboring states, then to Muslim traders and later to Fulani Islamic reformers, and finally to British imperialism. These long term processes led to considerable alterations in economic practices not only in Kano City and the surrounding countryside, but also in neighboring emirates, depending on where individual families were settled and what their specific family economic and status situation was. As part of the overall system of life in the subsistence village, the participation of women in agriculture was altered over time as well. Thus, Muslim Hausa women today may not work in the family fields while their pagan sisters (the Mugazawa) regularly do. Nor may Muslim Hausa women market family produce as Muslim Yoruba women and non-Muslim Hausa women do. Muslim Hausa women have less visible economic independence than do their nonsecluded sisters, although they do generally produce an income of their own.[9]

In the context of this continuously changing framework, the second problem with the stereotype set out above appears most striking. Not only were African villages responding to their changing environments, but villages as a genre could not be dealt with as if there were not major differences between the family and farming systems of different ethnic groups. What women do within one ethnic group at any particular point may be quite dissimilar to their role in any other group. In northern Nigeria there are approximately 135 ethnic groups.[10] Of northern Nigeria's sixty-seventy million people, about twenty million are Hausa/Fulani, but other large groups include the Nupe, the Kanuri, and the Tiv, each with a population of several million and quite distinct status positions and roles for women. Women in Muslim Hausa society live in seclusion, but they are economically active, principally in the sale of cooked food from within the confines of purdah or seclusion. Non-Muslim Hausa women may raise chickens and goats as well as vegetables and trade the products of both their farming and their animal husbandry along with other items of trade in the open markets in which their Muslim sisters are not present.

Finally, there are also wide variations among the many different farming peoples in relation to how responsibilities are allocated among family members and, of course, this allocation changes as the community (or a local subunit thereof) responds to changing circumstances. Thus, Hausa women traditionally did not have as much of a role in agriculture as did Igbo women, but took on increasing responsibility in processing food in order to feed people in the cities. In so doing they increased their economic independence although simultaneously they disappeared from public view as the practice of seclusion became the norm. Women in seclusion do plant gardens, raise poultry and sell eggs, process and sell food, and keep their own accounts, but not all women in all groups living in northern Nigeria do all of these things.

The point is that there is considerable variation among different peoples as to the exact tasks of women and their place in both the informal and agricultural economy. As cities grow and integrated rural development schemes take effect, the expected tasks of women will and do change. Therefore, it should be obvious that basic research is a prerequisite before prescriptions for effective assistance can be made. Yet, most development assistance projects proceed without the benefit of such research. To summarize, then, the problem with the stereotype derived from Esther Boserup's work is that there does not seem to be a linear pattern of progressive deprivation of women of the power and economic independence which they traditionally enjoyed in favor of men, nor is it always clear just what these were. Clearly, as markets grew, market women gained power in those societies where the market economy was strong and their roles in it clear. But, when the economy declined market women suffered disproportionately.[11] In the subsistence sector, men as well as women lost ground when cash crops were introduced. Consequently, a strategy of intervention cannot be made at any uniform point across a continuum.

Women and Development

The fact that most agricultural aid has been directed toward men is much criticized. Western agricultural extension workers all over Africa regularly approached only the male head of household with advice about new farming methods.[12] Tools, seeds, insecticides and fertilizer were most often given to the male head of household and loans were made in his name. Thus it is not surprising that most cash crops are controlled by men -- indeed where sophisticated machinery like tractors, or simpler hand or animal-driven tools like multi-purpose cultivators were available, these were also controlled by men. Only recently have extension workers been prepared to work with women in terms of their agricultural roles rather than simply in the areas of domestic or health activities. New projects, moreover, are all too likely to ignore the importance of women in overall production, and not allocate land to their use or otherwise allow for their needs.[13]

In lower northern Nigeria (or the Middle Belt) where extension workers assisted farmers with food crops (notably rice, where research has made dramatic gains), the extensionists tended to speak to husbands, even when women were the actual cultivators. Extensionists also fail to serve widows as well as women who are, due to their husbands' migration for work, *de facto* heads of household. One cause cited is the proscription against male strangers working with women: one solution proposed is the training of female agricultural extensionists.[14]

Despite the evidence that government policies and programs reinforce or disrupt the position of men farmers relative to women, it is still useful to look at the complex set of results which these programs have had. Here too the picture which emerges is not quite as simple as has been suggested. To begin with, women do grow cash crops, at least many women in many societies do -- for example among the Igbo in Nigeria and the Bambara in Senegal. Thus, some women do gain an income from commercial crops. Women not only grow cash crops in their personal plots, but they also work in the family fields in cash crop production for which they receive wages in cash (although, as noted above, these wages do not often equal the market value of similar male labor).[15] Their husbands, moreover, sometimes grow food crops as well, and also provide needed assistance in the women's fields as, for instance, in clearing the land. Where men receive the new tools, they often do use them in the women's fields. Women also sometimes gain in terms of receiving more money for their labor for example, at harvest time or in weeding, when men expand their cash crop production with the assistance of the new tools, better seeds, etc. Research on the Wolof of Senegal is indicative of the variety of possibilities which can be extrapolated to other societies. In one case it was demonstrated that farm mechanization did not decrease the income of women (in fact the reverse was true). However, the introduction of grain mills, which might be expected to alleviate an arduous chore for Wolof women, in fact did lessen income as they did not own or control the mills.[16]

Figures from East Africa also suggest that large numbers of women are in fact involved in cash and export crop production. Women provide 35 percent of the labor producing tobacco in Swaziland, 47 and 37 percent in two different areas of cotton production in Malawi, and 70 percent in coffee production in Rwanda.[17] There is evidence then that when given the same resource incentives, women are as productive and innovative in their work as men. Research suggests that women farmers are as responsive to new techniques as men who grow the same crops.[18]

Women in many African societies clearly understand the importance of an income of their own, separate from support provided by husbands. Gambian women rice farmers prefer to work on their own plots rather than work for their husbands, even for a wage. Women in northern Cameroon shift their work from their husbands' fields to their own when they feel they are not being adequately compensated for their labor. Women in Côte d'Ivoire refuse to provide free porterage of their husbands' crops to market.[19] Most women also work in food crop production, primarily to support themselves and their children. Women in southern Cameroon provide most of family food staples from their own fields and devote up to three-fourths of their cash income for household needs, and in four ecologically different areas in Côte d'Ivoire women supply between 48 and 63 percent of the most important food crops.[20]

Given the now known importance of women's labor in African agriculture, why is it nonetheless so consistently bypassed in assistance programs? One explanation is that women's involvement in farming is generally considered backward by the men who staff international assistance programs. By implication, from their point of view, women's farming and their independent enterprises are expected to disappear as development proceeds. Therefore, women's agriculture is not worth the investment of careful investigation or of scarce resources. In their world view, economic development occurs through the promotion of large-scale enterprise in which western scientific farming methods can be practiced without the incumbrances of family law and local custom, and in which men are visible and women are not. They emphasize that land fragmentation is already a troublesome issue without doubling the rate of miniaturization of holding by adding the fields of daughters and wives as legal receivers of assistance.

It is not only the emphasis on large scale agriculture per se that is wrong with this perception, but rather the elimination from consideration of women who currently farm the land and who will continue to do so in the foreseeable future. In fact, women's importance in rural economies continues to increase. It is not a question of whether or not women will still farm in the year 2000, but whether or not they will do so under more optimal conditions. The use of women's expertise in managing a difficult environment would seem crucial to proper development of the rural sector.

Hidden erroneous assumptions prevent constructive consideration of the possibilities for strengthening women's enterprise as a component in diversifying rural economies. Women's farming, processing and trade are not the entire answer to Africa's agricultural problems, but they are an important component of it. The realization in development circles that indigenous farming techniques have great adaptive strengths offers the possibility of productive engagement for the first time. Women's access to modern education offers the possibility of lifting some of the restrictions on women's enterprise.

Development policies which fail to address women's current economic activities are counterproductive and also contribute to serious ripple effects in children's welfare, fertility and the poor use of resources. Policies promoting women's economic well-being must also be varied and flexible enough to address different constraints in each particular national context, however. No single policy can possibly apply everywhere; alternative routes and strategies must be available to circumvent particular setbacks and limitations in order to avoid abandonment of the goals themselves.

For example, many production and/or sales cooperative projects for women are launched without adequate studies of economic feasibility, marketing alternatives or costs. If increased production cannot be sold or profits are small, participants are left with debts for inputs which have not really been of benefit to them. In Tanzania, when farmers received plows and thus tripled their farm size, women could not or would not weed the large planted area. Production losses resulted, and the innovation's results fell far short of expectations.[21] The failure to see the interconnectedness of men's work and women's work was crucial. If planners had established an accurate calendar of crop cycles, labor requirements and task allocation by gender, they would have seen that women could not weed the added acreage planted after the plows were introduced, and men would not do "women's work."

In this context and as another example, an evaluation of projects for women in Senegal sponsored by the United States Agency for International Development (USAID) was also discouraging. Village women did not understand what they were expected to accomplish. Their consequent lack of motivation was compounded by faulty analysis of the sustainability of the economic and social activities in the projects, shortage of supplies, poor credit and marketing arrangements, and unforeseen obstacles such as lack of support from the male village leadership and poor government backup.[22]

Over and above all this, another problem seldom addressed by development planners directly concerned with helping women in agriculture is that of population growth. Women are very much affected by unremittingly high fertility rates. African countries show a population growth rate of 2.5 - 4.4 percent. This is extremely high by both historical and contemporary standards. In contrast, agriculture grew 1.7 percent between 1970 and 1985 for the continent as a whole.[23] A population doubling every fifteen to twenty-five years requires a doubling of food production approximately every 16 years. This, too, is unprecedented in history. The fertility rate of 6.9 in Nigeria compares with 1.8 in the United States and 1.0 in Japan. The fact that there are virtually no effective family planning programs in West Africa obviously very profoundly affects women who are responsible for feeding their families. High fertility rates are related to poor nutrition, food shortages and short life spans. Development projects and policy analysts cannot ignore the need for population planning and control.[24]

In theory, women's wage employment is expected to promote anti-natalist incentives if work is in the formal sector and pro-natalist incentives if it is in the informal and peasant agricultural sector. This correlation does not hold true in Africa.[25] In Kano, where virtually no women were in the paid labor sector, the fertility rate was 6.5.[26] Three West African studies find virtually the same rate among women who do work in the wage sector.[27] Thus, the birth rate is likely to remain high wherever women have no alternative to children for support in widowhood or old age. Therefore, improving women's access to development resources may be one plank in developing an effective population policy in both rural and urban areas.

In addition to understanding population pressures and local economic constraints, roles and conditions, the question of local power structures is also a crucial part of these considerations. Who has power over whom (when power is defined as the ability to force someone to do something she/he would not otherwise do), and under what circumstances and to what extent is it exercised in a given situation? Political scientists have traditionally not dealt with the family in discussions of power because, as John Locke first argued, the family network is outside the arena of civil society.[28] But, trying to understand who has the authority and power to prevent another from doing something or to engage him or herself in a program of change requires conceiving of the family as a mutually interdependent system where the members all bargain and vie with each other to gain desired ends such as income, independence to make decisions, or access to good and plentiful land, etc. As such, the extended African family has to be viewed as a political unit. In those societies where men and women have separate economic and social concerns, as they do in much of Africa, gain to one member may imply loss or only limited gain to another. These become important political considerations in the design of development projects.

Unlike political scientists, anthropologists have looked at the politics of kinship groups and tribes for many years. Early writers distinguished between political society (civitas) founded on territory and property, and social society (societas) based on kinship relationships.[29] Later schools of anthropology reject this distinction and study the politics of tribal (ethnic) groups with increasing concern to refine the principles of organization and relationship.[30] In general, the major concern has been with kinship groups over a much broader area than in the confines of one family compound or even one village. The relevance of this broad anthropological research to the inquiry here is not always obvious. The point is, as discussed above, that ethnic groups differ greatly from one another in their organization. Further, change in the conditions and context of a particular family system will lead to changes in the allocation of responsibilities and the organization of the family that will vary from culture to culture. Thus, the analysis of the politics of the nuclear or extended family in which men control the money is only one model. It is opposed to others in which women are permitted to pursue their own income generating activities and pursue separate economic goals without male interference. In still other cultures both men and women believe the male head of household has economic responsibility and the right to exert his control and authority and be obeyed. Women in these societies may use the unhappiness of a raised consciousness as a prod to get some of what they want from their husbands, but this leaves them relatively weak compared with their peers in other family systems where men and women's economic activities are separate.

Certain concepts advanced in anthropological work are helpful for organizing a beginning approach to using the family system as a tool for understanding decision-making in the context of development. Perhaps most valuable is the distinction between economic and status control. Esther Boserup or, more correctly, those who have used the model she advances, have often written as if economic independence was all that is at stake in the declining position of African women. But status, in the sense of recognizing the superior authority of another, relates to, but is not determined by, economic power alone. A related issue of more than analytic significance is the issue of class. Political scientists and anthropologists have argued among themselves whether or not traditional African societies were classless. At issue is the Marxist assertion that traditional society was classless and only developed classes as it was pushed toward private ownership of property and pulled into capitalist relations of production.

This is not completely accurate. Traditional Hausa society, for example, was marked by both class and status distinctions. Slave were distinct from non-slave lineages, and commoner lineages (*talakawa*) were distinct from royal lineages (*surata*). Roles and status were determined by lineages, and there was hierarchical structuring of professions with butchers being at the bottom, traders in the middle, and teachers and judges at the top. Membership in a given lineage determined membership in a given skill or trade group. The issues of class and caste are beyond the scope of this chapter. Suffice it to note here the importance of these distinctions in assessing a given woman's ability to respond to or likelihood of participating in a given development project or of receiving other forms of assistance. It may not always be clear how this factor operates as either a facilitating or constraining influence. In the case of education, in both Igbo and Hausa areas in Nigeria, chiefs sent boys of lower status to school, thus making the social structure more fluid, at least at the beginning. It is conceivable that lower status women might similarly benefit from sensitive development strategies.

Despite the limitations of this approach, it is argued here that assessing the interrelationship of family and individual characteristics and relative political power of individual family members is a useful approach to a preliminary evaluation of how women will react to and benefit from new development programs. In the past insensitivity to these relationships has been a major factor explaining why programs have failed, or at least not met the originally set objectives. Women are admittedly difficult to reach. Understanding why may make it easier to devise incentives or to go around the barriers that block them. It could lead to more careful policy definition and implementation in a context where improvements are drastically needed to avert a deepening crisis situation as populations increase and land resources are pressed. The goal is to improve food production, health and family nutrition as well as to improve the social and political position of women.

In West Africa, the power implications of being male and head of family vary from society to society and under different economic and social conditions. Among differences which contribute to different statuses even within groups is religion. Within a society such as the Hausa, Muslims will differ from non-Muslims in the power they give to both men and women. The meaning of polygamy also differs according to religion. Muslim men must treat all wives equally. The spatial separation of men from women means, however, that Muslim women living in seclusion may have greater autonomy in their income-generating work than do their non-Muslim sisters. Generally, however, greater autonomy does not mean greater income because all work must be conducted from within the household. Thus, the complexity of the power structure even within the family is determined by such variables as isolation of the household, its wealth, religion, the number of wives, the number of children and their ages, as well as questions of lineage and economic standing. All of these factors suggest the construction of a matrix to suggest the type of constraints and enabling factors which policy makers might usefully identify in seeking to design projects to reach women effectively with useful inputs. These indices can be used to identify overriding characteristics of social structure, ethnic group and family in determining the independence of women and the likelihood of their participating effectively in specific development efforts.

Conclusion

In designing development projects, the connection between women's interest and community well-being must be stressed. Feminist policy makers in donor development agencies attempt to ensure that women farmers, now visible, can be more productive and less exploited. The effort is to include women's interests in project design. The argument is that women must be included if projects are to succeed. To be efficient, agricultural and rural development project design must take into account the gender division of labor and gender linked differences in access to and control of resources. The interconnectedness of family activities is stressed. One such effort is illustrative. The Women in Development Office (a very small component of a very large Agency, it must be noted)[31] of the USAID has offered the following guidelines:

-- both men's and women's roles should be analyzed;
-- analysis of the division of labor in project-related activities is not enough; it needs to be complemented by analysis of how project activities intersect with the other activities of men and women throughout the day or over the calendar year;
-- to predict whether either sex will be willing to innovate, the differential stakes and incentives -- with and without the project -- must be estimated.[32]

The Agency's Blueprint for Development (1985) stresses that understanding the sex division of labor and recognition of women's interests are requisites of project success. It stresses five sectors (agriculture, employment, education, energy and water supply/sanitation) as the means to achieve growth of national income and income of the poor, to reduce hunger and malnutrition, to improve health, and to reduce population pressure.[33]

The relevance of women to these goals is clear. The empirical link between education for women and population control is direct. The case for making women beneficiaries of agricultural aid in order to reduce malnutrition and hunger is straightforward. That women should be in the targeted population in project design is evident. To define the conditions of project success so that the project promotes women's control over their own production and thus empowers them is much more difficult.

African nations have widely varied constitutional provisions protecting women's rights and status. The constitution of Mozambique explicitly promotes women's equality in law, education and employment.[34] The Nigerian constitution just as explicitly exempts family law and the position of women from the protection of its human rights and anti-discrimination clauses.[35] The importance of the legal position of African women and African governments' responses to these goals are self-evident.

The concern of feminist scholars of Africa that women be empowered in the public domain has not changed as we enter the 1990s. The emphasis on economic avenues to such gains for women, and the concern that women's increased productivity translates into leverage for self-determination, are thus underscored. It is not clear, however, that more effective development assistance to women will lead to political or personal empowerment. This focus suggests only that gender related issues must be taken into account, but does not infer that women in fact have a veto power over projects that serve them ill. "Getting women on the policy agenda" suggests considerable effort to gain organizational legitimacy for feminist objectives. Equally important areas of policy which escape the project-centered and production-centered focus of agencies like USAID center upon legal, political, cultural and social questions. Diplomatic necessity as well as faith in the ameliorative effects of economic growth lead feminists in international donor agencies to focus on certain economic processes, while steering away from many other potentially conflictual policy questions.

The past decade has placed women in agriculture squarely on the policy agenda and has put what women do on the development research agenda. How and why women's status changes and how family relations shift with social change are still new, fertile fields of inquiry. Social historians are pursuing numerous avenues ranging from broad parameters such as mortality and fertility rates, cultural components of power, the cause and impact of legal change, and the link between changes in economic activity and independence to understand the lack of gender parity for women. These are not unrelated enterprises, and remain relevant, but they are beyond the scope of this particular chapter. All in all, the intricacy of the whole question of how women have fared from the introduction of cash crops in those areas where this has occurred, and from various efforts at rural modernization, together with the fluid and varied arrangements of women's roles in different ethnic groups and in different regions and localities, at different points in time, forces us to look more closely at each specific

situation as well as broad general historical trends. It is
not adequate, let alone feasible, to assume that all women
are being disadvantaged and therefore programs should be
directed at advancing all their specific interests. To make
these programs effective the exact impact of different types
of strategies on women in different situations must be
understood. In some cases what is advantageous in one
situation will be disadvantageous in another. The challenge
of assistance planning and giving is to set the parameters so
that in any given situation the results of planned
interventions can be predicted, at least more accurately than
they are now.

Notes

1. See Elizabeth Moen, Elise Boulding, Jane Lillydahl and
Risa Palm, *Women and the Social Costs of Economic Development*
(Boulder: Westview Press, 1982); Claire Robertson, *Sharing
the Same Bowl: A Socio-Economic History of Women and Class
in Accra, Ghana* (Bloomington: Indiana University Press,
1984); Judith Van Allen, "African Women, 'Modernization', and
National Liberation" in Lynne Eglitzin and Ruth Ross (eds.),
Women in the World: A Comparative Study (Santa Barbara: ABC
Clio Press, 1976); Section III, "Differential Aspects of
Development Policies" in Edna G. Bay (ed.), *Women and Work in
Africa* (Boulder: Westview Press, 1982).

2. See the landmark book in feminist scholarship edited
by Michele Rosaldo and Louise Lamphere, *Women, Culture and
Society* (Palo Alto: Stanford University Press, 1974).

3. See Denis Goulet, *The Cruel Choice: A New Concept of
Development* (New York: Atheneum, 1978); Peter Berger,
Pyramids of Sacrifice: Political Ethics and Social Change
(Garden City, NY: Anchor Press, Doubleday, 1974); and Timothy
M. Shaw (ed.), *Alternative Futures for Africa* (Boulder:
Westview Press, 1982).

4. Jean O'Barr, "Making the Invisible Visible: African
Women in Politics and Policy," *African Studies Review*, 18,
1975, pp. 19-28, was one of the first to make this point.
The World Bank echoes this invisibility theme in *Recognizing*

the 'Invisible' Women in Development: The World Bank's Experience in 1978; see also Barbara C. Lewis, Invisible Farmers: Women and the Crisis in Agriculture (Washington D.C.: USAID, 1980).

5. See Jane Guyer, "Women's Role in Economic Development" in Robert J. Berg and Jennifer Seymour Whitaker (eds.), Strategies for African Development (Berkeley: University of California Press, 1986). Guyer discusses the different measures of women's economic contribution, noting that while official figures of labor force participation put African women at slightly half of the rural labor force in Africa, detailed local studies in societies as diverse as Burkina Faso and Liberia find women's contribution in hours far exceed men's. See Ruth Dixon, "Women in Agriculture: Counting the Labor Force in Developing Countries," Population and Development Review, 8(3), 1982, pp. 539-566; and Brenda Gael McSweeney, "Collection and Analysis of Data on Rural Women's Time Use," Studies in Family Planning, 10(11/12), 1979, pp. 378-382.

6. See Ester Boserup, "The Position of Women in Economic Production and in the Household with Special Reference to Africa" in Clio Presvelou and Saskia Spijkers-Zwart (eds.), The Household, Women, and Agricultural Development (Wageningen: H. Veenman en Zonen, 1980), pp. 11-16; and Women's Role in Economic Development (New York: St. Martin's Press, 1970).

7. See Ibid. Also see Leslie Sophia McNeil, "Women of Mali: A Study of Sexual Stratification" (Cambridge: Harvard University B.A. Thesis, 1979); Kate Cloud, "Sex Roles in Food Production and Distribution Systems in the Sahel" in Lucy Creevey (ed.), Women Farmers in Africa: A Study of Rural Development in Mali and the Sahel (Syracuse: Syracuse University Press, 1986), pp. 19-51.

8. World Bank estimates of changes in productivity by crop over the past twenty years indicate that cassava, a crop grown almost entirely by Igbo women, has been the only West African staple to keep up with population growth; World Bank, Accelerated Development in Sub-Sahara Africa (Washington D.C., 1981), pp. 168-169.

9. See Polly Hill, Rural Hausa: A Village and a Setting (Cambridge: Cambridge University Press, 1972); M.K. Bashir,"The Economic Activities of Secluded Married Women in Kurawa and Lallokin Lemu, Kano City" (Zaria: Ahmadu Bello University, B.Sc. Thesis, 1979); Barbara Callaway, Muslim Hausa Women in Nigeria: Tradition and Change (Syracuse: Syracuse University Press, 1987); Enid Schildkrout, "Dependency and Autonomy: The Economic Activities of Secluded

Hausa Women in Kano, Nigeria" in Bay (ed.), *Women and Work in Africa*, pp. 55-83.

10. The largest ethnic group, the Hausa, number over fifteen million. The second largest, the Fulani, has four million. The greatest population concentration is in Kano State, which has approximately ten million people, 98 percent of whom are Hausa/Fulani, making this both the largest and the most homogenous state in Nigeria. It should be noted, however, that there are no reliable or generally accepted census figures for Nigeria, although a census is planned for 1991. For a comprehensive discussion of the volatile census issue in Nigeria, see Larry Diamond, *Class, Ethnicity and Democracy in Nigeria* (London: Macmillan, 1987).

11. See, for example, Claire C. Robertson, *Sharing the Same Bowl: A Socioeconomic History of Women and Class in Accra, Ghana* (Bloomington: Indiana University Press, 1984).

12. See the case studies presented in Creevey, *Women Farmers in Africa*.

13. See Kathleen A. Staudt, "Women Farmers and Inequities in Agricultural Services" in Bay (ed.), *Women and Work in Africa*, pp. 207-244; and Kate Cloud, "Sex Roles," pp. 19-51.

14. Jacqueline Ashby, "New Models for Agricultural Research and Extension: The Need to Integrate Women" in Lewis, *Invisible Farmers*. Ashby stresses the greater legitimacy that women extensionists will have with rural women, given the segregation and social distance between men and women. Even this solution would not necessarily work in places such as Kano, however, since even female extension workers are likely to be Christian, not Muslim.

15. A sample of Ghanaian female cocoa farmers hired 44.3 percent of the labor required on their farms, while only 33 percent of their husbands hired such labor. See Polly Hill, *Cocoa Farmers in Ghana* (Cambridge: Cambridge University Press, 1968).

16. Bernhard Vanema, "The Changing Role of Women in Agriculture in the Sahel" in Creevey, *Women Farmers in Africa*.

17. Food and Agriculture Organization, "Follow-up to WCARRD: The Role of Women in Agricultural Production" (Rome: FAO, 1982).

18. Peter Moock, "The Efficiency of Women as Farm Managers," *American Journal of Agricultural Economics*, 58, 1976, pp. 831-835; and Louise Fortmann, "Women Work in a Communal Setting" in Bay, *Women and Work in Africa*, pp. 191-205.

19. Jennie Dey, "Gambian Women: Unequal Partners in Rice Development Projects?" in Nici Nelson, *African Women in the Development Process* (London: Frank Cass, 1981), pp. 109-122; W.O. Jones, *Marketing Staple Food Crops in Tropical Africa* (Ithaca: Cornell University Press, 1972); Marguerite Dupire, "Planteurs autochtones et etrangers en Basse-Cote d'Ivoire orientale," *Etudes Eburneennes*, VIII, pp. 7-37; and Christine Obbo, *African Women: Their Struggle for Economic Independence* (London: Zed Press, 1980).

20. Jane Guyer, *Family and Farm in Southern Cameroon* (Boston: Boston University African Research Series #15, 1986) cited in Barbara Lewis, "Getting Women on the Agricultural Development Agenda" (forthcoming); and Ann-Jacqueline Berio, "The Analysis of Time Allocation and Activity Patterns in Nutrition and Rural Development Planning," *Food and Nutrition Bulletin*, 6(1), 1983, pp. 53-58.

21. Louise Fortmann, "Women's Work in a Communal Setting: The Tanzanian Policy of Ujamaa" in Bay (ed.), *Women and Work in Africa*, pp. 191-206.

22. Jeffalyn Johnson and Associates, *African Women in Development: Final Report* (Washington: Office of Regional African Affairs, USAID, April 1980); and Kathleen Cloud, *Women Farmers in Aid Agricultural Projects* (Evanston: Indiana University Press, 1987).

23. Carl Eicher, "Strategic Issues in Combating Hunger and Poverty in Africa" in Berg and Whitaker (eds.), *Strategies for African Development*, pp. 242-278.

24. In 1986, the United States decided to end American aid assistance to the one international family planning agency active in Africa -- the International Planned Parenthood Federation.

25. Mead Cain, "On Women's Status, Family Structure and Fertility in Developing Countries," (Washington: World Bank, 1984).

26. Barbara Callaway, *Muslim Hausa Women in Nigeria*, chapter two.

27. Eleanor Fapohunda, "The Child-Care Dilemma of Working Mothers in African Cities: The Case of Lagos, Nigeria" in Bay (ed.), *Women and Work in Africa*, pp. 277-288; Konia Kollehlon, "Women's Work-Role and Fertility in Liberia," *Africa*, 54(4), 1984, pp. 31-45; and Barbara C. Lewis, "Fertility and Employment: An Assessment of Role Incompatibility among African Urban Women" in Bay, *Women and Work in Africa*, pp. 249-276.

28. This is actually a theme in western political thought dating back to the ancient Greeks.

29.   See L.H. Morgan, *Ancient Society* cited in I. Schapera, *Government and Politics in Tribal Societies* (London: C.A. Watts, 1956), p. 3; and Georges Balandier, *Anthropologie Politique* (Paris: Presses Universitaires de France, 1967), p. 60.   Balandier also points out that Marxists make this same distinction.

30. See I. Schapera, *Ibid.*, and Georges Balandier, *Ibid.*; see also Max Gluckman, *Custom and Conflict in Africa* (Urbana: The Free Press, 1955); Marc Swartz, *Local Level Politics: Social and Cultural Perspectives* (Chicago: Aldine Publishing House, 1968); Michael S. Banton (ed.), *Political Systems and the Distribution of Power* (London: Tavistock Publications, 1965); M.J. Swartz, V.W. Turner and A. Tuden (eds.), *Political Anthropology Volume 2: Culture and Political Change* (New Brunswick: Transaction Books, 1983).

31. For an analysis of the work of this small office in USAID see Staudt, "Women Farmers and Inequities in Agricultural Services".

32. Alice Steward Carloni, "Lessons Learned 1972-1985: The Importance of Gender for AID Projects" (Washington: USAID, 1986), p. 27.

33. See Barbara C. Lewis, "Getting Women on the Agricultural Development Agenda" in Harvey Glickman (ed.), *The Crisis and Challenge of African Development* (New York: Greenwood Press, 1988), pp. 176-200.

34. Stephanie Urdang, "The Last Transition? Women and Development in Mozambique," *Review of African Political Economy*, 27/28, 1984, pp. 8-32.

35. Barbara Callaway and Enid Schildkrout, "Law, Education and Social Change: Implications for Hausa Muslim Women in Nigeria" in Lynne B. Iglitzin and Ruth Ross (eds.), *Women in the World: 1975-1985, the Women's Decade* (Santa Barbara: ABC Clio, 1986), pp. 181-206.

12

Trade Unions, Regionalism and the Contradictions of West African Political Economies

Jon Kraus

Development of Trade Unionism

It is possible to argue that there is a significant range of major economic and political forces that have promoted the development of regional relationships among trade unions in West Africa. Development -- the argument would go -- has been promoted in economic senses by migrant labor fulfilling varying regional demands for labor and in political-organizational senses by increasing the capabilities of trade unions. First, during the colonial period and continuing up to the 1980s, there has been a high level of labor migration in West Africa, with growth poles attracting unskilled and sometimes skilled and professional labor from countries of low or stagnant growth. Historically, labor has flowed from Mali and Guinea to Senegal-Gambia and from Mali and Burkina Faso to Ghana and Côte d'Ivoire to work both in cash crop agriculture (as wage or share tenant workers) and in the urban artisanal, commercial, industrial and port sectors. During the 1970s and 1980s there was massive migration from West African states to Nigeria's oil-driven economy.

Second, through extra-territorial ties under the British and French colonial empires, significant linkages developed between the trade unions in the diverse anglophone and, especially, francophone West African countries. In francophone colonial West Africa the trade unions that emerged in the post World War II period, apart from independent unions, were linked together as branches of the French communist-led union (CGT) and the smaller Socialist Party (CGT-FO) and Christian unions (CFTC). These regional linkages were transformed in the mid-1950s into African-led federations, especially the Confédération Générale du Travail-Africaine (CGT-A) and then the Union Générale du

Travail de l'Afrique Noire (UGTAN), organized by Sékou Touré of Guinea in 1957, and a smaller African Federation of Believing Workers (CATC). Postindependence efforts to form Pan-African union federations were disrupted by genuine differences in ideological orientations and power and leadership struggles between African state and union leaders, reducing several of these movements to instruments of political rather than union power.[1] Ultimately, in 1973, contending union federations agreed to form the Organization of African Trade Union Unity (OATUU), which in the mid-1980s was creating regional union organizations. OATUU has been an agency for union solidarity and cooperation.

Third, there has been a significant number of common extra-territorial private economic organizations in West African countries, most obviously transnational corporations (TNCs), operating primarily in either francophone or anglophone states. These TNCs are in agricultural export buying, commerce, transport, banking, construction and, more recently, industry. These could tend to promote intra-regional union cooperation and information sharing with regard to strategies and bargaining.

Other factors facilitated union cooperation. The common colonial cultures, institutions, roughly similar industrial relations frameworks and laws, and common colonial and now national languages have greatly facilitated linkages between trade unions and their leaderships as well as intraregional labor mobility. In addition, among trade union leaders at national and local levels there often develops a consciousness of the need for trade union solidarity and broad networks of support against oppressive employers and governments. The historical experiences of African unions during the independence struggle, when unions were often confronted with repressive state actions, and during postindependence travails have educated at least national union leaders regarding the importance of trade union solidarity from abroad, from African unions and Pan-African union groups as well as European and American unions, the western and communist labor internationals, the International Labor Organization (ILO), and the international trade union secretariats (organized by industry groups).

Of the several and contradictory implications of these factors for development, relatively free flows of intraregional labor migration can stimulate development in the recipient economy both by facilitating more rational supply responses to labor market demands than the many small West African economies could individually, and by generating employment. However, what is rational and beneficial for the individual migrant or the host economy is likely to be, over time, highly disadvantageous to the countries and regions serving as labor reserves, as has Burkina Faso for Ghana and Côte d'Ivoire. Alternative economic strategies are ignored; absent, youthful migrant labor leaves agriculture underdeveloped, and women and children become the primary farmers; this permits the persistence of low productivity, malnutrition and disease; and there are virtually no spillover effects in the labor reserves from the meager earnings of migrants in host economies.[2]

The thesis that will be argued here is that despite the factors that could promote (or have done so in the past) regional trade union cooperation, powerful countervailing factors have prevented significant union cooperation. These same factors have often disrupted and reversed sharply intraregional labor flows, though these are often driven by economic and social forces beyond the capacity of the states to contain. The mutual gains from such labor flows have been recognized by the states in the ECOWAS (Economic Community of West African States) Treaty of 1975, which permits, in its first phase, free, non-visa entry of migrants for ninety days to work and conduct business, after which residence permits must be obtained.[3]

Some key variables which explain the relative lack of regional trade union cooperation are: state imperatives; political authoritarianism; the growing predominance of a merchant-professional-bureaucratic bourgeoisie's perspectives and interests in political life; and the relative weakness of the proletariat and trade unions in Africa's agrarian and statist political economies, especially in an era of marked regional retrenchment. First, the newly independent West African states made relatively strong efforts to organize and regulate economic and political power at the national level, making it the major political arena in which economic, power and status demands are organized and resources sought. Although these states are not particularly powerful and authoritative (in the sense of being capable of eliciting widespread compliance with national laws and regulations), they have had the capacity over time to employ coercive sanctions and political measures to prevent or dismantle extra-territorial labor (and other) organizations, e.g., UGTAN and AATUF (All-African Trade Union Federation). Regional union interventions have been regarded as unwarranted, illegitimate intrusions in their sovereign affairs, although OATUU has intervened effectively on occasion to protest state actions against unions without being condemned as illegitimate.

Second, in most postindependence West African states, trade unions as well as other associational or political groups have not been permitted to organize freely and to develop organizational capacities and hence some political-economic influence, with some exceptions. Initially, dominant nationalist political parties established single-party regimes and sought to control and monopolize organized expressions of interest and also to determine ideologically (when necessary) the boundaries of legitimate participation in the political system and policy-making. Hence, the emerging union movements of the 1950s and 1960s were often repressed, strong union leaders jailed or exiled, new unions created and leaders coopted, e.g., in Senegal (up to 1975-76), Côte d'Ivoire, Togo, Benin since 1973-74, Guinea, Mali, Niger, Mauritania, Cameroon, Ghana during 1960-66, and Liberia under the Tubman regime.[4] This has also tended to be true where military regimes have seized power. There are some significant instances where the organizational capacity and strategic location of trade unions have prevented regimes from implementing key policies or have even prompted, by their strikes, the overthrow of regimes, e.g., on a variety of occasions in pre-1973 Benin and in Burkina Faso. Ghana's trade unions have also been intermittently successful in policy interventions and have retained their organizational autonomy since 1966.

Third, the nationalist movements and post-independence governments have been led largely by a petty-bourgeoisie, and since 1960 a merchant-professional-bureaucratic bourgeoisie has emerged in many countries with intimate ties to state power. It and its political expressions have been in a much stronger position to organize or pursue individually, or through ethnic and political linkages, their interests than has the formal sector proletariat and its political expression, trade unions, whose interests tend to conflict with this bourgeoisie. Although the merchant-professional-bureaucratic bourgeoisie in many West African countries is not well-organized, its members and groups tend to have significant influence, with ties to occupants of state institutions which are a major source of private capital accumulation.[5]

Fourth, the relative weakness of trade union organizations in most West African countries has meant that, with important exceptions, they did not possess the economic resources and political influence to threaten effectively politically repressive behavior against unions in their own or neighboring states. In most West African states less than 10 percent of the total labor force is in the modern wage/salary

labor force and hence available for organization into trade
unions (Ghana and Côte d'Ivoire are exceptions). In
addition, in virtually all states the largest single wage
employer is the state and parastatal organizations, where
sharp limitations on trade union activities (e.g., no
collective bargaining in the civil service) undermine support
for union membership and interest. In combination, these
variables have reduced the salience of the forces promoting
regional labor cooperation and solidarity.

In this chapter we will explore the following: the
relative weakness of the forces promoting regional labor
cooperation in light of the countervailing political and
economic forces; the extent to which regional and Pan-African
trade union organizations have promoted regional labor
solidarity, especially in protecting trade union rights; and
the relative power of trade unions in several West African
countries in terms of their relative development and
capabilities, which will illuminate the areas where regional
cooperation could be useful.

Migration and Trade Union Cooperation

Regional trade union cooperation could mitigate some of
the severe disabilities to which migrant workers, both
nationally and regionally, have long been subjected --
exploitative wages, harsh working conditions, job insecurity,
no bargaining power -- and to protect the capacities of the
unions themselves and the pressure on wages in the face of a
non-organized reserve army of unemployed. Both migrant
workers and trade unions, however, have confronted
contradictions with the rise of nationalistic African states.
These have, generally, obstructed intermittently and harshly
the prior relatively unrestricted flow of migrant labor
across state borders in West Africa. The ability of unions
to organize workers' power to protect wages and employment
has been limited by several forces: the impact of the
international political economy which structures levels of
national economic activities by its pricing of African
commodity exports; state and class interests which have
sought to delimit and contain union organization and its main
leverage, strikes, and public policies which, by making much
immigration illegal, discourage migrants from participation
in union activities and protests; and nationalist tendencies
among politicians, the public, and sometimes unions which
relegate migrant workers to lesser beings. Some argue that
union organization of migrant workers (who are otherwise most

frequently employed at substandard wages) would impede economically rational uses of labor and discourage private investment and employment. The fatuousness of this idea is easily seen when one extends it to all labor and argues that economic rationality and development would be best served by having a labor force with no organized capacity to bargain. The benefits and spheres of "development" would then be limited to the upper class and macro-economic indicators, while most workers would be ill-paid, often laid off, and their families malnourished, illiterate, and without medical help. Union organization of migrants could obstruct economic rationality only where unions could command a price for labor in excess of its productive contributions, which is true in West Africa only where excessive labor is employed in the public sector for political purposes.

Historically, migrant labor in Africa was created to meet the labor demands of colonial powers and foreign capital in mines, railways and European farms. Although initially there were forms of forced labor in virtually all West African colonies, this ended in anglophone West Africa in the late 1920s and in francophone Africa after World War II.[6] Forced labor in francophone West Africa was itself a source of migrant labor as workers and even villages fled to British colonies.[7] Forced and quasi-forced labor was much more extensive in the settler colonies of southern Africa with their much higher labor demands. By the early 1930s and often earlier, workers were responding to income opportunities in the key coastal and forest areas of West Africa in a voluntary or quasi-voluntary way with seasonal migrations. Extremely depressed wages, poor working conditions (especially in mines), and migrants' retention of land rights meant that much of the wage labor force remained migrant well into the 1950s. In 1921, 41 percent of the mineworkers in Ghana were foreign migrants, in 1931, 30 percent, and in 1960, 41 percent. In the early 1950s, labor turnover in Ghana's mines was over 70 percent annually, 90-100 percent among underground workers.[8] Foreign and northern Ghana migrant labor constituted 39 percent of the work force in forestry, and 37 percent in construction in 1951.[9] The high labor turnover which prevailed up to the 1950s in many countries made trade union organization in many sectors extremely difficult.

The major historical pattern of regional migration, which was relatively unrestricted, was from interior countries (Burkina Faso, Mali, Niger, interior Guinea) to the southern zones (plantations, cities) of Ghana and Côte d'Ivoire, with a lesser stream from Mali and interior Guinea to the Senegal-

Gambia groundnut area. In addition, there were lateral, east-west migrations, especially from Nigeria and Togo to Ghanaian urban areas and cocoa zones as well as a small number of skilled workers (Dahomeyans, Sierra Leoneans) and merchants. Nigeria prior to 1960 had a much smaller number of regional migrants and experienced primarily internal migration.[10] Among varying estimates of the size of regional migrant flows, involving primarily unskilled workers, one suggests 300,000 per year into Ghana in the late 1950s, mostly seasonal.[11] The surveys by Rauch in 1958-59 estimate 400,000-500,000 regional migrants for the group of countries comprising Niger, Burkina Faso, Mali, Ghana and Côte d'Ivoire. Amin estimates that among these countries there were around 180,000 migrants annually during 1920-40, with 75 percent seasonal, roughly 250,000 a year during 1950-60, with 70 percent seasonal, and around 300,000 a year in 1960-70, with perhaps 67 percent seasonal.[12] Migrant workers from Guinea and Mali to the Senegal-Gambia groundnut area are estimated at 60,000 annually in 1935-40, 40,000 annually during 1940-58, falling to 11,000 during 1958-61 and almost none thereafter. Mabogunje argues that there were two million migrants per year in West Africa before 1960; an OECD study estimates migrants in West Africa in 1975 involved 4.4 million people (both presumably include internal migration).[13] There is no doubt that the seasonal and permanent regional migrant labor made major contributions to the agricultural and other development of southern Ghana and Côte d'Ivoire.

There are at least two significant changes in migrant labor patterns (internal and regional) since the 1960s. First, to an increasing extent, labor migration has become medium and long-term in character, the latter in effect permanent. Simultaneously in all countries there has been massive rural-urban internal migration, leading to a large labor reserve army of unemployed and underemployed, with a vast expansion of the informal sector of small-scale enterprises and self-employment (hawking, artisanal). Second, there has been a major flow of both unskilled and skilled and professional labor, short to medium term migrants, pushed from low growth economies in the 1970s to the high growth economies in West Africa, primarily Nigeria and Côte d'Ivoire.

Regional migration in the postindependent period has confronted problems created by new nationalist states: increased restrictions on migration by many states, hence rendering either migration itself or working illegal (under ECOWAS, after ninety days, without a state work permit), thus exposing migrant workers to exploitation by employers and harassment, brutality and extortion with impunity by police and border officials and sometimes by host state citizens. In addition, there have been state regulations or laws giving preference to citizens in employment or through indigenization decrees, giving exclusive rights to citizens in major business sectors, especially commerce, taxis and other transport, and small-scale construction and contracting.[14]

The legal restrictions on migration and preferences in hiring give rise in host economies to a dual labor market (DLM), which includes a primary sector where wages are relatively high, employment secure, advancement possible, and a secondary sector (where most migrants, it is argued, work) which has low wages, unstable employment, poor working conditions, and few advancement opportunities.[15] Fashoyin argues that in Nigeria, apart from skilled and professional labor on contract, most migrant workers have been confined to the secondary market, which may include some formal sector jobs at low levels (e.g., construction, dock workers, transportation, clerical) but mostly has involved informal sector employment, i.e., relatively small family-run businesses outside state regulation and enumeration, or self-employment. The DLM thesis argues that workers in these two sectors are non-competing groups, which Fashoyin argues with regard to Nigeria in the 1970s and 1980s. Hence, he argues that the expulsion of aliens in 1983 and 1985 was largely if not wholly irrelevant to improving employment opportunities for the indigenous people.[16] Those employed in the secondary sector, primarily Nigerian businesses, were not organized by unions, because of the incapacities of Nigerian unions, employer resistance, difficulties in organizing small businesses (e.g., two to twenty employees), and the disinterest of migrants in unions or unwillingness to act with sufficient militancy, given their illegal status and short-term goals.[17] However, not all migrant workers are employed in the secondary labor market (which partly coincides with the informal sector). In Ghana in 1960, when 12.3 percent of the population was of foreign origin (57 percent Togolese and Nigerian), in mining 41 percent of workers were foreign migrants, in manufacturing 11 percent (among males, 15 percent), in construction 21 percent, in electricity-gas-sanitary services 22 percent, and in transport-storage-communications 14 percent (32 percent of longshoremen).[18] Virtually all these sectors were very largely unionized and became more so in the early 1960s, including Ghanaian firms, and were in the primary sector.

In Côte d'Ivoire, in the private and state corporate domains, 82 percent of workers in agriculture in 1971 were foreign African migrants, 38.4 percent in manufacturing-utilities-mining-construction, and 34 percent in the tertiary sector.[19] Undoubtedly many of the migrants in manufacturing-mining-construction, and some in agriculture (in parastatals), occupied primary sector jobs which were covered by the minimum guaranteed wage levels mandated by the state; but not all these would have been unionized (Ivorian unions are less extensively organized than in Ghana).

Nonetheless, except when African states have badly needed foreign migrant workers, they have tended to possess less secure jobs, at lower rates of pay, and to be subject to the caprices of government policies and intermittent expulsions. Côte d'Ivoire repatriated Togolese, Dahomeyans and Nigerians in 1958. The French West African federation permitted the hiring of non-nationals in the civil services of individual states, but many francophone states expelled to their countries of birth African civil servants in 1960-61, following independence. Ghanaian fishermen have been expelled from Guinea, Côte d'Ivoire, Nigeria and Sierra Leone. Nigerian traders have been banished from Cameroon, Côte d'Ivoire, Ghana and Niger. All Dahomeyan citizens were expelled from Niger following a 1964 border dispute. Senegal expelled Guineans in 1967. In the 1960s, migrant labor to Nigeria faced great difficulty in entry without work permits. The two most notable cases involved the Busia government's expulsion of over 200,000 aliens from Ghana in November 1968, with two weeks notice, and the January 1983 expulsion of over two million migrants from Nigeria, of whom a million were Ghanaians.[20] This caused enormous suffering, material losses and deaths. In 1985, Nigeria again expelled an estimated 700,000 migrants, while in 1989 many thousands of Mauritanians and Senegalese were repatriated after skirmishes between their respective countries.

Most expulsions of migrant workers have been initiated by governments on the basis of anticipated political and economic benefits. Economic benefits involved expected opportunities for increased indigenous employment and, especially, for business or trade. There were no pressures for the expulsions by Ghanaian and Nigerian unions. In Ghana during 1966-68, following the Nkrumah government's overthrow, there were an estimated 60,000 government layoffs. There were high estimates of unemployment among Ghanaians in 1969; Prime Minister Busia suggested (incorrectly) 500,000. In July 1969, the then military government warned foreign embassies that all aliens should be registered in nine months. Then, the elected Progress Party government, under Busia, suddenly ordered in November 1969 that all aliens must have working papers in two weeks or leave the country. The major pressures for alien expulsion were in the business community, where a National Crusade for the Protection of Ghanaian Enterprises fomented a campaign to give Ghanaians greater control over business. The National Crusade was formed to speed the implementation of the Ghanaian Enterprises Decree of 1968, issued by the then military government, which required (over five years) large alien wholesale and retail traders to sell their businesses to Ghanaians and eliminated entirely aliens from petty trading, commercial transport, printing, baking, butchering and other artisanal and small manufacturing occupations (aliens were important as traders, bakers and millers, 46 percent; and tailors, 25 percent). The National Crusade worked with Ghanaian cattle dealers, sawn timber and spare parts dealers, butchers, and women traders to spur pressures for the removal of alien traders and businesses. There was also rural support for such measures, where Yoruba and Hausa traders from Nigeria were prominent.[21]

The expulsion order elicited strong nationalist support in the (state) media and in some spheres of public opinion, though surveys note a high tolerance of alien workers among Ghanaian workers. There is little evidence of the reactions of the trade union movement, which at this point had friendly relations with the Busia government.[22] In the next year, 1970, the Ghana Trade Union Congress (TUC) gave a large financial donation in response to the appeal of a Nigerian labor federation for assistance in rebuilding the unions after the civil war.[23] Although alien mine workers (41 percent of the total in 1960) and agricultural labor were exempted, many left Ghana in the face of nationalist outcries, creating labor shortages.

The two-week deadline for the expulsion of aliens in Nigeria in 1983 was even more outrageous, inflicting gross hardships, given the problem of two million workers finding transport. The action was decreed by the Nigerian government in January 1983, as the downturn in Nigeria's rentier economy was starting to produce unemployment and hardship. The beleaguered Shagari government hoped to divert Nigerians from their economic woes and held forth prospects for increased employment, since national and state elections were due in seven months. The recent violent revolt of a puritanical Muslim sect composed of largely Niger nationals in northern cities may also have been an additional (security) factor in the expulsion decision. The state initially exempted all workers in federal, parastatal and state employment (including 35,000 Ghanaian teachers); employer pressures induced Nigeria to give skilled workers an extra month deadline in which to obtain work permits.

There was an outpouring of support from the Nigerian press and parts of the public.[24] The Nigeria Labor Congress (NLC) criticized only the manner in which the expulsion was announced but was silent on the rightfulness of the action itself. The dockworkers' union unsuccessfully sought replacements for the 7,000 aliens employed; the textile union which faced a drastic decline in employment and union-busting employers was indifferent to the alien expulsion, which might preserve some jobs for Nigerians.[25] One union general secretary, reflecting the incapacity and perhaps indifference of union leadership, suggested that since most migrant workers labored in the informal sector, which was non-unionized, there was little the union movement could do.[26] The Secretary General of the Organization of African Trade Union Unity (OATUU), Dennis Akumu, appealed to the Nigerian government to exercise caution in its expulsion order and not to victimize African workers; he later asked OATUU to deplore the action.[27] There were relatively few employment benefits from this massive expulsion of workers, most of whom were unskilled, or skilled but working as traders or in more menial jobs.[28]

In conclusion, regional migration has become more difficult and less legal since independence. In West Africa migrants tend to be employed in the secondary labor market or informal economy and hence are not organized by trade unions; Ghana was a partial exception. There is no evidence that regional migration contributes to trade union cooperation in the postindependence period. Poor treatment of nationals may incite hostile sentiments among home country unionists. Migrant workers with illegal status in a host economy will tend to be reluctant to join trade unions or support union protests, fearing job loss or visibility to authorities. In the past, however, where labor was scarce and migrants legal, they often supported militant worker protests, without necessarily joining unions.[29]

State and Class Formation, Labor Controls and the Contraction of Regional Trade Union Linkages

As African states became independent, new political leaders were anxious to secure their political kingdoms in the face of insecure support, weak national sentiment, political competition for state offices and resources which mobilized ethnic opposition, and low institutional capabilities. This had profound consequences for existing intraregional trade union linkages and the capacity of unions to establish their institutional autonomy and strength. Development and budgetary imperatives were also perceived as major reasons to control union demands on scarce resources in regimes pursuing either capitalist or state socialist strategies. Where the government was often the largest employer, increased wages inevitably cut into state resources available for development programs. But public employment was greatly expanded in all regimes to provide services (e.g., education) and jobs for the party faithful and the urban unemployed in order to reduce discontent. In the thirty years after independence, there has also developed a significant commercial-professional-bureaucratic bourgeoisie intimately linked to state resources, whose interests and perspectives conflict with those of the trade unions and working class. Lastly, regional Pan-African trade union groupings were often perceived as -- and were -- expressions of a striving for power and influence by other African states or Cold War superpowers and hence to be opposed or employed opportunely for resources that could be extracted.

The important regional trade union movement developed in French West Africa (FWA) and Togo in the preindependence period was broken up by interstate conflicts over decolonization and nationalist security fears in 1959-60. The trade union movement in FWA was created after World War II by French trade unions as subsidiary branches of the French unions (themselves linked to French political parties), amalgamated on a territorial basis, with hierarchical links to Paris headquarters and, initially, no horizontal linkages. The French unions included: the communist-led CGT (Confédération Générale du Travail), which started earliest (1944-45), created the most unions, and linked them to the communist-led (by 1948) World Federation of Trade Unions (WFTU), which, with the CGT, provided great financial and other assistance to the small, weak unions; the CFTC (Confédération Française des Travailleurs Chrétiens), starting in 1946; and the Socialist Party's CGT-FO (CGT-Force Ouvrière), starting in 1948, linked to the western International Confederation of Free Trade Unions (ICFTU).[30] African political leaders created the Rassemblement Democratique Africaine (RDA) as an interterritorial party which linked the key nationalist parties in all states (except Senegal). Union leaders were active in many of the parties. The RDA was linked to the French Communist Party

(PCF) in the French National Assembly.

The movement towards union cooperation and autonomy had several roots. After the Cold War began, the communist ties subjected the RDA and the African CGT unions to harsh colonial repressive measures, especially during 1948-51. The RDA broke with the PCF in 1950. Senghor and Houphouët-Boigny (RDA) in 1952-53 started to urge and pressure union leaders to break with the French CGT and create autonomous unions, in part in order to reduce French colonial antagonism and permit greater African influence with the French government. African CGT leaders were reluctant to do so because of the CGT assistance in its organization and strikes to compel the French to pass the Overseas Labor Code (1952) -- designed to create greater equity in African and French wages -- and then to implement it.[31] Second, African union leaders themselves sought more coordination and autonomy. They demanded and received a regional CGT coordinating committee in 1951, and in 1954 unsuccessfully demanded the integration of the territorial CGT unions into one federal union, without French CGT influence. Starting with the Senegal CGT union in November 1955, and followed by the Guinean CGT, an autonomous CGT-Africaine (CGTA) was established in 1956, despite French and African CGT resistance. In January 1957, CGTA, CGT, and now autonomous ex-CFTC unions met and created a single federal union, UGTAN (Union Générale des Travailleurs de l'Afrique Noire), which included 85-90 percent of FWA's unionized workers (183,000, 36 percent of the wage force). UGTAN, led by Sékou Touré, who was also head of Guinea's dominant party, strongly advocated more powerful federal institutions and independence.[32]

A strong countervailing current was the *loi cadre* of 1956, which mandated the devolution of federal power in FWA to individual territories. The dynamics of consolidating national parties and power now overwhelmed regional cooperative efforts, despite the resistance of the "federalists" among African political leaders (chiefly in Senegal and Soudan/Mali). After the 1957 territorial elections, the dominant parties or coalitions formed territorial governments with substantial internal powers. African union leaders were elected to twenty of the 474 assembly seats in eight states; ten were made ministers, of whom two were (in effect) heads of government, Touré in Guinea, Bakary Djibo in Niger.[33] The clash between UGTAN affiliates and the dominant parties climaxed in the 1958 referendum called by President De Gaulle. States were asked to choose between autonomous membership in a French-African community and independence (a "non"-vote). After some discussions, UGTAN and Touré in Guinea urged a vote for independence and organized UGTAN affiliates in FWA to support this, while all dominant parties except Touré's in Guinea supported a "yes" vote. Guinea alone became independent in 1958. The serious split between dominant parties and UGTAN unions was exacerbated immediately after as Touré and other UGTAN affiliates sought to maintain UGTAN as cohesive and militant, though its head (Touré) was now leader of an independent foreign country and was denouncing other FWA leaders as colonialist stooges. It was also widened as new territorial governments faced the demands of civil servants and others for equality in wages and benefits with French workers, a traditional demand but one the new governments could not afford, given the relatively small number of French and large number of African civil servants. Strikes were launched, with both political and economic objectives, to resist a new civil service statute which curtailed strike rights and many benefits.

Thereafter, in most FWA states, all of which ultimately became independent in 1960, the unions were "nationalized," as unions themselves broke with UGTAN or the state forced the break and exiled non-national union leaders (Mali, Côte d'Ivoire, Burkina Faso, Niger) or abolished the UGTAN affiliates.[34]

In the next year or so, most of FWA trade unions were forced to merge into a single union and roughly subordinated to the ruling party and, often later, a military regime (Guinea, Mali, Côte d'Ivoire, Mauritania, Niger). Strikes became illegal in most states. This pattern fluctuated intermittently in Senegal with periods of plural union centers which, since 1976, have remained and coincided with the reemergence of party competition, though the largest union remains linked to Senegal's ruling party. Only in Benin and Burkina Faso in ex-FWA did multiple union centers, relative autonomy, and militant union action persist, and these were obliterated in Benin in 1973-74. Although the struggle between UGTAN and African governments was articulated in part by UGTAN and Touré in terms of radical change versus conservative interests and neocolonialism, in fact unions suffered as much if not more severe losses of autonomy under "radical" regimes (Guinea, Mali) as in others.

The justification for union subordination to single parties was the need for national unity and the irrelevance of class struggle. In practice, these governments refused to permit the organizational autonomy of a relatively large organized group which might oppose its policies. As the largest wage employer, it justified sharp limits on wage/salary increases by the need to allocate scarce capital for development. This was an important problem in the weakest economies, such as Burkina Faso's and Benin's, where the efforts to repress the real wages of civil servants and teachers was occasioned by repeated financial crises and vigorous, sometimes effective union strikes.

However, wage/salary workers have confronted two major contradictions. First, real wages since independence have deteriorated in many regimes, and labor pressures and protests have largely been to halt this wage loss. In 1975, in ex-FWA the real minimum wage index was above the 1960 level only in Senegal, Mauritania and Côte d'Ivoire, slightly below that level in Niger and Togo, and well below it in Guinea (24 percent of 1960 wages), Mali (59 percent), Benin (66 percent) and Burkina Faso (80 percent). Real wages have deteriorated considerably in all but Côte d'Ivoire since then,[35] especially with the economic crisis in the late 1980s.

Second, in both francophone and anglophone West Africa, the hypocrisy of state repressive strategies has been evident in the behavior of civilian and military leaders who individually and in concert with members of the rising bourgeoisie have engaged in massive forms of corrupt private accumulation of public resources and high levels of economic mismanagement for short-term political ends. High state regulations and the weak economic bases of the bourgeoisie have meant that a major route to private capital accumulation has been through close access to state offices and to state resources. This has occurred through import and foreign exchange licenses, land allotments, construction and contracting bids, credit, disproportionately large benefits for political leaders and parastatal managers (cars, housing, large allowances), the reservation of business sectors and foreign company stock through the indigenization decrees in many states, and the corrupt diversion of public resources to private use.[36]

A major contradiction between bourgeois and worker-union interests has occurred preeminently in the sphere of allocations of state resources rather than wage repression for indigenous bourgeois employers. However, where a significant merchant-industrial bourgeoisie has emerged -- in Nigeria and, less so, Côte d'Ivoire and Senegal -- low wages and union/labor control policies have been a major contributor to private capital accumulation.

Pan-African Labor Organizations and Regional Conflict

Throughout the 1950s, the competition for alignment of African unions in FWA between the French CGT and WFTU, the CGT-FO and ICFTU, and the CFTC and the (Christian) World Confederation of Labor reflected the struggle for African labor support in the Cold War. A similar competition was occurring in anglophone West Africa between the WFTU and ICFTU. In all cases, the labor internationals provided some union organizing funds, scholarships and travel grants to assist African labor centers, which had few financial resources, and favored union leaders. The poverty of African union federations came from non-payment of union dues by members or by member unions. The ICFTU was the most well-established international, with some twenty affiliates in Africa in 1960. The ICFTU sponsored three regional conferences during 1956-60 before establishing an African Regional Organization (AFRO) in 1960. It had made some real contributions in supporting nascent union movements against colonial opposition, especially in Kenya and Tunisia.

However, the financial assistance of the ICFTU, the AFL-CIO's African-American Labor Council (AALC), and WFTU to favored leaders and federations had side effects: it drastically reduced union leaders' reliance upon rank and file support for dues and reduced labor unity by the intrusion of foreign union, political and ideological interests. In Nigeria between 1963 and 1965 the United Labor Congress (ULC), the largest labor center, received 92-98 percent of its revenue from the ICFTU and was still receiving large sums in the 1970s; during 1966-75 the Nigerian Workers' Council received 99 percent of its revenues from foreign internationals; the Nigerian TUC received relatively slight sums from the WFTU.[37] During the 1956-61 period, foreign labor internationals confronted a growing belief that African unions should disaffiliate with all labor internationals and their Cold War associations. This was a somewhat more favorable tendency for the WFTU than the ICFTU, because of the former's fewer affiliates and greater use of covert funding.

With the effective collapse of UGTAN, Touré and other proponents of African trade union solidarity launched a new effort which included anglophone countries. Touré and John Tettegah, Secretary General of the Ghana Trades Union Congress (TUC), sought to rally countries or unions by employing a radical analysis of the neocolonial situation to create an All-African Trade Union Federation (AATUF). This involved Ghana, Guinea, Mali, Egypt, Algeria, and the labor

center in Morocco. The fact that unions in the first four
states were increasingly under party/state control, and
possessed little autonomy, made it clear that AATUF
represented more of an effort of the most militant anti-
imperialist states to pursue their foreign policies through
an inter-African union movement than it did the attempt of
independent trade unions to collaborate.[38] By 1960-61, the
newly independent African states were increasingly divided on
foreign policy issues, including the extent of their break
with the ex-colonial power, nonalignment, Algeria's
liberation struggle and the Congo issue: by May 1961, they
were divided into ostensibly "radical" and "conservative"
blocs.

Trade unions from most African states attended the
inaugural conference of AATUF in Morocco in May 1961. Many
were deeply opposed to its manipulation by the conveners:
the latter received six delegates each, other unions two,
including unrepresentative splinter unions seeking AATUF
support, while many ICFTU affiliated unions were denied
delegate status; proceedings were closely controlled; and
many unions, especially ICFTU and WCL affiliates, were
opposed to the demand that there be only one union federation
in each country and that all AATUF members would have to
disaffiliate from any non-African labor internationals.
There was also concern from well-established unions which
still possessed organizational autonomy -- including those
from Kenya, Tunisia, Nigeria and Sierra Leone -- that AATUF
appeared to be indifferent to union freedom within each
country. Most unions withdrew from AATUF and were taunted by
Ghana's Tettegah that AATUF would "break them, enter their
countries, and form AATUF unions there."[39] The dissident
unions met in January 1962 in Senegal, forty national centers
from thirty countries, and formed the African Trade Union
Confederation (ATUC), which stressed free trade unionism
(though most lacked autonomy), African liberation, and the
right to affiliate internationally. Intermittent efforts to
unify the two organizations always foundered on the question
of disaffiliation with internationals and contending
leadership interests. The AATUF member unions were
intransigent on disaffiliation from ICFTU, a disingenuous
position since some unions had close ties to the WFTU. And
Ghana under Nkrumah secretly depended on Soviet and WFTU
funds (and the Ghana government's) to run AATUF activities.
Ghanaian/AATUF funds were used repeatedly to support splinter
trade union groups -- in Kenya, Nigeria, Congo/Brazzaville,
Benin, Senegal, Togo and Burkina Faso, which the major unions
in these countries deeply resented.[40] None of the

organizations -- AATUF, ATUC, AFRO -- were continuously active, for lack of funds. In 1966, AATUF headquarters were moved to Tanzania.

With the assistance of African labor ministers, a single Organization of African Trade Union Unity (OATUU) was inaugurated in 1973, merging the prior organizations. Although the OATUU Charter dictated non-affiliation of African union centers with other labor internationals (Article 8),[41] no sanctions have been taken against those centers which retained affiliations with ICFTU, WCL or WFTU. OATUU also permits as members, with the right to vote and contest for OATUU offices, only a single trade union center per country. Where there are plural centers, none are admitted or, after investigation, only the one with greatest union support. Only those with paid up dues are permitted to vote in and contest OATUU offices. In the 1985 Extraordinary Congress, only fifteen of fifty members had fully paid their OATUU dues, though another nine in arrears by only one year were permitted to vote.[42] The non-dues payments reflected more the desperate shortages of foreign exchange by African states (and unions) than disinterest. And OATUU offices were arranged to provide broad representation of member countries among the leading offices and General Council membership until the 1985 Fourth Congress, when the attempt by the Nigeria Labor Congress (NLC) to challenge Dennis Akumu for the Secretary General position made voting more important and helped foment a split in OATUU which lasted two years. In the mid-1980s, regional OATUU organizations were being established, and one was set up for thirteen West African states. But OATUU remains the primary organization for trade union cooperation, not least because of the legitimacy it has acquired over time with unions and African governments.

OATUU as an organization has sought to become a major voice for African labor and coordinator of African labor views in all international arenas, including the Organization of African Unity (OAU), the ILO, specialized economic organizations (e.g., the European Community [EC]) and, especially, African governments. It has concerned itself with a wide range of issues, including Africa's economic crisis, migrant and women workers, rural development, workers' education and the struggle against apartheid. By 1983 there were, under OATUU, eight distinct Pan-African federations of specific union sectors, e.g., commerce, mine worker, teacher, agricultural, and transport unions, which shared information on the specialized problems of their sectors. But undoubtedly the most important and difficult issue has been the protection of the rights of trade unions and union leaders in African states. The subordination of African unions to the state and the regular denial of union rights has made this a delicate issue. OATUU has been compelled to accommodate itself to the subordination of unions to parties and of unions' advocacy of this course, though OATUU's Secretary General (until 1986), Dennis Akumu, argued that was a mistake for governments and unions.[43]

OATUU seeks to defend the rights of trade unionists to freedom from arbitrary arrest, freedom of opinion and expression through any media, of assembly, to fair trial, and protection of union property.[44] The protection of these rights has been a major preoccupation, the coordination of protests from African unions a major form of union cooperation. Although such protests are initially not conducted publicly, to reduce giving offense, OATUU officers seek a meeting with the head of state involved and coordinate protests from African unions. If this is not successful, public condemnation and the filing of charges with the ILO follow. During 1975-76, there were fifteen trade union leaders in jail in African states. While OATUU helped free some of these, in 1977 another fourteen were jailed. By 1977, OATUU had only sought to have the ILO "blacklist" one country (Liberia) and was on the verge of seeking this regarding Ethiopia's suppression of unions.[45] Since then, OATUU has been more vigorous in bringing charges against African countries before the ILO when initial mediation is unsuccessful.

Representative protests organized among African unions by OATUU against violations of union rights during 1981-85 included: right to form trade unions (Equatorial Guinea); dissolution of a trade union center (Gambia); banning of specific unions and arrests of trade unionists (Kenya, Morocco, Sierra Leone); banning of union activities and arrests of union leaders (Tunisia, Burkina Faso, Central African Republic); death sentences against trade unionists (Sudan); ouster of union leaders, takeover of union center (Ghana).[46] In many of these protests, OATUU was somewhat successful, especially in those countries where some degree of political freedom existed. Even where OATUU was not immediately successful, it has increased its legitimacy to intervene on behalf of trade unions and leaders in member countries, obtaining meetings of OATUU delegations with heads of state, making it clear to political leaders that inter-African and international campaigns will be organized against countries where severe violations of union rights occur.

Trade Unions and Development in West Africa

In many West African countries, trade unions enjoy few of the rights possessed by unions in industrial democracies: to organize freely, strike, protest, speak out effectively, and avoid unjust arrests and banning of unions. Development that does not entail the creation and control of organizations by the working class and peasants effectively eliminates those classes from participation in the political system and from access to public resources, renders them less willing to accept as legitimate state laws and regulations, confines important dimensions of human development to the middle and upper classes, and permits the benefits of the economy to be appropriated by occupants of state offices and the rising merchant-professional-bureaucratic bourgeoisie. Trade unionists share these conditions of little freedom with other citizens in those regimes which are civilian or military dictatorships, e.g., Guinea, Mali, Togo, Mauritania, Benin, Niger, Central African Republic and Côte d'Ivoire, all ex-French territories in which there are few degrees of freedom, as well as Burkina Faso, Ghana and Nigeria when under military regimes, where greater conditions of liberty prevail for associational groups. In ex-FWA, national unions (between union centers and locals) have always tended to be weak: what little collective bargaining occurs does so on a national level in accords comprising all sectors, sometimes with annexes for specific sectors; major wage setting is undertaken in terms of periodically revised state agricultural and industrial wage scales, sometimes in consultation with unions. All these reduce the roles of unions.[47]

Historically, the True Whig regime in Liberia only permitted trade unions to form in the 1960s. It consistently obstructed their organization, permitted union busting (e.g, mineworkers union), and controlled the labor federations by ensuring that leading members of the American-Liberian bourgeoisie, often in direct collaboration with key firms in which they had interests, were elected as the heads of the labor centers (e.g., the sons of Presidents Tubman and Tolbert).[48] In two small anglophone states, Gambia and Sierra Leone, union movements have retained some autonomy, although in Sierra Leone clientelist politics effectively coopted many union leaders in the Sierra Leone Labor Congress (SLLC) during the 1970s, obstructing public criticism of a corrupt and authoritarian regime. The increasingly severe economic conditions in both countries led to general strikes in the mid-1970s and in 1981 in Sierra Leone. In both countries the union movements have survived, despite the temporary deregistration of the Gambia Workers Union (GWU) in 1977 and its dissolution in the early 1980s and the banning of the SLLC Secretary General in 1982, actions protested by OATUU.[49]

Nigeria, with the largest population, wage labor force and unionized membership in Africa, offered unions substantial freedom from state controls to organize and protest until 1967. Despite intermittent cooperation for national wage protests and strikes, however, its union centers were historically weak and divided by ideology and personal rivalries. During the 1967-70 civil war and after, state controls on strikes and unions increased. In the late-1970s, the military government abolished the four major labor centers, established a single NLC and forty-two industrial unions in place of hundreds, provided the check-off, and created a new, more restrictive conciliation-industrial court process for industrial disputes. Ultimately, this created a stronger, more cohesively organized labor movement, but one whose political capacities remained weak.

With a relatively numerous commercial and industrial (construction, contracting) bourgeoisie, unions have confronted a relatively high level of resistance to union organizing and collective bargaining in the private sector. Despite great increases in unionization in the 1970s and early 1980s, the unions have been unable to prevent drastic layoffs, wage non-payments, and real wage losses in the late-1980s as the oil recession deeply depressed the Nigerian economy.[50] The NLC executive was itself disbanded by the government in February 1988 and many of its leaders arrested, so underlining its continuing weakness. Efforts to increase NLC influence occurred in 1989 as it attempted to organize its own political party, but the NLC was unsuccessful because of government hostility.

Ghanaian trade unions have waged a long, continuous struggle to retain their autonomy and develop their capabilities. Soon after independence, a pro-Convention People's Party (CPP) wing of the TUC led it into an alliance with the CPP and obtained passage of the largely TUC-designed Industrial Relations Act, which had substantial benefits: it required collective bargaining of employers, reorganized the many small unions into (eventually) seventeen industrial unions, and mandated a check-off and union shop, which gave the unions the ability to pay full-time leadership to organize the unions and pursue grievances. These enabled union membership to grow from 100,763 in 1959 to 351,711 in 1965. However, the legislation also banned strikes except after a conciliation-mandatory arbitration process (used by many unions advantageously) and was the instrument for CPP domination over TUC leadership. Union power and wages were initially increased but plummeted in 1963-65; political controls demoralized the unions.[51]

After the CPP's ouster in 1966, in a more liberal polity new trade union leadership from the ranks reasserted the TUC's independence, reestablished internal democratic procedures, reduced TUC control over national unions, and challenged the economic policies and attacks upon unions of the successor military and civilian governments (1966-71) with a wave of strikes, organizing, and a complaint to the ILO.[52] Though the TUC itself was legally dissolved by the Busia government in 1971 (the unions reformed it voluntarily), it sprang back to life in 1972 under the Supreme Military Council (SMC) military regime (1972-79) and fought off efforts to intervene in its internal affairs. Although constrained initially by military rule in strikes and wage bargaining gains, the TUC managed to expand greatly union membership (550,000 in 1977, 60 percent more than in 1974) and until the mid-1970s to increase workers' wages and benefits through vigorous collective bargaining, which now exceeded government wages and benefits. While it refused to openly support opposition to SMC rule in 1977-79, strong and repeated labor protests against economic conditions helped to erode SMC rule.[53] Union leadership was politically cautious and economically reformist, but it repeatedly pressed the civilian government (1979-81) on behalf of workers' wages, price controls on essential commodities, and favorable economic policies.

The union movement embodied substantial tensions as it was unable to prevent workers from suffering great real wage losses during Ghana's sustained economic depression and hyperinflation in 1977-83. It confronted its greatest challenge when the Provisional National Defense Council (PNDC) government of Jerry Rawlings (1981-) came to power in a December 1981 coup. The PNDC mobilized an angry populist rebellion and, in the process, permitted dissident unionists and others to oust forcefully the trade union leadership and seize control of the TUC. Despite workers' awareness of the shortcomings of their unions, they deeply resented and protested widely this undemocratic takeover and the challenge at the workplace from non-union workers' defense committees. OATUU leaders, with headquarters in Accra, Ghana, protested repeatedly to the PNDC this illegal violation of union rights. With the pressures and protests from rank and file Ghanaian unionists, former union leaders now released from jail, OATUU, and other foreign unions, the PNDC regime was forced to require an immediate national delegates' conference, where union representatives demanded that unions and the TUC quickly hold elections in early 1983. These elections returned both old and dissident unionists as leaders of the seventeen unions and a prominent ousted union leader, A.K. Yankey, as TUC Secretary General.[54] While the union leaders were divided on some issues, they were united by their demands for trade union independence, the right to bargain collectively (against regime attempts to freeze wages), and their strong and consistent criticisms of the impact of the PNDC's IMF-style economic reconstruction policies. However necessary to end Ghana's bankrupt economic policies and performance, these policies have involved significant pain and layoffs for workers. Despite intermittent arrests of lower level unionists, the unions have created their political autonomy for the defense of worker interests within the highly authoritarian regime, repeatedly protesting regime efforts to scale back important benefits.

Conclusion

The relatively unfettered regional labor migration and developing regional trade union organizations (e.g., CGTA, UGTAN) and cooperation during 1946-58 contracted sharply when confronted with the dynamics of national politics of new states and the imperatives of political leaders in securing their political kingdoms and eradicating autonomous trade union organizations and power. Early postindependence efforts to create Pan-African movements foundered (e.g., AATUF) partly because they were manipulated by political leaders for foreign policy purposes, none related to working class/union interests, and partly because they represented defensive formations by unions and states to prevent encroachments on their prerogatives and domains (e.g., ATUC). Moreover, African unions were without the financial resources to maintain regional union organizations. OATUU was initially forged along lines of a minimal program, African trade union unity, that obscured some basic cleavages between and within states. But by the 1970s a greatly sobered African trade union leadership understood that OATUU could be employed for the protection, and in the interests, of the unions themselves.

In most West African states, trade unions enjoy relatively few freedoms in the early-1990s to act forcefully on behalf of worker-union interests. OATUU has increasingly involved itself in efforts to secure minimal trade union rights from those forces seeking to control union activities: states with their imperatives, especially economic ones, and notably privatization of government-owned parastatals; political authoritarianism; and the interests of a rising merchant-professional-bureaucratic bourgeoisie. Through OATUU, trade union centers cooperate to protect minimal freedoms -- fuller demands for democratic and radical unionism would divide them -- and to articulate broad union concerns with the impact of the world economy upon Africa. But the contradictions of national chauvinism and worker-union interests remain.

Notes

1. On Pan-African labor groups, see Ioan Davies, *African Trade Unions* (Baltimore: Penguin, 1966), pp. 188-218; I. Wallerstein, *Africa, The Politics of Unity* (New York: Random House, 1967), pp. 176-212; Wogu Ananaba, *The Trade Union Movement in Africa* (New York: St. Martin's, 1979), pp. 21-38 and 120-140; G.E. Lynd, *The Politics of African Trade Unionism* (New York: Praeger, 1968), Chapter 4; A. November, *L'Evolution du Mouvement Syndical en Afrique Occidentale* (Paris: Mouton, 1965), pp. 133-244.

2. Sharon Stichter, *Migrant Laborers* (New York: Cambridge University Press, 1985), pp. 29-57.

3. E. Bunting, "The Economic Community of West African States -- ECOWAS: the First Six Years" in Colin Legum (ed.), *Africa Contemporary Record, 1981-82* (New York: Holmes and Meier, 1983), p. A130. The second phase permits right of residence up to five years (without other permits), while the third phase will permit (if ever brought into effect) the right of permanent residence.

4. On the establishment of state controls over, and repression of, trade unions in the postindependence period, see the following: Davies, *African Trade Unions*, Chapter 8; Richard Sandbrook, *Proletarians and African Capitalism: The Kenyan Case, 1960-1972* (Cambridge: Cambridge University Press, 1975); George Martens, "Industrial Relations and Trade Unionism in French-Speaking West Africa," and Jon Kraus, "The

Political Economy of Industrial Relations in Ghana," both in U. Dimachi, H.D. Seibel and L. Trachtman (eds.), *Industrial Relations in Africa* (London: Macmillan, 1979) pp. 34-49 and 118-146, respectively; Elliot Berg and Jeffrey Butler, "Trade Unions" in James Coleman and Carl Rosberg (eds.), *Political Parties and National Integration in Tropical Africa* (Berkeley: University of California Press, 1964), pp. 340-381; Jon Kraus, "The Political Economy of Trade Union-State Relations in Radical and Populist Regimes in Africa" [Tanzania, Ghana, Algeria, Ethiopia] in Roger Southall (ed.), *Labour and Unions in Asia and Africa* (London: Macmillan, 1987); Nicole Grimaud, "Les Relations du Travail en Algerie: Le Cinquième Congrès de L'UGTAN," *Maghreb-Machrek*, 80, April-June 1978, pp. 57-62; Paschal Mihyo, "The Struggle for Workers' Control in Tanzania," *Review of African Political Economy*, 4, November 1975, pp. 62-84.

5.   See Richard Joseph, "Class, State, and Prebendal Politics in Nigeria," *Journal of Commonwealth and Comparative Politics*, 21(3), November 1983, pp. 21-34; see chapters on indigenization in Zambia, Ghana, Nigeria, Kenya, Tanzania and Senegal in Adebayo Adedeji (ed.), *Indigenization of African Economies* (New York: Africana Publishing Company, 1981); Richard L. Sklar, "The Nature of Class Domination in Africa," *Journal of Modern African Studies*, 17(4), December 1979, pp. 531-552; Ankie Hoogvelt, "Indigenization and Foreign Capital: Industrialization in Nigeria," *Review of African Political Economy*, 14, 1979, pp. 36-55.

6.   Strichter, *Migrant Laborers*, pp. 96-98; Roger Thomas, "Forced Labour in British West Africa: The Case of the Northern Territories of the Gold Coast, 1906-1927," *Journal of Modern African Studies*, 14(1), 1973, pp. 79-103; Davies, *African Trade Unions*, pp. 31-40.

7.   Stichter, *Migrant Laborers*, pp. 96-98; D. Cordell and Joel Gregory, "Labour Reservoirs and Populations: French Colonial Strategies in Koudougou, Upper Volta, 1914-1939," *Journal of African History*, 23(2), 1982, pp. 205-224; Myron Echenberg, "Military Migrations in French West Africa, 1900-1945," *Canadian Journal of African Studies*, 14(3), 1980.

8.   J.I. Roper, *Labour Problems in West Africa* (Harmondsworth: Penguin, 1958), pp. 30, 39.

9.   *Ibid.*, p. 33.

10.   Samir Amin, "Introduction" in Samir Amin (ed.), *Modern Migration in West Africa* (London: Oxford University Press, 1974), pp. 71-74.

11.   J.C. Caldwell, "Migration and Urbanization" in W. Birmingham, I. Neustadt and E.N. Omaboe (eds.), *A Study of Contemporary Ghana*, vol. II.   *Some Aspects of Social*

Structure (Evanston: Northwestern University Press, 1967), p. 114.

12. Amin, *Modern Migration*, pp. 74-75.

13. Cited in Tayo Fashoyin, "Trade Unions, the State, and Labour Mobility in the ECOWAS," paper presented to a conference on Third World Trade Unionism, Ottawa, Canada, 25-27 October 1984, p. 7.

14. See country studies in Adedeji, *Indigenization of African Economies*.

15. Fashoyin, "Trade Unions," pp. 2-4.

16. *Ibid.*, pp. 9-14.

17. *Ibid.*, pp. 19-25. On the importance of industrial structure for unionization, see Peter Waterman, *Aristocrats or Plebians in African Unions* (The Hague: Waterman, 1983), pp. 39-96.

18. Ghana, *1960 Population Census of Ghana, Advanced Report of Volumes III and IV*, computed from Table 38, p. 59.

19. World Bank, *Ivory Coast: The Challenge of Success* (Washington D.C.: World Bank, 1978), p. 130.

20. See E.P. Skinner, "Strangers in West African Societies," *Africa*, 32, 1963, pp. 307-320; Margaret Piel, "Ghana's Aliens," *International Migration Review*, 8(3), 1974, pp. 367-368; Margaret Piel, "The Expulsion of West African Aliens," *Journal of Modern African Studies*, 9(2), 1971, pp. 205-207; Fashoyin, "Trade Unions," pp. 1, 5; *West Africa*, 29 April 1985, pp. 821-822, and 20 May 1985, pp. 988-989.

21. Piel, "The Expulsion of West African Aliens," pp. 209-213.

22. There is no comment on the expulsions in the union leadership report to the TUC's delegates' congress or the Maritime and Dockworkers Union's delegates' conference, both in 1970. See TUC Secretary-General, *Report of the Activities of the TUC (Ghana) to the Third Biennial Congress*, 31 July-2 August 1970 (TUC, mimeograph, 1970); Maritime and Dockworkers Union General Secretary, *Report on Activities 2nd Biennial Conference*, 4-6 September 1979 (MDU, mimeograph, 1970).

23. TUC, *Third Biennial Congress*, pp. 12-13.

24. *Africa Research Bulletin* (Political), 15 February 1983, p. 6698.

25. Fashoyin, "Trade Unions," pp. 24-26.

26. *West Africa*, 26 September 1983.

27. *Africa Research Bulletin* (Political), 15 February 1983, p. 6698. *OATUU, Report of Activities (March 1982-February 1983) of OATUU by the Secretary General to the Eighth Session of the General Council*, 26-27 April 1983 (Accra: OATUU, mimeograph), p. 33.

28. Fashoyin, "Trade Unions," pp. 9-19.

29. Fashoyin cites the unwillingness of Ghanaian and other non-native teachers on contract to support the strikes of the Nigeria Union of Teachers against irregular and non-payment of salaries, undermining the effectiveness of the strikes (p.23). Strichter, pp. 122-138, cites the historical support of migrants for strikes among dockworkers and miners in Zambia, Zimbabwe and South Africa. In Ghana, mineworkers, who included many migrant workers, went on strike frequently in the 1950s -- both in rank and file wildcat solidarity strikes with workers whose rights were abridged and for wage increases -- but were difficult to organize into the mineworkers' union.

30. An excellent account is in George Martens, *Trade Unionism in French-Speaking West Africa during the Colonial Period* (Lomé: Regional Economic and Documentation Center, September 1983), pp. 4-20.

31. *Ibid.*, pp. 28-36.

32. *Ibid.*, pp. 39-57.

33. *Ibid.*, pp. 58-60. Martens' careful documentation of the level of trade union representation in the national assemblies and governments of the francophone colonies after the 1957 elections refutes the comments of Berg and Butler ("Trade Unions," in Coleman and Rosberg, p. 362) that the trade union leaders were politically insignificant. Berg and Butler indicate that there were only four unionists in these assemblies, while Martens notes twenty.

34. Martens, *Trade Unionism*, pp. 68-84; Ananaba, *The Trade Union Movement in Africa*, pp. 25-28; Aristide Zolberg, *One Party Government in the Ivory Coast* (Princeton: Princeton University Press, 1964), pp. 238-239, 278-279, 296-305.

35. Martens. *Trade Unionism*, p. 61.

36. Joseph, "Class, State, and Prebendal Politics in Nigeria"; Sklar, "The Nature of Class Domination in Africa," pp. 531-552; chapters on Ghana, Nigeria and Senegal in Adedeji, *Indigenization of African Economies*; Paul Collins, "Public Policy and Indigenous Capitalism: the Nigerian Experience," *Journal of Commonwealth and Comparative Politics*, 15(2), 1977; Bonnie Campbell, "Ivory Coast" in John Dunn (ed.), *West African States: Failure and Promise* (Cambridge: Cambridge University Press, 1978), pp. 105-116.

37. Tayo Fashoyin (ed.), *Industrial Relations in Nigeria* (London: Longman, 1980), p. 30.

38. Algeria was convulsed in a colonial war with France; the Union Générale des Travailleurs Algerien (UGTA) was banned in Algeria and had no active organizational life in the country; it was closely linked to the National Liberation

Front.   Only the Union Morocain du Travail (UMT) was an independent union.

39. See Ananaba, *The Trade Union Movement in Africa*, pp. 124-128; Wallerstein, *Africa: The Politics of Unity*, pp. 190-197.

40. See Benjamin Bentum, *Trade Unions in Chains* (Accra: TUC, 1966), in which the successor to Tettegah as Ghana TUC Secretary General published documents of the TUC and Ghana government which revealed AATUF's secret reliance on Soviet and WFTU funding.

41. OATUU, "Charter," (mimeograph).

42. "Why the OATUU Split," *West Africa*, 3 March 1986, p. 456.

43. Anthony Hodges, "Interview -- Dennis Akumu," *Africa Report*, November-December 1977, p. 50.

44. *OATUU, Report of Activities (Part One) of OATUU by the Secretary General to the Fourth Congress*, Lagos, 1985, pp. 14-15.

45. Hodges, "Interview -- Dennis Akumu," p. 51; Ananaba, *The Trade Union Movement in Africa*, pp. 101-118.

46. *OATUU, Report of Activities to the Eighth Session of General Council*, 1983, pp. 13-32.

47. George Martens, "Industrial Relations and Trade Unionism in French-speaking West Africa" in Dimachi, Seibel and Trachtman (eds.), *Industrial Relations in Africa*, pp. 49-62.

48. Ananaba, *The Trade Union Movement in Africa*, pp. 101-119; Dew Tuaw-Wleh Mayson and Amos Sawyer, "Labour in Liberia," *Review of African Political Economy*, 14, January-April 1979, pp. 3-15; Gus Liebenow, *Liberia, The Quest for Democracy* (Bloomington: Indiana University Press, 1987), pp. 73-75.

49. See David F. Luke, *Labor and Parastatal Politics in Sierra Leone* (Washington D.C.: University Press of America, 1983), especially pp. 179-220; Ananaba, *The Trade Union Movement in Africa*, pp. 16-21.

50. See Fashoyin, *Industrial Relations in Africa*, pp. 20-39, 73-104; Paul Lubeck, "Unions, Workers and Consciousness in Kano, Nigeria," and D. Remy, "Economic Security and Industrial Unionism: A Nigerian Case Study," both in Richard Sandbrook and Robin Cohen (eds.), *The Development of an African Working Class* (Toronto: University of Toronto Press), pp. 139-160 and 161-177, respectively; Waterman, *Aristocrats and Plebians in African Unions*; Adrian Peace, *Choice, Class and Conflict* (Atlantic Highlands, N.J.: Humanities Press, 1979); Nicholas Van Hear, "Recession, Retrenchment and Military Rule: Prospects for Nigerian Labor in the Later

1980s" in Roger Southall (ed.), *Trade Unions and the New Industrialization of the Third World* (London: Zed Press, 1987).

51. Richard Jeffries, *Class, Power and Ideology in Ghana: The Railwaymen of Sekondi* (London: Cambridge University Press, 1978), pp. 58-101; Jeff Crisp, *The Story of an African Working Class: Ghanaian Miners' Struggles 1879-1980* (London: Zed Press, 1984), pp. 94-149; Jon Kraus, "The Political Economy of Industrial Relations in Ghana" in Dimachi, Seibel and Trachtman (eds.), *Industrial Relations in Africa*, pp. 118-136.

52. Jon Kraus, "Strikes and Labor Power in Ghana," *Development and Change*, 10(2), April 1979, pp. 259-286; Jeffries, *Class, Power and Ideology in Ghana*, pp. 102-139.

53. Kraus, "The Political Economy of Trade Union-State Relations" in Southall (ed.), *Labor and Unions in Asia and Africa*; TUC, "Report of the Activities of the TUC (Ghana) to the 2nd Quadrennial Congress, 1978" (mimeograph).

54. TUC, "Report of the Interim Management Committee of the TUC (Ghana) Presented by Brother E.E. Aboagye to the Extraordinary Delegates' Congress, 1983"; TUC, "Position Paper on the Present National Situation by the Executive Board of the TUC" (mimeograph, 18 February 1985).

Abbreviations

AATUF	All-African Trade Union Federation
ACP	African, Caribbean and Pacific States
ADB	African Development Bank
AFRO	African Regional Organization
AID	Agency for International Development (US)
ASEAN	Association of South East Asian Nations
ATUC	African Trade Union Confederation
BADEA	Arab Bank for Economic Development in Africa
BCEAO	Banque Centrale des Etats de l'Afrique de l'Ouest
BHN	Basic Human Needs
CACM	Central American Common Market
CATC	African Federation of Believing Workers
CBC	Chad Basin Commission
CEAO	Communauté des Etats de l'Afrique de l'Ouest
CFA	Communauté Financière Africaine
CGT	Confédération Générale du Travail
DLM	Dual Labor Market
EAC	East African Community
EAMA	Etats Africaine et Malgache
EC	European Community
ECA	Economic Commission for Africa (UN)
ECCAS	Economic Community of Central African States
ECOWAS	Economic Community of West African States
FAO	Food and Agriculture Organization
FCD	Fonds Communautaire de Développement
FOSIDEC	Fonds de Solidarité et d'Intervention pour le Développement de la Communauté
FWA	French West Africa
GDP	Gross Domestic Product
GNP	Gross National Product
ICFTU	International Confederation of Free Trade Unions
IDB	Islamic Development Bank

ILO	International Labor Organization
IMF	International Monetary Fund
KFAED	Kuwait Fund for Arab Economic Development
LAFTA	Latin American Free Trade Association
LDC	Less Developed Country
LLDC	Least Developed Country
LPA	Lagos Plan of Action (OAU)
MRU	Mano River Union
NIC	Newly Industrializing Country
NIEO	New International Economic Order
OATUU	Organization of African Trade Union Unity
OAU	Organization of African Unity
OCAM	Organisation Commune Africaine et Mauricienne
OIC	Organization of the Islamic Conference
OPEC	Organization of Petroleum Exporting Countries
PNDC	Provisional National Defense Council (of Ghana)
PQLI	Physical Quality of Life Index
PTA	Preferential Trade Area
RDA	Rassemblement Democratique Africaine
RNC	River Niger Commission
SADCC	Southern African Development Coordination Conference
SDF	Saudi Development Fund
SENEGAM	Senegal-Gambia Confederation
SITC	Standard International Trade Classification
TCR	Taxe de Coopération Régionale
TNC	Transnational Corporation
UAM	Union Africaine et Malgache
UAMPT	Union Africaine et Malgache des Postes et Télécommunications
UDEAO	Union Douanière des Etats de l'Afrique de l'Ouest
UGTAN	Union Générale du Travail de l'Afrique Noire
UMOA	Union Monétaire de l'Ouest Africaine
UN	United Nations
WACH	West African Clearing House
WFTU	World Federation of Free Trade Unions
WMC	World Muslim Congress

Contributors

DANIEL C. BACH gained his doctorate at the University of Oxford, and taught political science at the University of Ife, Nigeria, from 1978-80. Since 1980, he has been chargé de recherche of the Centre national de la recherche scientifique at Bordeaux University's Center for Black African Studies. He was a founding member of *Politique Africaine*, and author of several articles on regional cooperation and French policy in Africa. He is editor of *Le Nigeria Contemporain* (Paris: CRNS, 1986) and coeditor of *Nigeria: un pouvoir en puissance* (Paris: Karthala, 1988). He was a Visiting Senior Research Fellow at St. Antony's College, Oxford, from 1986-88, and a Visiting Professor at the University of Montreal in Spring 1990.

MARY BURFISHER is an economist in the Developing Economies Branch, Agriculture and Trade Policy Division, Economic Research Service, US Department of Agriculture. She received a M.S. Foreign Service from Georgetown University and is a Ph.D. candidate in economics at the University of Maryland. Ms. Burfisher has written extensively on issues related to African agricultural development, including the impact of development projects on women's productivity, and the Cameroonian agricultural sector.

BARBARA CALLAWAY is a Professor of Political Science and Acting Dean of the Graduate School at Rutgers University in New Brunswick, New Jersey. Her early research was on processes of change and development in African societies and her field research was conducted in Nigeria and Ghana. In recent years she has focused on women and social change. During 1981-83 she was Senior Lecturer and Fulbright Professor of Political Science at Bayero University in Kano,

Nigeria. Her articles have appeared in the *Journal of Modern African Studies, Comparative Politics, African Studies Review* and the *Journal of Politics*.

OLIVER S. KNOWLES B. Litt., M.A. (Oxon) is a retired international civil servant who worked for several international organizations and specialized in dealing with cooperation problems among developing countries and groupings, including ECOWAS, the Mano River Union, the Communaute Economique des Pays des Grand Lacs, the South Pacific, and the Association of South East Asian Nations, where he was Deputy Leader of the UN Advisory Team from 1970-72. Prior to joining the UN he worked for the Kenya Government where, as a senior Treasury officer, he specialized in economic planning, foreign aid, and regional cooperation problems.

PHOEBE KORNFELD has been teaching most recently in Paris. She received her doctorate in political science at Duke University in 1984. She is the author of several articles on the uses and abuses of bilateral and multilateral aid in Africa.

JON KRAUS is a Professor of Political Science at the State University of New York/College at Fredonia. He has written on Ghanaian political economy, African trade unionism, and military regimes. Among his most recent publications are: "The Political Economy of Agricultural Regression in Ghana" in M. Lofchie and S. Commins (eds.), *Africa's Agrarian Crisis* (1986), "Political Party Failures and Political Responses in Ghana" in K. Lawson and P. Merkl (eds.), *When Parties Fail* (1987), "The Political Economy of Trade Union-State Relations in Radical and Populist Regimes in Africa" in R. Southall (ed.), *Labour and Unions in Asia and Africa* (1987), and "The Political Economy of Food in Ghana" in N. Chazan and T. Shaw (eds.), *Coping with Africa's Food Crisis* (1988).

WILLIAM F.C. MILES is Assistant Professor of Political Science at Northeastern University in Boston, and chair of the graduate program in Development Administration there. He has spent three and a half years in West Africa with the Fulbright Program, State Department and Peace Corps. His book on Nigerian Hausa politics was published in 1987 by Lynne Rienner under the title *Elections in Nigeria: A Grassroots Perspective*. Dr. Miles is also the author of *Elections and Ethnicity in French Martinique: A Paradox in Paradise*.

MARGARET MISSIAEN is an agricultural economist in the Developing Economies Branch, Agriculture and Trade Policy Division, Economic Research Service, US Department of Agriculture. She received a B.A. degree in political science from Indiana University and has done graduate work in economics. She has fourteen years experience in analyzing developments in African agriculture with emphasis on West Africa. Recent work has included development of a data base on African agriculture and coordination of food needs assessments for African countries.

JULIUS EMEKA OKOLO was an Associate Professor of Political Science at Howard University, Washington D.C. Since 1979, he has taught at the University of Sokoto (now Usman Dan Fodio University), Nigeria, where he was previously Chair of the Department of Political Science and is currently Dean of the Postgraduate School. He has written extensively on the problems of and prospects for West African cooperation, and his articles have appeared in journals such as *International Organization, The World Today, World Affairs, Comparative Strategy, Journal of Social and Behavioral Sciences* and *Terrorism.*

AMADU SESAY gained his doctorate at the London School of Economics, and is currently a Senior Lecturer in International Relations at the Obafemi Awolowo University (Ife), Nigeria, where he has taught since 1978. He has published widely on the politics of Africa, and is coauthor of *The OAU after Twenty Years* (Westview Press, 1984), coeditor of *The Future of Regionalism in Africa* (Macmillan, 1985), and editor of *Africa and Europe: From Partition to Interdependence or Dependence?* (Croom Helm, 1987).

TIMOTHY M. SHAW is Professor of Political Science and Director of the Center for African Studies at Dalhousie University, Canada. He has published extensively on the international political economy of Africa, and his most recent coedited volumes are *Economic Crisis in Africa, Confrontation and Liberation in Southern Africa* and *Corporatism in Africa.*

CLAUDE E. WELCH, JR. is Professor of Political Science at the State University of New York at Buffalo, and has specialized in the study of African militaries for more than twenty years. Among his major books on the subject are *Soldier and State in Africa, Military Role and Rule, Civilian Control of the Military,* and *No Farewell to Arms?;* other books include *Anatomy of Rebellion, Human Rights and Development in Africa* and *Political Modernization*, in addition to over fifty book chapters and articles in professional journals.

STEPHEN WRIGHT gained his doctorate at the London School of Economics, and taught political science at the University of Sokoto, Nigeria, from 1977-82. After a period teaching in London, he has, since 1985, been at Northern Arizona University, where he is an Associate Professor of Political Science. He is coeditor of *Africa in World Politics: Changing Perspectives* (Macmillan, 1987).

Index